The Elements
of Trial

The Elements of Trial

Rick Friedman
and
Bill Cummings

Trial Guides, LLC

Trial Guides, LLC, Portland, Oregon 97210

Copyright © 2013 by Rick Friedman and Bill Cummings. All rights reserved.

TRIAL GUIDES and logo are registered trademarks of Trial Guides, LLC.

RULES OF THE ROAD is a trademark of Trial Guides, LLC.

ISBN: 978-1-934833-88-9

Library of Congress Control Number: 2013939867

These materials, or any parts or portions thereof, may not be reproduced in any form, written or mechanical, or be programmed into any electronic storage or retrieval system, without the express written permission of Trial Guides, LLC, unless such copying is expressly permitted by federal copyright law. Please direct inquiries to:

Trial Guides, LLC
Attn: Permissions
2350 NW York Street
Portland, OR 97210
(800) 309-6845
www.trialguides.com

Interior design by Laura Lind Design

Illustrations and jacket design by Theodore Marshall

Printed and bound in the United States of America.

This book is printed on acid-free paper.

10 9 8 7 6 5 4 3 2 1

ALSO BY RICK FRIEDMAN

Rules of the Road: A Plaintiff Lawyer's Guide to Proving Liability (Pat Malone, co-author)

Polarizing the Case: Exposing and Defeating the Malingering Myth

Rick Friedman on Becoming a Trial Lawyer

Moral Core Advocacy: Finding the Heart of Your Case (CD/DVD)

Stop Your Whining and Go to Trial (with Don Bauermeister; CD/DVD)

To my parents, who always said I could be anything I wanted, and never once suggested what that should be.

—Rick Friedman

To Mom and Dad, who believed I should be a lawyer, and made it (and everything else) possible.

—Bill Cummings

Contents

Publisher's Note xi
Acknowledgments xiii
Introduction 1
   1. An Overview 5
   2. Jury Instructions 11
   3. Investigation 27
   4. Fighting Chaos 35
   5. Assessing Your Case-in-Chief 47
   6. Trial Briefs and Motions *in Limine* 57
   7. The Pretrial Hearing 65
   8. Jury Selection (Voir Dire) 73
   9. Opening Statement 93
  10. Presenting Your Case-in-Chief:
      Direct Examination 107
  11. Cross-Examination 127
  12. Making a Record 145
  13. Directed Verdict 161
  14. Rebuttal Case 171
  15. The Charging Conference 177
  16. Closing Argument 181
  17. Jury Questions and Taking the Verdict 201
  18. Posttrial Motions 207

19. You 217
Conclusion 227
Index 229
About the Authors 253

Publisher's Note

This book is intended for law students and practicing attorneys. This book does not offer legal advice and does not take the place of consultation with an attorney or other professional with appropriate expertise and experience.

Attorneys are strongly cautioned to evaluate the information, ideas, and opinions set forth in this book in light of their own research, experience, and judgment; to consult applicable rules, regulations, procedures, cases, and statutes (including those issued after the publication date of this book); and to make independent decisions about whether and how to apply such information, ideas, and opinions to a particular case.

Quotations from cases, pleadings, discovery, and other sources are for illustrative purposes only and may not be suitable for use in litigation in any particular case.

The cases described in this book are composites, and the names and other identifying details of participants, litigants, witnesses, and counsel (other than the authors of this book) have been fictionalized except where otherwise expressly stated.

All references to the trademarks of third parties are strictly informational and for purposes of commentary. No sponsorship or endorsement by, or affiliation with, the trademark owners is claimed or implied by the authors or publisher of this book.

The authors and publisher disclaim any liability or responsibility for loss or damage resulting from the use of this book or the information, ideas, or opinions contained in this book.

Acknowledgments

This book is better than it otherwise would be because of generous help and comments from Bill Bailey, Don Beskind, Roger Dodd, Professor Nora Freeman Engstrom, Steve Fury, Larry Roberts, and Trina Tinglum. Thank you.

Thanks also to Tina Ricks, the pit-bull editor who fought for this book as if it were her own. It is.

Introduction

The trial process is infinitely complex, bafflingly subtle, and frustratingly unpredictable. Years of experience, study, and discipline can improve your performance, but *no one* ever *masters* the complexity, subtlety, and randomness of trial.

Like many great truths, the truth about trial practice is a paradox. While it is true that the process of trying cases is complex, subtle, and unpredictable, it is also simple and straightforward. The purpose of this book is to provide the simple and straightforward principles and concepts involved in trying a case. This is more than most of today's trial lawyers had when they tried their first case. Understanding these simple principles and concepts is necessary before you can productively struggle with the complexities of trial practice.

For the practicing lawyer, this book is designed to be analogous to a pilot's or surgeon's checklist. You will be reminded of issues to consider, and provided legal research leads to address those issues for each trial stage. Each major stage of the trial process is addressed in a chapter. Many chapters are divided into six subsections: "Purpose," "Advocacy Goals," "Applicable Law," "Implementation," "Questions to Ask," and "Suggested Reading." Here is an overview of what each subsection will address.

Purpose

Trials are a process by which we resolve disputes. Every aspect of the process serves one or more legal or procedural purposes. Motions *in limine,* for example, give the judge and the parties an opportunity to resolve evidentiary issues before the trial actually starts. The judge and each side can make decisions without the time pressure that often exists once the trial begins. The purpose of jury instructions is to inform the jury of the applicable law and encourage decision making in accordance with that law. This subsection describes the purpose behind each stage of trial.

Advocacy Goals

At every stage of trial, you must think about the opportunities you have for advancing your case—increasing your chances of winning the trial. This subsection describes common opportunities available at each stage.

Applicable Law

You must be familiar with the basic controlling legal principles applicable at each stage of trial. This subsection gives you these principles.

The law of trial practice and procedure varies between jurisdictions. While there are important similarities, there are also important differences. This book presents leading cases on each topic from six jurisdictions—Florida, New York, Illinois, California, Arizona, and Washington—and also touches regularly on federal law. It is hoped this will give you efficient research leads no matter where you practice.

Implementation

This subsection discusses some ideas for implementing your advocacy goals and trial strategy.

QUESTIONS TO ASK

Trial practice and procedure varies from federal to state court, from state to state, from county to county, and even from courtroom to courtroom in the same courthouse. Many beginning trial lawyers are unaware of this fact, assuming they are the only ones who do not know the proper practice.

The easy response to this reality is to *ask questions* of the court personnel and judges, as well as other lawyers who have practiced before them. This is what experienced lawyers do. Inexperienced lawyers sit quietly, hoping no one will notice how little they know. This subsection suggests the right questions to ask.

SUGGESTED READING

Much has been written about many of the individual topics covered briefly in this book. A good way to improve your skills as a trial lawyer is to read what other trial lawyers have written. Some of the chapters will have a subsection giving you suggestions for further reading on the chapter's topic.

• • •

This book is designed to be your "basic training" manual. It will not transform you into a brilliant advocate, but it should help you do a credible job for your clients. "Credible job" is a good place to start on your journey to trial excellence.

1

An Overview

In a trial, you are trying to tell a story. You are trying to convince the jury or judge that your story is true. You are trying to convince them that your story entitles you to a favorable verdict.

Unlike the storytelling we all engage in every day, storytelling at trial is sharply constrained by legal rules. We can't necessarily tell the story we would like to tell in the way we would like to tell it. Perhaps more importantly, there is a competing story; our adversary is fighting to convince the judge or the jury that our story is false and his is true.

Throughout the litigation and throughout trial, keep the following questions in mind:

1. What is the story I want to tell?

2. How believable is this story?

3. What parts of the story are vulnerable to legal attack (exclusion) or factual attack (discredit)?

4. Does the story entitle my client to the legal result he seeks?

5. How does the story's credibility (as I will be permitted to tell it in court) compare with the credibility of the other side's story?

6. Out of all possible stories I could tell, is there another one that could increase the chance of success?

With these questions in mind, your discovery and motion practice will be more efficient focused on the end game of your trial presentation. Constantly revisit these questions as new facts come to your attention and the court makes new legal rulings.

What Is the Story I Want to Tell?

You *should* want to tell the story that will cause you to win the case. Instead, lawyers often want to tell a story to satisfy their own ego or ideological needs. If you represent a man charged with murder, you may want to tell a story involving his mistreatment at the hands of the police. This part of the story may be accurate. It may be compelling to you. It may feel very satisfying to attack the police officers in open court and take them to task for their misconduct. And it might well leave the jury unimpressed.

A good advocate keeps her eye on the ball: what it will take to win the case. What is important or significant to her may be very different than what is important and significant to the jurors. She understands that trial is a time for self-discipline, not self-indulgence. The best story is the one that guides the jury to a verdict in her client's favor. She can vent her anger or promote her causes on her own time.

Ideally, your story will cause the jurors to want your client to win the case. If you represent a man accused of murder, hearing the decedent was a drug dealer and rapist may well convince the jurors that your client did the world a favor. They may *want* your client to win.

How Believable Is Your Story?

With credible witnesses to testify, or documentary evidence establishing the deceased was a drug dealer and rapist, your story may be believable. If such evidence is lacking, and the deceased was a forty-year-old suburban father of three, your story loses credibility. Evaluate each available fact. Does it make your story more or less believable? Almost every trial will have a mix of available facts, some that add to and some that detract from your story's credibility. If all the facts were in your favor, there would be no need for a trial.

WHAT PARTS OF THE STORY ARE VULNERABLE TO LEGAL ATTACK (EXCLUSION) OR FACTUAL ATTACK (DISCREDIT)?

There are innumerable reasons why your evidence of the decedent's bad conduct may not be admitted. To take just one example, suppose he was killed after a minor traffic accident, during which he and your client got into a shouting match that escalated into violence. The court might rule that the decedent's drug dealing and rape convictions are irrelevant or too prejudicial for the jury to consider and exclude them from evidence.

If all of your witnesses are biased against the decedent and the prosecution has character witnesses showing he was a saint, your story is vulnerable to factual discredit. Or, if the jury hears your client is also a drug dealer, and the death occurred as part of a business dispute, you may get in all the evidence about the decedent's bad character, but the power of your story is greatly diminished. Your client's presumed moral superiority over the decedent has evaporated.

DOES THE STORY ENTITLE YOUR CLIENT TO THE LEGAL RESULT HE SEEKS?

If your client's story is that he approached the decedent and shot him without provocation because your client hates drug dealers, the story does not legally entitle your client to acquittal. Your story needs more facts. It must either credibly rebut one of the elements the prosecution must prove to secure conviction (perhaps the intent to kill) or establish a recognized legal defense (perhaps self-defense).

This is why the best place to start case analysis—in *any* case—is with the legal instructions the jury will likely be given at the end of the trial. Only then will you know if the facts of your story can support your desired verdict.

How Does Your Story Compare to the Other Side's Story?

In life, and in trials, there are always two or more possible stories or explanations for an event or series of events. You are going to trial because the other side has an alternative story. Subject your opponent's story to the same analysis you applied to your own:

1. What story does he want to tell?

2. How believable is his story?

3. What parts of the story are vulnerable to legal or factual attack?

4. Does his story entitle his client to the legal result he seeks?

5. How does the credibility of his story compare to the credibility of your story?

And then ask one more question about your own case:

6. Is there a different story (or part of a story) I could tell that would increase my chance of success?

Good trial lawyers are constantly thinking and rethinking these questions at every stage of the litigation process—from their first contact with the client or case, until the verdict is announced. This book's goal is to help you do this with your own cases, while introducing you to the legal structure within which you must consider these questions.

SUGGESTED READING

Bettinger, Carl. *Twelve Heroes, One Voice: Guiding Jurors to Courageous Verdicts*. Portland, OR: Trial Guides, 2011.

McComas, James. *Case Analysis: Winning Hard Cases Against the Odds*. Portland, OR: Trial Guides, 2011.

Perdue, Jim. *Winning with Stories: Using the Narrative to Persuade in Trials, Speeches and Lectures*. Austin, TX: Texas Bar Books, 2006.

Spence, Gerry. *Win Your Case: How to Present, Persuade, and Prevail—Every Place, Every Time*. New York: St. Martin's Griffin, 2006.

2

Jury Instructions

Most judges don't give the important jury instructions until the *end* of trial. So why does the *first* substantive chapter of this book address the subject of jury instructions? *Because you cannot make a reasoned decision about any aspect of your trial presentation until you know what you must prove to prevail on each issue in the case.*

A prosecutor must prove elements of a crime; a plaintiff's lawyer must prove elements of a cause of action. Failure to prove a single element can result in total failure of the case.

The defense often has affirmative defenses. These can be a complete defense, even if the opponent proves all elements of his claim. But affirmative defenses have elements too, and the affirmative defense fails if each element is not proven.

Unless you know what elements each side must prove to prevail, you cannot know which story will entitle you to relief, what evidence to present, what evidence is admissible, or what motions or objections to make. *Drafting substantive jury instructions is the only logical place to start your trial preparation.*

Drafting instructions will help even when there will be no jury. Judges, arbitrators, and hearing officers all need to know the basic elements of the claims and defenses. Before or during trial, it is a good idea to show them what the instructions would be, were a jury deciding the case.

Please note that although this chapter talks about *drafting* instructions, it may be more accurate to say *assembling*. In most jurisdictions, there are pattern or model instructions covering most common issues that you need to address in your instructions. The terms *pattern instructions* and *model instructions* are used interchangeably in this book. A committee of lawyers or judges usually drafts these pattern or model instructions in order to provide a standard approach to reoccurring situations. As a result, in many cases, "drafting" the instructions will mean selecting the appropriate instructions from the available model instructions, modifying them with names and dates from your case facts, and *maybe* writing a handful of additional instructions to address the particularities of your case. In simple cases, no instructions beyond the models may be needed.

Where there are model instructions on a point, most trial judges will look with suspicion on any attempt to draft a new instruction covering the same ground. This is not to say that you should always accept the model instructions as the final word, but you must pick your battles and be prepared to defend the changes you suggest.

Purpose

Instructions the court gives to the jurors fall into three general categories, those that:

1. Orient the jurors to trial procedures

2. Give orders and suggestions on how jurors should approach their tasks

3. Provide substantive instruction on the law jurors must follow and apply

Think of the first category of instructions as "housekeeping" instructions. They inform jurors of things like the trial schedule, the sequence of the trial stages, and how to ask for help from the bailiff.

Think of instructions in the second category as "standard" or "boilerplate" instructions. They tell jurors what they can and cannot do as they perform their job. These instructions commonly include an order not to discuss the case with anyone or form an opinion about it until after deliberations begin. Instructions to avoid media accounts of the trial, to refrain from using social media, and to not do independent research on the case outside the courtroom are also common. Boilerplate instructions may also include suggestions on such topics as how to evaluate testimony or conduct deliberations.

These two categories of instructions are often collectively referred to as "standard" or "boilerplate" instructions. Many (though not all) judges have a set of these instructions they give in every trial. Examples of standard or boilerplate instructions can usually also be found in a state's pattern or model instructions.

The third category consists of substantive instructions. These tell jurors the law that applies to the parties' dispute and that should control the jury's decision. These are the instructions that drive your trial preparation and strategy. In a breach of contract case, the substantive instructions will explain what facts must be present for a contract to exist, what must be proven to establish a breach, and how to calculate damages. Here is a breach of contract instruction commonly given in California:

> **CACI[1] 303. Breach of Contract—Essential Factual Elements**
>
> To recover damages from [*name of defendant*] for breach of contract, [*name of plaintiff*] must prove all of the following:
>
> 1. That [*name of plaintiff*] and [*name of defendant*] entered into a contract;
>
> 2. That [*name of plaintiff*] did all, or substantially all, of the significant things that the contract

---

[1] CACI is shorthand for the Judicial Council of California Civil Jury Instructions.

required [*him/her/it*] to do [*or that he/she/it*] was excused from doing those things;

3. That all conditions required by the contract for [*name of defendant*]'s performance had occurred;

4. That [*name of defendant*] failed to do something that the contract required [*him/her/it*] to do; and

5. That [*name of plaintiff*] was harmed by that failure.

In a murder case, the substantive instructions will list the elements the prosecution must prove to establish the crime. In Florida, a first degree murder elements instruction looks like this:

7.2 MURDER—FIRST DEGREE
§ 782.04(1)(a), Fla.Stat.
To prove the crime of First Degree Premeditated Murder, the State must prove the following three elements beyond a reasonable doubt:

1. [*Victim*] is dead.

2. The death was caused by the criminal act of [*defendant*].

3. There was a premeditated killing of [*victim*].

Definitions
An "act" includes a series of related actions arising from and performed pursuant to a single design or purpose.

"Killing with premeditation" is killing after consciously deciding to do so. The decision must be present in the mind at the time of the killing. The law does not fix the exact period of time that must pass between the formation of the premeditated intent to kill and the killing. The period of time must be long enough to allow reflection by the defendant. The premeditated intent to kill must be formed before the killing.

The question of premeditation is a question of fact to be determined by you from the evidence. It will be sufficient proof of premeditation if the circumstances of the killing and the conduct of the accused convince you beyond a reasonable doubt of the existence of premeditation at the time of the killing.
Florida Standard Jury Instructions for Criminal Cases.

Here, the Florida pattern instruction for first degree premeditated murder includes definitions of "act" and "killing with premeditation." It is common to give additional substantive instructions to provide definitions of terms used in the elements instruction.

Housekeeping and boilerplate instructions are often given at the beginning of trial as well as at the end. Substantive instructions are almost always given at the end. A growing minority of judges now give basic substantive instructions before opening statements. These judges believe that jurors are better able to understand the significance of evidence if they have been told the legal rules of decision they must apply.

Advocacy Goals

Draft jury instructions early in the case—ideally, when you first get involved. A litigator working on a case without draft jury instructions is like a driver in an unfamiliar city with no directions, map, or GPS. You may ultimately get to your destination, but not without a lot of needless stress and wasted energy.

Draft jury instructions for your opponent's claims and defenses as well. This will educate you on the strengths and weaknesses of his legal positions and give you an advantage in objecting to his proposed instructions.

An important benefit from drafting jury instructions early in the case is the help they provide in writing briefs. When you are able to say to the judge, "Here are the elements we must prove to prevail on this claim," you focus her attention where it belongs, and can save yourself a lot of unnecessary research and writing.

Return to your draft instructions as the litigation proceeds. You will be surprised at how much insight your factual development will provide for new or modified instructions. Conversely, reminding yourself of the legal issues will continue to benefit your factual investigation and development.

You would like the instructions to favor your case as much as possible. But if you leave out elements or unfairly shade legal meaning in your favor, you will either lose credibility with the judge (when she finds out) or create appellate issues for your opponent (if you win). It is not worth it. When a model or pattern instruction accurately addresses a point, use it. Where your case requires that you substantially modify a pattern instruction, or write an instruction on a new cause of action or a special definition, be prepared to defend your instruction with supporting authority and argument.

If you want to make your case easier to prove, write your jury instructions in plain, easy-to-understand English. This can be a challenge when you are dealing with complex legal principles, but you can and must do it. The simpler, the better.

If the judge has decided against you on a legal theory, drafting and submitting jury instructions on that theory serves two goals: first, it may cause the judge to change her mind or at least modify her previous ruling, and second, it helps preserve your position on appeal. (In some states, it may be *required* to preserve your position on appeal.)

APPLICABLE LAW

◆ Each party is entitled to have its legal theory of the case presented to the jury in the form of jury instructions, if the theory is supported by evidence.[2]

---

[2] *Gemstar Ltd. v. Ernst & Young*, 917 P.2d 222 (Ariz. 1996) (trial court has a duty to instruct on all legal theories supported by the evidence); *Soule v. General Motors Corp.*, 882 P.2d 298, 311 (Cal. 1994) ("A party is entitled upon request to correct, nonargumentative instructions on every theory of the case advanced by him which is supported by substantial evidence."); *Seaboard*

♦ If a jury instruction is not submitted on an issue or no objection is made to an instruction offered by the other side, the issue is waived.[3]

Coastline R.R. Co. v. Addison, 502 So.2d 1241, 1242 (Fl. 1987) (recognizing the "established rule of law that a party is entitled to have the jury instructed upon his theory of the case when there is evidence to support the theory"); *Mikolajczyk v. Ford Motor Co.*, 901 N.E.2d 329, 348–49 (Ill. 2008) (parties are entitled to instruction on each theory supported by some evidence); *Barrett v. Lucky Seven Saloon, Inc.*, 96 P.3d 386, 389 (Wash 2004) ("Failure to permit instructions on a party's theory of the case, where there is evidence supporting the theory, is reversible error.").

In New York, the court is required to state the fundamental legal principles and give a balanced charge, not necessarily instruct on each party's theory of the case. *See People v. Croskery*, 695 N.Y.S.2d 788 (N.Y. App. 1999).

[3] For example, Federal Rule of Civil Procedure 51(d)(1) provides that a party may assign error to the giving of an instruction only if the party properly objected, and to the failure to give an instruction only if it requested the instruction and properly objected to its exclusion. Similarly, in criminal proceedings, Federal Rule of Criminal Procedure 30(d) requires a party to make a specific objection and offer grounds for the objection and bars appellate review if there was no proper objection except in the case of clear error.

Many state rules and cases provide similarly. *See, e.g.*, Ariz. R. Civ. P. 51(a); Ariz. R. Crim. P. 21.3(c); Fla. Civ. Pro. R. 1.470(b); N.Y. CVP. LAW § 4110-b; N.Y. CPL § 470.05; Wash. Civ. R. 51(f); Wash. Crim. R. 6.15(c); *Walker v. State*, 848 P.2d 721, 723 (Wash. 1993); *Deal v. Byford*, 127 Ill.2d 192, 202–03, 537 N.E.2d 267, 271 (Ill. 1989) ("To preserve an objection to a jury instruction a party must both specify the defect claimed and tender a correct instruction."); *People v. Thurman*, 104 Ill.2d 326, 472 N.E.2d 414 (1984) ("The general rule is that where no objection is made at trial to an erroneous jury instruction, the issue is waived."). *See also* Illinois S.Ct. Rule 451 (addressing instructions in criminal proceedings).

In California civil cases, however, California Civil Code § 647 provides that a party is deemed to have objected to "giving an instruction, refusing to give an instruction, or modifying an instruction requested," so waiver, at least with respect to legal error, does not easily occur. *See, e.g., McCarty v. State of California Dept. of Transp.*, 79 Cal. Rptr. 3d 777, 797 (Cal. App. 2008). A litigant cannot, however, complain about the failure to give an additional instruction that it did not propose. *See Jamison v. Lindsay*, 166 Cal. Rptr. 443 (Cal. App. 1980). In California criminal cases, a similar rule applies. *See* Cal. Penal Code § 1259 ("The appellate court may also review any instruction given, refused or modified, even though no objection was made thereto in the lower court,

- In some jurisdictions there is a requirement or presumption that if there is a pattern instruction on point, it is error not to give it.[4] In other jurisdictions, the patterns are simply persuasive authority and trial judges rely heavily on them.[5]

---

if the substantial rights of the defendant were affected thereby."); *People v. Milosavljevic*, 107 Cal. Rptr.3d 792, (Cal. App. 2010) (objection or request required where substantial rights not affected).

[4] Florida Rule of Civil Procedure 1.470(b) provides, "The Florida Standard Jury Instructions appearing on the court's website at www.floridasupreme court.org/jury_instructions/instructions.shtml shall be used by the trial judges of this state in instructing the jury in civil actions to the extent that the Standard Jury Instructions are applicable, unless the trial judge determines that an applicable Standard Jury Instruction is erroneous or inadequate."

Illinois Supreme Court Rules of Civil Proceedings in the Trial Court, Rule 239 similarly provides, "Whenever Illinois Pattern Jury Instructions (IPI) contains an instruction applicable in a civil case, giving due consideration to the facts and the prevailing law, and the court determines that the jury should be instructed on the subject, the IPI instruction shall be used, unless the court determines that it does not accurately state the law." *See also* Illinois Supreme Court Rules of Criminal Proceedings in the Trial Court, Rule 451 (providing similarly).

[5] *See, e.g., Mora v. Phoenix Indem. Ins. Co.*, 996 P.2d 116, 120 n.4 (Ariz. App. 1999) (citing to instructions to support proposition and noting that while the Revised Arizona Jury Instructions are not law, "they reflect the practicing bar's understanding of the current state of the law"). California Rule of Court 2.1050, "Judicial Council Jury Instructions," provides that the CACI instructions are the official instructions for use in the state and "strongly encourage[s]" the use of appropriate CACI instructions, but they are not mandatory. The New York Pattern Civil and Criminal Instructions are not mandatory, *see* N.Y. Pattern Jury Instructions, Civil, Second Edition (2011 ed.), at xix, but are commonly given. In Washington, the Civil Rules specifically address how pattern instructions should be cited to the trial courts, but do not mandate that the pattern instructions be given. As the Co-Chairs of Instruction Committee carefully point out in the preface to the 5th edition of the Washington Pattern Jury Instructions, Civil, "While often commending the committee's work to the bench and bar, the [Washington Supreme Court] does not review the instructions in advance of its consideration of them in cases before it on appeal."

- Parties are not entitled to argumentative instructions.[6] Argumentative instructions include instructions that, although proper in themselves, overemphasize one party's position.

- Judges usually disfavor putting quoted passages from legal opinions into instructions because the passages are either too complex or too argumentative.[7] Use care in quoting

---

[6] *See, e.g., Stephens v. State*, 176 P. 579, 581 (Ariz. 1918) (stating that giving of argumentative instruction is error). The *Stephens* court described an argumentative instruction as one that "directs the attention of the jury especially to certain portions of the evidence, and suggests to them certain inferences of fact to be drawn therefrom—thus singling out for their consideration particular facts favorable to the defendant, and ignoring, by failing to particularize, other evidence having a contrary tendency." *Id.; People v. Earp*, 978 P.2d 15, 54 (Cal. 1999) (proposed instruction that "invite[s] the jury to draw inferences favorable to one of the parties from specified items of evidence" was argumentative and "therefore should not be given"); *Major v. Western Home Ins. Co.*, 87 Cal. Rptr. 3d 556, 573–74 (Cal. App. 2009) (instructions should not amount to an argument to the jury); *see also* California Rule of Court 2.1050(e) (stating that any instructions not taken from the judicial council model instructions "should be accurate, brief, understandable, impartial, and free from argument"); *Sierra v. Winn Dixie Stores, Inc.*, 646 So.2d 264 (Fla. App. 1994) (rejecting instruction which tended "to endorse an argumentative position of the defendant" and which was otherwise unnecessary); *Lauman v. Vandalia Bus Lines, Inc.*, 681 N.E.2d 1055, 1062 (Ill. App. 1997) ("In Illinois, jury instructions must be 'simple, brief, impartial, and free from argument.' 134 Ill.2d R. 239(a). Argumentative instructions are unacceptable because they are not fair and impartial statements of the law but are adversarial statements highlighting favorable and unfavorable evidence with partisan overtones."); *Watson v. Hockett*, 727 P.2d 669, 673 (Wash. 1986) (stating that courts should "avoid slanted or argumentative instructions. A jury instruction should be a statement of the law only.").
 As noted above, in New York, a trial court is required to state the fundamental legal principles and give a balanced charge, not necessarily instruct on each party's theory of the case. *See People v. Croskery*, 695 N.Y.S.2d 788 (N.Y. App. Div. 1999).

[7] For example, the Arizona Supreme Court has noted, "Words used in an opinion discussing legal principles are not necessarily the best words to be used in instructing the jury. Jury instructions are better when framed in clear, comprehensible, everyday English." *Petefish by and through Clancy v. Dawe*, 672

from statutes, as well, although judges usually accept quoting from statutes more than quoting from cases.[8] The language you quote should be clear and not misleading.

P.2d 914, 921 n.6 (Ariz. 1983); *see also Merlo v. Standard Life & Acc. Ins. Co.*, 130 Cal. Rptr. 416, 424 (Cal. App. 1976) (stating that judicial opinions are unreliable in providing language for jury instructions); *Bankers Multiple Line Ins. Co. v. Farish*, 464 So.2d 530, 533 & n.3 (Fla. 1985) (criticizing instruction language taken from prior opinion); *Kingston v. Turner*, 505 N.E.2d 320, 326 (Ill. 1987) ("The practice of lifting sentences from court opinions and converting them into instructions . . . is not a good one, as it often leads to serious error."), quoting *De Rosa v. Albert F. Amling Co.*, 404 N.E.2d 564, 573 (Ill. App. 1980); *Stryzinski v. Arnold*, 141 N.Y.S.2d 11, 14 (N.Y. App. 1955) (discussing difficulty of using words taken directly from decision to frame instruction); *Anfinson v. FedEx Ground Package System, Inc.*, 244 P.3d 32, 37 (Wash. App. 2010) (noting that "[t]he fact that a proposed jury instruction includes language used by a court in the course of an opinion does not necessarily make it a proper jury instruction."); *Turner v. City of Tacoma*, 435 P.2d 927, 930 (Wash. 1967) (describing instruction as reading like a jury argument, and stating "[t]hat we may have used certain language in an opinion does not mean that it can be properly incorporated into a jury instruction").

[8] *See, e.g.*, *State v. Maloney*, 416 P.2d 544 (Ariz. 1966) (stating that better practice would be not to instruct in language of statute, which was somewhat ambiguous); *California v. Estrada*, 904 P.2d 1197, 1200 (Cal. 1995) (stating that if the statutory language can be understood without further guidance, the court can instruct in the statutory language, but an additional instruction may be required if a word or phrase is used in a technical legal sense that differs from its ordinary meaning). In the civil context, the California Supreme Court has similarly explained that an instruction in the language of the statute is acceptable if the language is clear, but is not sufficient if reasonable people could disagree on the proper construction of the statute. *Torres v. Parkhouse Tire Serv., Inc.*, 30 P.3d 57, 61 (Cal. 2001). In Illinois, "it is well established that jury instructions may quote portions of statutes and ordinances" where supported by evidence and relevant to the claims. *Mayol v. Summers, Watson & Kimpel*, 585 N.E.2d 1176, 1186 (Ill. App. 1992). Florida courts have recognized that an instruction taken directly from a statute "is not necessarily erroneous," so long as it is justified by the evidence, pertinent, confined to the issues of the case, and not misleading. *Brown v. State*, 11 So.3d 428, 433 (Fla. App. 2009), quoting *Ruskin v. Travelers Ins. Co.*, 125 So.2d 766, 769 (Fla. App. 1960). In Washington, an instruction incorporating the words of a statute is "appropriate only if the statute is applicable, reasonably clear, and

IMPLEMENTATION

Pattern instructions address boilerplate topics as well as substantive topics such as breach of contract, tort causes of action, and each criminal offense. Here are the titles to the model or pattern instructions in the jurisdictions frequently referenced in this book:

- Arizona: Revised Arizona Jury Instructions (RAJI (Criminal) 3rd)[9] and Revised Arizona Jury Instructions (RAJI (Civil) 4th)[10]

- California: Judicial Council of California Civil Jury Instructions (CACI)[11]

- Judicial Council of California Criminal Jury Instructions (CALCRIM)[12]

- Florida: Florida Standard Jury Instructions,[13] which provides links to both civil and criminal instructions

- Illinois: Illinois Pattern Jury Instructions—Civil[14]

- Illinois Pattern Jury Instructions—Criminal[15]

- New York: New York Pattern Jury Instructions—Civil[16]

---

not misleading." *Barrett v. Lucky Seven Saloon, Inc.*, 96 P.3d 386, 389 (Wash 2004) (citation omitted).

[9] http://www.azbar.org/SectionsandCommittees/committees/criminaljuryinstructions

[10] http://www.azbar.org/SectionsandCommittees/committees/civiljuryinstructions

[11] http://www.courts.ca.gov/partners/documents/caci_2013_edition.pdf

[12] http://www.courts.ca.gov/partners/documents/calcrim_juryins.pdf

[13] http://www.floridasupremecourt.org/jury_instructions.shtml

[14] http://www.state.il.us/court/CircuitCourt/CivilJuryInstructions/default.asp

[15] http://www.state.il.us/court/circuitcourt/CriminalJuryInstructions/default.asp

[16] Published by Thomson West Reuters.

- New York State Unified Court System Criminal Jury Instructions 2d[17]

- Washington: Washington Pattern Instructions[18]

- Federal: Run the words "jury instructions" and the name of the jurisdiction you are interested in through your favorite search engine.

You can often find pattern instructions in other states through a simple Web search, although in some states, the pattern instructions are only available through proprietary sources.

Chances are, these pattern instructions will cover any topic you need to address. They are also a good place to start on any research project having to do with your case. How can you argue a summary judgment motion, for example, without knowing what elements must be proven at trial? Pattern instructions are the quickest and easiest way to determine those elements.[19] You should, of course, always double-check pattern instructions to make sure they accurately state the law and continue to comply with recent decisions and statutory changes.

Trial judges are well aware that instructional error is one of the most common reasons they get reversed. Nothing feels safer to a trial judge than a pattern instruction. If you are going to propose a non-pattern instruction, explain why it is necessary for a fair trial, and how the law supports it.

If you are in a jurisdiction with no pattern instructions, or no pattern instruction on a needed topic, go to a nearby jurisdiction with law similar to yours. Why reinvent the wheel? Someone else has already struggled with the task of converting a legal

---

[17] http://www.nycourts.gov/cji/

[18] Can currently be found at http://government.westlaw.com/linkedslice/default.asp?SP=WCCJI-1000. This website is maintained by Thomson West under contract with the Washington Supreme Court Committee on Jury Instructions to provide free public access to the Washington Pattern Jury Instructions for use in the practice of law and legal research.

[19] Most pattern instructions cite the leading cases or statutes in the jurisdiction supporting the instruction.

principle into plain, understandable language. Take advantage of their work; that's what it's there for. Just be careful that the law is indeed sufficiently similar, and modify the instruction to account for any differences that do exist.

Cite to the court the authorities supporting any instruction you propose. This can be as simple as citing the pattern instruction your instruction is based upon, or as detailed as listing quotations from cases explaining why the instruction is required. Complex cases may warrant a brief in support of your instructions.

If you have to draft your own instruction, be careful not to make it argumentative. The temptation can be almost irresistible. From the judge's perspective, an argumentative instruction is unfair, even unprofessional. Given a choice between your argumentative instruction that accurately states the law, and your opponent's neutral-sounding instruction that inaccurately states the law, there is a good chance the judge will chose your opponent's.

Some judges will ask the parties to prepare an instruction briefly summarizing the claims and defenses in the case. This is sometimes called a *statement of the case* or *summary of the case* instruction. There are no patterns or models that will help you here. The judge is looking for something to read to the prospective jurors before jury selection begins to tell them generally what the case is about. Here is a statement of the case instruction to give you an idea what they look like:

> John Smith is the plaintiff in this case. He entered into a contract to purchase a 1999 Jaguar sports car from the defendant, Acme Motors. The parties agree that the contract required the Jaguar to be delivered by May 19, 2013.
>
> Mr. Smith claims the contract was breached because Acme delivered the Jaguar on June 25, 2013, and because the car lacked seat belts, making it unsafe. As a result, he claims to have suffered a loss of $1,000 due to having to rent a car between May 19 and June 25, and another $2,000 from having to pay to have seat belts installed.

> Acme admits it delivered the car on June 25, 2013, but denies that Mr. Smith suffered any damages as a result of late delivery. It also denies that the contract required it to provide a car with seat belts.
>
> Acme has a claim of its own, called a "counterclaim," for $4,000 it says Mr. Smith still owes it under the contract.

Your opponent will submit proposed jury instructions. It is a good idea to file written objections to those you oppose, whether the judge requires written objections or not. These written objections will focus your thoughts on the precise reasons each instruction is unsound. The judge, or her clerk, may read your objections and be persuaded. The written objections will also give you a good outline for your oral argument at the instruction conference.

Note that in most courthouses, giving the judge a pleading or document is not the same as *filing* that pleading or document. For the document to be *filed,* and therefore part of the record on appeal, you must give it to the court clerk, and the clerk must file-stamp it. You may still give the judge her own copy of a document you have filed or intend to file (sometimes called a *bench copy*); just don't forget to file with the clerk as well.

In some jurisdictions, cases are assigned to trial judges shortly before trial begins. Your jury instructions may be the first impression the judge forms of you and your case. Did you think through your instructions, organize them, and present them professionally? Or are they filled with misspellings, formatting errors, and lacking citations? Who can the judge rely upon to make her job easier?

Judges usually hold an instruction conference toward the end of the trial to discuss jury instructions with the attorneys.[20] This is part of the judge's decision-making process to determine which instructions to actually use. With some judges, this is a very informal, off-the-record exchange. The judge allows attorneys to put their formal objections to instructions on the record later. Other

---

[20] See chapter 15.

judges conduct a formal hearing similar to any oral argument. Either way, be prepared to argue in support of your own instructions and against the infirm instructions offered by your opponent.

Questions to Ask

Frequently, the judge has a standing order that answers some or all of the questions below. If there is no standing order, there is usually at least one person, besides the judge, who can answer these questions. That person might be the judge's secretary, law clerk, or bailiff. Call or stop by the courthouse and simply ask the judge's secretary who would be the best person to ask these questions. If all else fails, ask them of the judge when you appear before her. Judges and court personnel understand that a lawyer asking these questions is trying to get things right—which makes things easier on court personnel.

- Does the judge have a standing order addressing how she would like jury instructions presented?

- Does the judge have a standard set of instructions she likes to give the jury in every case?

- In what format would the judge like the proposed instructions to appear? (Type size? Citations to authority at the top or bottom? Numbered or unnumbered?)

- Would she like an electronic copy as well? If so, in what format?

- When would she like you to submit the proposed instructions?

- Does the judge hold formal or informal jury instruction conferences to decide which instructions to give the jury?

- Does the judge give any substantive jury instructions before opening statements?

- Does the judge give jury instructions before or after closing arguments?

Suggested Reading

All the annotations, notes, or commentary to the pattern or model instructions that you or your opponent cite.

3

INVESTIGATION

At the most basic level, a trial is a series of witnesses sitting in a chair and telling jurors "this is what I saw," "this is what I heard," or "this is what I did." In a case with expert witnesses, jurors might also hear "this is what it means." These are the building blocks of the coherent story and argument you are trying to put together. Along with jury instructions, these witnesses should be the center of your trial lawyer universe. This is not meant to denigrate the importance of documents and photographs, but using them effectively at trial usually requires a witness's involvement.

How to find witnesses, and documents to support or attack them, is beyond the scope of this book. This chapter is titled "investigation" to emphasize the point that the quality of the pretrial investigation has an enormous impact on the quality of your trial presentation. Lack of attention to finding and working with witnesses is a major failing in many otherwise excellent trial lawyers.

How you work with witnesses once you find them is also crucially important, and *not* beyond the scope of this book. Once you find witnesses, you have to talk to them—sometimes for twenty minutes, sometimes for hours. That is the only way to determine whom you should call for trial—and what you should ask them. Once you have decided whom to call, you need to spend more time to help them prepare for deposition and trial.

Spending more time with witnesses—including clients—is probably the single most important thing *any* trial lawyer can do to improve his or her performance in the courtroom. Yet it is difficult. Everything about our practices conspires to keep us from spending the time we need with our witnesses. As a result, almost every lawyer is deficient in this area.

The deficiency is understandable and human. If we don't respond to discovery requests on time, opposing counsel will punish us. If we don't respond to motions or pretrial deadlines on time, the judge will punish us. If we don't appear for status conferences or oral arguments, the judge will punish us again. If we don't respond to our employees' concerns in a timely manner, they will punish us. If we don't pay our bills on time, our creditors will punish us.

Yet, if we fail to spend the time we need with witnesses, no one punishes us—at least not immediately. With no one breathing down our neck to interview witnesses, it is easy to put this task low on the list of priorities. But when you step into the courtroom, you are totally dependent on your witnesses, your knowledge of what they can say, and how well they can say it.

Witnesses may have helpful or harmful things to say. Shouldn't you know these things before the trial starts? Walking into court without learning everything each available witness has to say is like walking into a boxing match with one eye taped shut.

Working with Witnesses

Here are some ideas to keep in mind as you investigate your case and work with the witnesses.

Interview All Important Witnesses Before the Case Is Filed

Of course, you won't always be able to do this, but it is an important aspiration. The closer you come to this goal, the better you will handle the case. Early interviews will help you recognize weak points in your case, frame the issues and causes of action, and focus your discovery. Prefiling interviews may even reveal this is not a case you wish to be involved in at all.

Form Relationships with Witnesses

You don't need to become their new best friend, but you should impart a sense that you are reliable and will treat them with respect. The two of you are going to be going through a unique experience together. Even for experienced witnesses and lawyers, every case is different and unique. The witness needs your help in understanding an unfamiliar and sometimes frightening process. You need her to show up for interviews, depositions, and trial.

A relationship with the witness means you treat her like a fellow human being and gain some understanding of how she views the world and her place in it. This will help her become a more effective witness.

Spend Time with Your Witnesses

Try not to be in a rush. Force yourself to slow down, and try to ignore all the deadlines crowding in on you. The more time you spend with your witness, the more you will each learn, and the better you will each do in court.

Tell the Witness How She Fits into the Case

You know (or think you know) the whole case and how the pieces fit together. However, each witness sees only a small piece of the case. Unless you tell her, she will have no idea how she fits into the larger whole. We are all uncomfortable if we feel out of context. When an inexperienced witness comes into the courtroom, for her it is like coming into a classroom for the first time, halfway through the third lesson.

If the witness has an overview of the case and feels respected, the chances of her willing participation increase. In addition, a witness who knows something about the big picture may make connections or volunteer information you would have never found without her help.

Ask Open-Ended Questions

One mistake most lawyers make is to be goal-driven when interviewing a witness. They have a preconceived idea of how the witness fits into the case, and try to extract the facts the witness has as quickly and efficiently as possible—before moving on to the next legal task. By approaching the interview this way, lawyers often miss key facts the witness knows.

Instead, try questions like:

- What stands out most in your mind about the accident? The situation? The drivers?

- Who knows more about this than you do? Was anyone else around?

- How did it feel to witness this?

- If I wanted to have a picture in my mind about what happened, what would help me the most?

- What do you think are the most important things for a jury to know about this situation?

Obviously, you will want to follow up and ask for specific details, but you will be amazed at the things you will learn by asking questions that invite the witness to express what she considers important.

Invite witnesses to tell you the "bad stuff" about your client or the facts. You might even ask: "What is the worst thing you can tell me about my client?" Or "Do you think he did the right thing in filing this lawsuit?" Better to hear it first outside of court than during a deposition or trial.

Spend More Than One Session with the Witness

After your first interview, go back and spend some more time with the witness. This might be before he or she is deposed, and again before trial. Every time you meet with the witness, you strengthen your relationship. Chances are, you will learn more facts each time as well. That's just the way human nature works.

Go to Different Locations to Meet the Witness

Depending on the case and the importance of the witness, consider going to different locations to meet with the witness. Think about meeting her at her office, her home, a coffee shop, or the scene of the accident. Each location may bring out different memories or responses from the witness. Yes, you can also meet at your office, but with many witnesses, the responses you get will not be as revealing as they would be at other locations.

Remember That Your Client Is Often a Witness

You won't forget this of course, but you might overlook it. Our conversations with a client or client representative often focus on procedural updates and discussions of litigation tactics and strategy. It is easy to assume that the client has told you everything important that he knows, while the client assumes that if it was important, you would ask. Set aside time to talk to the client as a witness, following all of the above recommendations.

Don't Ignore Adverse or Potentially Hostile Witnesses

Don't just interview "friendly" witnesses. Make the effort to interview witnesses you think may be neutral or even hostile to your case. They may not be as hostile as you suppose; and even hostile witnesses may disclose helpful information. If the witness refuses to talk to you, just bringing out that fact in the courtroom may be useful in itself to demonstrate bias on the witness's part.

Of course, you cannot interview the opposing party or its managing agents or employees. Most states, including all of the states focused on in this book, except California, have adopted professional ethical rules based on the *ABA Model Rules of Professional Conduct.*[1]

A common issue is whether a particular employee of a corporation or government agency is represented by the entity's lawyer. Different states answer this question differently, and even those

---

[1] In California, see California R. Prof. Conduct 2-100.

states that use similar language (referring to "managerial responsibility" or "control group") may differ from each other when they apply this language to particular facts. Answering this question for any specific jurisdiction is beyond the scope of this book, so check your local rules, ethics opinions, and case law.

In interviewing any third-party witness, also be familiar with your local rule on dealing with unrepresented persons.

Some lawyers refuse to meet with witnesses—especially potentially adverse or hostile witnesses. These lawyers claim they are afraid of becoming witnesses themselves and therefore becoming disqualified from trying the case. A simplistic fact pattern can illustrate the problem and its easy solutions.

Problem: You are defending a man accused of rape. You meet with the victim's sister, who confirms your client's story that earlier in the evening of the alleged attack, the three of them were at a bar together and the victim was flirting with your client.

At a later date, perhaps from the witness stand, the victim's sister not only denies any flirtation, but also says you tried to get her to lie about this issue.

Solutions: If you think there is any risk that a witness will change her story, try one or more of the following approaches:

- Have a paralegal or investigator go with you to the interview. That person can then be a witness for you if a dispute occurs about who said what.

- If you think the witness will allow it, ask to record the interview.

- If you don't ask to record the interview, ask the witness if she would be willing to write out and sign a statement regarding the most crucial facts—or sign a statement you will bring to her the following day.

- Send an investigator or paralegal to conduct the interview and write you a memo recounting the conversation.

Your fear of becoming a witness *never* justifies failure to contact a witness who may testify at trial.

Of course, when dealing with an adverse or third-party witness, remember the applicable ethical rules.[2] These include:

- The duty of fairness to the opposing party and counsel[3]
- The requirement of truthfulness in statements to others[4]
- The restrictions on communicating with people represented by counsel, either individually or in the course of their job duties[5]
- The requirements for dealing with unrepresented people[6]
- The duty to show respect for others and "not use means that have no substantial purpose other than to embarrass, delay, or burden" another person, or violate his or her rights[7]
- The duty not to falsely impugn the qualifications or integrity of a judge[8]

Obviously, this is not a book on ethics, but ethical behavior is not only our obligation as lawyers, it is essential to good trial advocacy.

When all is said and done, the witnesses are the essence of your case. Give them the time and attention they deserve, and you will be paid back many times over. Treat them as an afterthought, and you will suffer.

---

[2] In California, Rule of Professional Conduct 5-310 directly addresses contact between a lawyer and a witness.

[3] ABA Model Rule 3.4; Cal. R. Prof. Conduct 5-220, 5-310; Cal. Civil Code § 6068(d) (general duty to be truthful).

[4] ABA Model Rule 4.1; Cal. Civil Code § 6068(d).

[5] ABA Model Rule 4.2; Cal. R. Prof. Conduct 2-100.

[6] ABA Model Rule 4.3.

[7] ABA Model Rule 4.4.

[8] ABA Model Rule 8.2; Cal. Civil Code § 6068(b).

Suggested Reading

Barton, William A. *Recovering for Psychological Injuries.* 3rd ed. Portland, OR: Trial Guides and the American Association for Justice Press, 2010.

Friedman, Rick. *Rick Friedman on Becoming a Trial Lawyer.* Portland, OR: Trial Guides, 2008.

Pozner, Larry, and Roger Dodd. *Cross-Examination: Science and Techniques.* 2nd ed. New York: LexisNexis, 2004.

Spence, Gerry. *Win Your Case: How to Present, Persuade, and Prevail—Every Place, Every Time.* New York: St. Martin's Griffin, 2006. See especially chapter 9, "Discover the Story," and chapter 10, "Discovering the Story through Psychodrama."

4

FIGHTING CHAOS

Your most fearsome trial adversary is not your opponent, it is lack of organization. Even in simple cases, there is a lot to keep track of: exhibits, pretrial orders, motion *in limine* rulings, jury instructions, witness statements, and more. The ability to find the right document at the right time—which usually means immediately—is critical. It would be false to say that in trial, organization is everything. But it is true that without good organization, nothing else will go well.

Over time, you will develop a system of organization best suited to your personal style and the types of cases you try. Below is an easy system to get you started. It is the product of stealing ideas from scores of trial lawyers over the years.

ORGANIZE FOR TRIAL FROM THE BEGINNING

As soon as you begin the case, start organizing for trial. As documents come into your possession, put them where you will want them during trial. In other words, have one organizational system—a trial system—that you use for your case from beginning to end.

If you fail to do this, there will come a time when you must transition from your original filing system to your trial filing system. This transition will not come at a convenient time. It will likely come as you and your staff are trying to draft and respond to motions *in limine,* issue trial subpoenas, draft jury instructions, engage in last-minute settlement discussions, reinterview witnesses, prepare opening statement, prepare notes for direct examination of witnesses, attend pretrial hearings and arguments, and get your suits cleaned.

Then there is the risk that exists in any transition—whenever it occurs—of documents being lost or misfiled.

Another benefit of having a trial-oriented filing system from day one is that you will always be thinking about your case like a trial lawyer. The end result—presenting your evidence to a judge or jury—will be woven into the fabric of your activities and thinking on the case.

Use a Notebook System

"Notebook system" does not mean you must use paper or ignore electronic organization systems. In this context, "notebook" means a separate file—paper or electronic. If using an electronic system, try to mimic the paper notebook system described below, as best you can. Remember, even if you have a simple and efficient electronic system, you will still need a paper copy of exhibits to introduce into evidence—at least for the next several years. This means you need a way to organize your paper exhibits. Simple three-ring notebooks are the easiest way to work with paper in court.

Three-ring notebooks are easier than files to move in and out of the courtroom. They are easier to handle at counsel table or when examining a witness. And when you drop them—and you *will* drop them—they are more likely to keep your documents safely in order than other systems. Another advantage of a notebook system is that a staff member or fellow lawyer is less likely to take a page out and fail to return it.

Whether you prefer paper or electronic, the main point is that you must develop a system for organizing all of your material in a trial-centric way—and then develop the discipline to *always* use it.

In some cases, the material for an entire trial can be contained in one notebook. In others, the material on a single witness may fill fifteen four-inch notebooks. But the basic system remains the same for any case.

Here are the major categories of information you will be filing. In a large case, each category of information will have one or more notebooks devoted to that category, with subcategories separated by divider tabs. In a small case, all categories may be in one notebook, with each category separated by divider tabs. For illustrative purposes, let's look at the organization of a medium-size case, one that could be tried in one or two weeks.

You will have approximately seven types of notebooks:

1. Pleadings books

2. Discovery books

3. Witness books

4. Unique discovery books

5. Research books

6. Trial brief books

7. Exhibit books

Again, in a simple case, these might be tabs in a single book rather than separate books.

Pleadings Books

Starting with the complaint, put the pleadings in a notebook with *Pleadings Book 1* written on the spine. Place the oldest document—usually the complaint—at the front, with a tab labeled *1*. The next pleading goes right behind that, with a tab labeled *2*. When the first pleadings notebook is full, put the next pleading at the beginning of *Pleadings Book 2*.

In the front of each pleadings book, create a table of contents that looks like this:

Pleadings Book 1

Complaint
    4/17/13 1

Motion to dismiss
    6/1/13 2

Opposition to Mtn. to Dismiss
    6/15/13 3

Reply to Mtn. to Dismiss
    8/15/13 4

Order Denying Mtn. to Dismiss
    9/15/13 5

Answer
    9/30/13 6

As you read the pleadings that come in, keep alert for documents that you might wish to use at trial to cross-examine witnesses—or that the other side might use to cross-examine your witnesses. If an affidavit is attached to a search warrant or a motion, make an additional copy and file it behind that witness's tab in the witness book (see below). The same is true if a letter or report that a potential witness has written is attached to a pleading.

Discovery Books

As discovery comes in, it will be organized very much like pleadings. A table of contents for a discovery book might look like this:

Plaintiff's 1st Interrog. to Def.
    8/1/13 1

Plaintiff's 1st RFP[1] to Def.
    8/10/13 2

---

[1] RFP stands for "request for production."

Def's Resp. to 1st Interrog.
   10/14/13 3

Def's Resp. to 1st RFP
   10/14/13 4

In a criminal case, the discovery book table of contents might look like this:

1st Set of Police Reports
   Produced 8/1/13 1

Supplemental Police Repts.
   Produced 11/10/13 2

State's Expert Report of Dr. Smith
   Produced 12/12/13 3

The expert report would also go into the witness book for that witness. The same is true for any statements in the police reports—make copies of those statements and place them in the witness book for those witnesses. Similarly, if a witness signed interrogatory answers, those answers also belong in that witness's witness notebook.

This may seem like needless duplication and a shameless waste of paper, but it is not. This organization system simply reflects the reality that a single document may have multiple roles in litigation.

Let's take the example of a letter produced in discovery and attached to a summary judgment motion. When working on the summary judgment motion, you need to know what evidence has been submitted to the court to support or oppose that motion. Months after the court decides the motion, you may need to determine what the court had before it when it ruled on the motion. You must maintain the pleadings notebook's integrity; that letter must stay in the pleadings notebook.

Similarly, it may be important to know when that letter was produced in discovery. You never know when that could become an issue—maybe even during trial. You must keep the integrity of the discovery notebook intact. If you take pieces out of this notebook, it will be next to impossible to re-create who produced what, or when.

But you are a trial lawyer. You are preparing for trial from day one. When you first see that letter, you know there is a chance you or your opponent will be questioning the witness about it at trial. If you don't make a copy now, and place it in the witness notebook, there is a very good chance you will overlook it when you prepare to handle that witness at deposition or at trial.

Witness Books

Organize witness notebooks in alphabetical order. Create a tab for John Adams, then one for David Atkins. Depending on the amount of material you have, you can subdivide each witness's section by tabs such as *Interview Notes, Letters* (written by or to the witness), or *Deposition*.

Create a witness section for any person who could possibly be a witness at trial. Even witnesses who are not called at trial can be important during the course of litigation. You will be grateful that you have all material related to each witness in an easy-to-find location. And, of course, trials are full of surprises. The unimportant witness may suddenly loom large at trial. Again, you will be grateful you have all the material related to this "unimportant" witness collected in one place.

File depositions in the witness books, not in the discovery books.

If the witness testified at grand jury or in a prior trial, file transcripts of this testimony in the witness's section of your witness book.

After you take or attend a deposition, take ten minutes to dictate or write a quick memo summarizing your impressions of the witness and the key points she covered. Put that in your witness notebook as well.

Unique Discovery Books

It is not uncommon to have a large paper record that is too unwieldy to put into discovery books or witness books. For example, in a personal injury case, the medical records may come from dozens of doctors and amount to hundreds or even thousands of pages. In an insurance bad faith case, the defense may produce a five-thousand-page claim file. In a products liability case, the defense may produce ten thousand pages of testing results in discovery, but less than one hundred pages are likely to be relevant. Keep such massive files in their own set of notebooks. If the pages of these files have not already been numbered, you should do so.[2] As you review this material, take notes on a separate page as to which pages are relevant to which witnesses, and simply put those notes in the witness's section of the witness notebook.

Research Books

In some cases, you will be doing extensive research on a particular subject. Perhaps you will have medical articles on diabetes, engineering articles on metal failure, or forensic articles on gunshot analysis. Whatever the subject matter, you need to keep this unique, specialized knowledge organized separately, in a way that makes sense to you. You can label the notebook *Diabetes Research* or something similar.

Likewise, your case may involve complex legal principles, requiring quick and easy access to cases, statutes, or regulations. You can label your notebook *Legal Research,* or even have different notebooks for different legal topics.

Trial Brief Books

Immediately before and during trial, you are almost certain to refer to particular pleadings. These belong in what can be called the *Trial Brief Book*. Make yourself one or more notebooks to contain these categories of documents:

- Court's pretrial order
- Any court orders you may need to argue about at trial

---

[2] The numbering of documents produced in discovery is commonly known as *Bates numbering* or *Bates stamping* in reference to an automatic numbering stamp invented over a hundred years ago. Now, numbering is usually computerized and includes the option of placing identifying words or letters before the numbers. The claim file pages received from Acme Insurance, for example, could be numbered "Acme-1," "Acme-2," and so on.

- Motions *in limine* and resulting orders
- Jury instructions proposed (or to be proposed) by each side
- Leading authorities supporting your jury instructions or that you will use to attack the other side's instructions
- Trial brief
- Each party's exhibit list
- An outline of the bases to challenge potential jurors for cause in your jurisdiction, and the authority supporting those challenges
- Any standing order of the court or local rules that may be relevant during your trial[3]

At times, all of this material will not fill even a two-inch-thick notebook. At other times, it will fill six four-inch notebooks. The important point is that it is all organized together in a system that makes sense to you.

Exhibit Books

Exhibits are the documents, photographs, videos, and tangible objects you want the jury to look at during the trial. It is easy to describe what your exhibit books should ideally look like as you go into trial: each exhibit should be in a notebook, with the chronologically oldest exhibit marked as Exhibit 1, and the most recent marked as your last exhibit.

Thus, ideally, the table of contents section of your exhibit book would look something like this:

Ex. 1 . . . . . Letter from R. Smith to D. Jones 4/6/09

Ex. 2 . . . . . FAA report 4/23/09

---

[3] Many courts have standing orders or local rules that differ from the Civil Rules and Rules of Evidence. These are a trap for the unwary. Always read the local rules and ask the court personnel for any standing orders from your judge before heading to trial. If relevant, put copies in your trial brief book.

Ex. 3 . . . . . Police photos taken on 1/24/10

* * *

Ex. 115 . . . . . Letter from S. Smith to D. Ogg 6/23/12

Ex. 116 . . . . . Letter from D. Jones to D. Ogg 7/1/12

Keeping documents and exhibits in chronological order is by far the easiest and most efficient method of organization. The human brain is wired to put facts into chronological order. Give a person a set of facts about an event without telling her the order in which they occurred, and her first questions will be about chronological order. What happened first? What happened next? This is how we make sense of things.

Because of this, the chances are that you will be presenting your case story and supporting evidence along chronological lines.

A trial lawyer is constantly searching for context. When did this occur? How does it relate to the other events that occurred before and after? A trial lawyer is also constantly searching for documents. An opposing witness just referred to a conversation that occurred between Dave Ogg and Sally Smith in June of 2012. I know there is a letter between these two witnesses around that time; how do I find it? If you organized your documents and exhibits chronologically, it is easy. If you didn't, it may be difficult, even impossible.

Some documents will not lend themselves to chronological order. In a medical malpractice case, for example, it might be too confusing to try to separate each medical record into an individual exhibit. You might want all of Dr. Smith's records in one place, as one exhibit. There is nothing wrong with that, as long as the system makes sense to you and your staff.

The exhibit book is the one book that does not lend itself to preparation during the course of litigation. This is because new documents will be coming in throughout the case. If you chronologically order your original documents, you will have to reorganize and renumber every time you discover new documents. In addition, documents that at first appeared critical may lose their relevance as the case progresses, and you will need to remove them.

Here are suggested steps for preparing your exhibit books.

1. As documents come to your attention as being possible exhibits, put copies in an exhibit book, with a tab separating each one. Do this throughout the litigation.

2. As you near trial, copy all documents from discovery, all documents attached as exhibits to depositions, and all exhibits from pretrial hearings. Put the copies in your exhibit book if they are not already there.

3. You should now have the universe of potentially relevant exhibits. Put them in chronological order, with a tab separating each one. *Do not mark them yet.*

4. Read through the exhibits in chronological order. As you read through the exhibits, do three things:

   a. Pull out any exhibits you are certain you will not want to use at trial.

   b. Mark the remaining, chronologically ordered exhibits as required by your court.[4]

   c. Make notes in your computer or hard-copy files as to which exhibits you may want to discuss with each witness. For example, for witness Dr. J. Smith, you might have an entry that reads: "Exhibits 2, 17, 54, and 78." When you begin your preparation for Dr. Smith's examination, you will immediately know which exhibits to review.

Most courts leave the order of exhibits up to the attorneys. Some, however, have orders that require exhibits to be marked in the order in which they will be introduced at trial. If you have more than thirty exhibits, ask the court for permission to mark them in chronological order instead. Explain that with the

---

[4] Courts commonly require that prosecution or plaintiff exhibits be marked numerically, "1– . . ." and the defense exhibits alphabetically, "A–Z, AA, BB, etc." But this is by no means universal. Ask the court clerk how the judge prefers exhibits to be marked.

volume of exhibits, it is difficult to know which order you will introduce them in, and it will be easier for everyone to keep track of them if they are in chronological order. Most judges, if you ask, will allow you to mark exhibits in chronological order, even in the face of a standing order to the contrary. It is worth the trouble to get the permission.

Different Colored Spines

Each type of notebook should have a different colored spine. All pleadings notebooks, for example, might have light blue spines; all witness books might have red spines. This makes them easier to keep track of in the office, but more importantly, easier to quickly find the right book in the heat of trial.

Discipline

This system is flexible enough to work in any case. Don't be afraid to modify it to take into account your own working style or the particularities of your case. But whatever form of organization you adopt, that system must be followed *without fail* by *everyone who touches the file.*

In the modern law office, it is common for many people to work on a file. *They all must follow the same system, without fail,* or chaos will result.

Staff members, once they know the system, are happy to follow it. Most often, the problems arise when a lawyer thinks that just this once, he can make an exception and take a document out of a book without copying it and replacing it. Or, he simply gets distracted and forgets to put a key letter his client just showed him into the witness book.

Any case or trial organizational system requires discipline from all participants. At first, the discipline may feel onerous, even counterproductive. In fact, this discipline will pay huge dividends before and during trial.

Create a Timeline

List every date and time involved in your case, and annotate with the exhibits, documents, depositions, police reports, or witness statements that support each entry. When you list all important dates and times, it is almost certain that new ideas will occur to you. Take the timeline to court with you. It will be one of your most important references.

One-Page Trial Summary

Some lawyers find it helpful to create a one-page summary consisting of the elements that each side must prove and the witness and documents they will use to address each element. This list is like a pilot's checklist. It ensures you will not forget something in the heat of battle. It is surprising how often you might overlook a "minor" element because it is not hotly contested. It is also common for a witness to be excused from the witness stand without having addressed an important issue, simply because a lawyer forgot to ask about it. A one-page summary can help you avoid these mistakes.

Questions to Ask

Ask the court clerk:

- How does the judge prefer exhibits be marked?
- Will the judge want his own bench copy of exhibits in addition to the original exhibits that will be admitted?
- Once the exhibit is admitted into evidence, will the clerk hold the original exhibit throughout the rest of the trial, or are the lawyers expected to do that?

5

Assessing Your Case-in-Chief

Someone has to go first. If you are the prosecutor or the plaintiff's lawyer, it's you. You have to try to prove something. The witnesses and other evidence you intend to present to the jury is your *case-in-chief*.

The defense is not required to have a case-in-chief; it can win by presenting no evidence and arguing the opposition failed to prove its case. If the defense decides to present evidence, that evidence—all of it—is considered the defense case-in-chief.

As you approach trial, step back from the individual pieces of your case and look at the whole picture. By this time, you have completed discovery (or the end is in sight). You have identified all possible witnesses you could use, and every document even arguably relevant to the action. You have done your research and know every possible legal theory you might employ. It is time to decide what your case will look like at trial. Here are some things to think about as you consider your case-in-chief.

When writing a law school exam, there is no penalty for including too many issues. Writing about every issue you can think of means you are more likely to hit on the answers most important to your professor. It feels safer to include more legal concepts, more facts, and more arguments in your answer. One of the most common mistakes trial lawyers make is to carry this mind-set into trials. Generally speaking, at trial, *fewer* witnesses, fewer exhibits, and fewer arguments make for a stronger case. There are exceptions, of course, but there is probably a ten to one ratio between lawyers who lose by presenting too much evidence and those who lose by presenting too little.

The problem of presenting too much of a case is so common there is a name for it: *overtrying the case*. It means you have put on too much evidence, put too many issues in play, made too many arguments, and talked too long to the jury. This is one of the most common mistakes trial lawyers make.

A whole book could be written on this subject, and one has: *Winning Jury Trials*.[1] Read it. It might pound home the point made here in just a few pages. It explains in detail how and why too much evidence or argument can hurt your case. Experienced trial lawyers have known this for years. Many of the largest verdicts come from remarkably short trials. Multimillion-dollar verdicts can come from trials lasting less than a week. Criminal defense lawyers can obtain acquittals after presenting no case at all.

To understand how too much evidence can hurt your case, let's go back to the basics. To win a case, you must present a story that is easy to understand, consistent, believable, and compelling. These qualities overlap, of course. The jury won't likely believe a story that is inconsistent. A story that is hard to understand is not likely to be compelling. But let's look at these qualities one at a time and examine how too much evidence can undercut your case's effectiveness.

Ideal Qualities of Your Case

The following qualities are what you are striving for in your case.

---

[1] Robert Klonoff and Paul Colby, *Winning Jury Trials: Trial Tactics and Sponsorship Strategy*, 3rd ed. (New York: LexisNexis, 2007).

Easy to Understand

Ultimately, we are trying to get the jury to *do something*. If we want jurors to do something, they need to understand *why* they are doing it. And to understand why they are doing it, they need to understand your story. The more complicated your story, the more they will resist.

Think of yourself trying to learn something new, complicated, and not particularly interesting. Your first reaction is probably to just give up. "I don't need to know organic chemistry anyway." You have this reaction even if you would very much like to learn organic chemistry.

As you add witnesses, exhibits, and arguments to your case, your story almost always becomes more complicated, and thus more difficult to understand.

Consistent

Inconsistencies make a story harder to understand, less believable, and less compelling. That much is obvious. What is less obvious is that every new piece of evidence you introduce has the capacity to create inconsistencies in your story. Let's use a simple fact pattern to illustrate this problem.

> Your client is hit from behind while stopped at a traffic light. The driver who hit her comes up to her and asks if she is all right. Your client testifies that she told him, "I feel OK, but my neck got yanked." There are two witnesses on the sidewalk when this exchange occurs. Witness A tells you he heard your client say, "OK, but my neck hurts." Witness B tells you he heard your client say, "OK, but my back got yanked."

Suppose the defense claims your client simply said she was OK, and not hurt, immediately after the accident, and you want to introduce testimony to show that your client was immediately aware she might have been hurt. The differences between your client's version and Witness A's version are not significant enough to cause any problems.

Some lawyers might also have Witness B testify out of a desire to hammer home that the plaintiff was aware from the beginning she was hurt, and her present claims are not later fabrications. Now your story becomes inconsistent. Did she say "back" or "neck"? Did she say two different things right after the accident? Are the witnesses lying out of a desire to help the plaintiff, and unable to keep their stories straight?

Every time you call an additional witness to prove a point, you create a very real risk of inconsistencies. People at the same event focus on different things, remember things differently, and use different words to express the same ideas. The problem is even worse with experts. Two qualified experts will almost always disagree on certain points, and competent opponents will seize on this to make your case appear inconsistent: "The plaintiff's own hired experts can't even agree on these points . . ."

Even if two witnesses are consistent on the points that most interest you, they may be inconsistent on other points. These inconsistencies may come out inadvertently on direct examination. They are even more likely to come out on cross-examination. A well-known cross-examination tactic is to question adverse witnesses on collateral matters, hoping to discover and capitalize on inconsistencies.

Suppose Witness A says there was a passenger in the plaintiff's car, and Witness B says there wasn't. All of the sudden, the jury is wondering about your client's credibility, what was going on in the car, or why the "passenger" disappeared from the scene. These sorts of inconsistencies can range from being merely distracting to utterly destroying your case. Every time you add an additional witness or document, you risk compounding this effect.

Documents, in fact, have a particularly pernicious way of creating inconsistencies. Let's keep using our simple car crash example to illustrate. It may be undisputed that your client went to the emergency room the day after the accident. After the ER exam, she was referred to an orthopedist, who became her treating doctor. Many lawyers will introduce the emergency room records just because they think they should, or because they believe the records will make the client's injuries look more substantial.

The problem is that many doctors are poor historians—especially about facts not material to medical diagnosis or treatment. So while your client testified that the accident happened on the way to the grocery store, the medical record might say, "Patient was on her way to pick up her children at school when she was hit from behind . . ." "So," the defense lawyer says, "why would she tell us one thing and her doctor something else?" Of course, he doesn't even need to say that: jurors are very likely to pick up on such inconsistencies on their own.

It should be obvious that the more complex the case, the more opportunities for inconsistencies to arise. This is yet another reason to keep your case as simple and straightforward as possible.

Believable

If the jury does not believe your version, your story, then you lose.

A simple story or explanation is almost always more believable than one that is complex. This is why politicians gravitate toward slogans and sound bites.

Compare "We will fight the terrorists in Iraq so we don't have to fight them here at home," with "The causes of terrorism are numerous and complex, requiring us to address cultural and economic forces that span the globe and are centuries old . . ." Regardless of your views of the Iraq war, the instant appeal of the first argument over the second should be obvious—to everyone except some lawyers.

Some lawyers have a natural affinity for complex stories, arguments, and explanations. Law school cultivates and encourages this natural affinity. For some types of law, this may be an asset; for trial law, it is deadly. If you cannot take complex facts and concepts and convey them simply and directly, you have no business trying cases.

Remember, as a trial lawyer, you are laboring under an additional handicap when it comes to complex explanations. Our culture conditions jurors to expect that a trial lawyer will try to obscure the truth by facilely manipulating complex concepts and words—double-talk. The jurors come to court believing you are the evasive, slippery lawyer trying to lead them astray. The more complex and wordy your presentation, the less credible it will be.

This point cannot be emphasized strongly enough. If there is anything remotely close to a formula for effective trial advocacy, it is that the simpler the explanation (or story), the more likely it is that the jury will believe it.

Compelling

Ultimately, as a trial lawyer, you're looking for a way to make your case compelling. What is it that makes a jury want to act? A likable client? A rags-to-riches life story? A David and Goliath battle? An evil defendant? There is no single answer to this question. The essence of advocacy is discerning and presenting what is compelling about your client's case. Trial lawyers, social scientists, and jury consultants are constantly grappling with this question—and will be for centuries to come. For now, there is no framework or formula to make every case compelling.

There *is* a formula for sucking anything that might be compelling right out of your case: overtry it. Present three witnesses when one will do; present an expert on every conceivable issue; offer a thousand documents into evidence when you only need ten; make complicated, convoluted arguments; take two weeks to present a case that you could present in two days. It happens every day: lawyers lose strong, compelling cases under the weight of too much evidence.

It is worth noting that there is a particular form of overtrying a case that civil lawyers are particularly prone to: burying the case in mounds of documents. Even the most complex cases rarely have more than a dozen important documents. Simpler cases may only have one or two. The fact that you spent months of your time discovering, reading, and organizing thousands of pages of documents does not mean you should present all, most, or even some of them to the jury. The jury's boredom increases in direct proportion to how many documents are introduced, discussed, or read.

A prominent movie director was once asked which characteristic sets great directors apart from merely good directors. He replied that a *great* director is willing to edit out his favorite scene for the good of the movie. As a trial lawyer, you need this same sense of discipline. *When in doubt, cut it out.*

Addressing Bad Facts

Every case has facts you will wish did not exist. Many lawyers get so uncomfortable thinking about these "bad facts" that they simply *stop* thinking about them. This is a bad idea, because these facts will not go away. The other side *will* use them against you.

Other lawyers obsess about the bad facts in their case. These lawyers can hardly see anything in their case other than the bad facts. This approach often leads to discouragement and a self-fulfilling thought pattern that ends in defeat.

The truth is that good lawyers often find ways to make bad facts help their case. Let's look at a simple example.

> Your client is a sixty-year-old high school English teacher. She was in her car, waiting for the light to change, when the defendant's car hit her from behind at twenty miles per hour. She has back and neck injuries.
>
> When in her thirties, the plaintiff went to a doctor and a chiropractor complaining of back and neck pain and was eventually diagnosed with a herniated disc. The doctor the defense hired to examine your client says that herniated discs don't heal, and that your client's present problems relate to the herniated disc from twenty-five years ago.

Traditionally, trial lawyers would regard the prior herniated disc as a bad fact. They would be discouraged and defeated by the defense's argument: "The defendant didn't cause this injury; the plaintiff was diagnosed with this injury twenty-five years ago." Eventually, plaintiffs' lawyers began to understand that this type of bad fact is actually a good fact. It allows them to argue:

> You might wonder how such a minor impact could change someone's life so profoundly. To understand that, you need to understand Mrs. Smith's medical history. You see, when she was thirty-five, she fell down some stairs and hurt her back. She received treatment for a herniated disc for over a year.

Eventually, the pain receded and she learned to live in a way that would not cause her problems. She was careful about the strain she put on her neck and back.

You will hear that she lived a full and active life. She bowled with her husband every Saturday; she worked in her garden every weekend and most summer nights. She coached the girls' volleyball team at her high school.

The collision might not have hurt a young healthy man or woman, but she had a weakness. She was more fragile than most. It took only a moment of carelessness to destroy the careful balance she had maintained for twenty-five years. Her disc and the ligaments around it were injured again, and even the defense doctor agrees she is unlikely to get much better. She will not be bowling with her husband or working in her garden anymore . . .

In this example, the preexisting condition explains how a minor impact could hurt the plaintiff—often the toughest thing to overcome in a minor impact case. The bad fact has become a good fact. Further, this argument fits well with the damage law in all states. The defendant is not responsible for preexisting conditions, but *is* responsible for making preexisting conditions worse.[2] The difference between the quality of the plaintiff's life before and after the accident is the heart of any personal injury case. Here, the bad fact shows why such a minor impact caused such a major change in the quality of the plaintiff's life.

You can neutralize a bad fact, or even support your case with it, if you have the discipline to thoughtfully evaluate the fact in the context of your entire case. It helps to discuss the bad fact with as many people as possible—family, friends, or legal staff. Good ideas can come from any source. What you cannot afford to do is ignore the bad fact.

---

[2] Check your state's model or pattern instructions for "preexisting condition."

SUGGESTED READING

Klonoff, Robert, and Paul Colby. *Winning Jury Trials: Trial Tactics and Sponsorship Strategy.* 3rd ed. New York: LexisNexis, 2007.

6

Trial Briefs and Motions *in Limine*

Purpose

A trial brief's purpose is to give the judge a preview of the evidence and legal issues that you will present at trial. Local rules or the judge's standing order may specifically describe what should be in the brief. In the absence of such guidance, a four-part structure for the brief will usually get the job done:

1. Provide a brief overview of the facts, highlighting where the factual disputes lie.

2. Identify legal rulings, whether through summary judgment or motions *in limine,* that have already been made.

3. Identify pending motions that have not yet been ruled upon.

4. Identify logistical, evidentiary, or jury instruction issues the judge might wish to hear about ahead of time. (Most judges do not like surprises.)

A trial brief is particularly useful in jurisdictions where the trial judge has not been working on the case prior to trial. Many times, a judge will have had no contact with a case until she is assigned to preside over the trial. Even judges who have previously been assigned and ruled on motions in the case may remember little or nothing about it by the time trial is about to begin.

In limine means "at the threshold." The purpose of *in limine* motions is to give the court and the parties an opportunity to have the judge decide evidentiary issues before the trial, out of the presence of the jury.[1]

There are three common justifications for filing *in limine* motions. First, if the evidentiary issue is particularly complicated, it may require briefing and extended argument for resolution. Rather than delay the trial, it is more efficient to address the issue before the trial begins. The trial judge will appreciate the opportunity to become familiar with the issue and the relevant authorities before making a decision.

A second justification for *in limine* motions occurs when the issue involves evidence of such a nature that even mentioning it in front of the jury may cause prejudice: "Isn't it true that you have three convictions for domestic violence for beating your wife?" Regardless of the court's ruling and subsequent instructions to the jury, such questions can cause harm that cannot be undone.[2]

---

[1] *See, e.g., Kelly v. New West Federal Savings,* 56 Cal. Rptr. 2d 803, 808 (Cal. App. 1996) (explaining that while "the usual purpose of motions *in limine* is to preclude the presentation of evidence deemed inadmissible and prejudicial by the moving party," they also "permit more careful consideration of evidentiary issues than would take place in the heat of battle during trial . . ., minimize side-bar conferences and disruptions during trial, allowing for an uninterrupted flow of evidence . . . [and] by resolving potentially critical issues at the outset, . . . enhance the efficiency of trials and promote settlements").

[2] *Hyatt v. Sierra Boat Co.,* 145 Cal. Rptr. 47, 54 (Cal. App. 1978) (stating the advantage of motions *in limine* "is to avoid the obviously futile attempt to 'unring the bell' in the event a motion to strike is granted in the proceedings before the jury") (citations omitted).

A final practical benefit of *in limine* motions is that each side can more efficiently and clearly structure their case presentation if they know in advance what evidence the judge will admit.

Advocacy Goals

For the trial brief, your advocacy goals are to:

- Familiarize the judge with the facts and legal issues she will see and hear during trial. A well-prepared judge is more likely to give correct rulings.

- Predispose the judge toward seeing the issues in a favorable light.

- Demonstrate to the judge that she can rely on you to accurately present the facts and the law.

This last point deserves elaboration. Judges are constantly evaluating the lawyers before them to determine their reliability and credibility. Are you someone whom the judge can rely on to present the issues and facts fairly and accurately? If so, the judge is likely to be receptive to your positions; if not, she will be suspicious—maybe even hostile.

Your advocacy goals for motions *in limine* are straightforward:

- Resolve evidentiary issues before trial begins so you can better plan your trial presentation. This most often involves motions to exclude evidence, but can include a motion asking to preadmit exhibits or evidence so you know what you can use at trial.

- Limit or exclude evidence that can harm your case.

- Make a record (for appellate purposes) of your objections to particular aspects of your opponent's evidence.

- Demonstrate to the judge that she can rely on you to accurately present the facts and the law.

APPLICABLE LAW

- Court rules, local practice, and your individual judge's standing orders control the need for, content of, and time for filing trial briefs. There is no overarching legal principle.

- The purpose of motions *in limine* is to promote trials free of prejudicial material while avoiding disclosure of prejudicial material to the jury through offer and objection.[3]

- A judge can change an *in limine* ruling at any time before entering final judgment.[4]

- When a judge overrules a motion, you usually need to object to the introduction of the evidence at trial to preserve the objection for appeal.[5] It is important to know the

---

[3] *State ex. rel. Berger v. Superior Court*, 499 P.2d 152, 153 (Ariz. 1972); *Kelly v. New West Federal Savings*, 56 Cal. Rptr. 2d 803, 808 (Cal. App. 1996); *Dailey v. Multicon Development, Inc.*, 417 So.2d 1106, 1107 (Fla. App. 1982); *Konieczny v. Kamin Builders, Inc.*, 709 N.E.2d 695, 699 (Ill. App. 1999); *State v. Metz*, 671 N.Y.S.2d 79, 83 (N.Y. App. 1998); *State v. Evans*, 634 P.2d 845, 847–48 (Wash. 1981).

[4] *Ohler v. United States*, 529 U.S. 753, 758 n.3 (2000) ("[*I*]n limine rulings are not binding on the trial judge, and the judge may always change his mind during the course of a trial."). *People v. Yarbrough*, 278 Cal. Rptr. 703, 705–06 (Cal. App. 1991); *Hawker v. State*, 951 So.2d 945, 950 (Fla. App. 2007); *Cunningham v. Millers General Ins. Co.*, 591 N.E.2d 80, 83 (Ill. App. 1992); *Innovative Transmission & Engine Co., LLC v. Massaro*, 879 N.Y.S.2d 856, 857 (N.Y. App. 2009). *But see State v. Latham*, 667 P.2d 56, 59 (Wash. 1983) (stating that although some rulings on motions *in limine* may be tentative and therefore subject to change, "[w]hen a trial judge makes a clear nontentative ruling on such an issue, the defendant is entitled to rely upon that ruling").

[5] *Swan v. Florida Farm Bureau Ins. Co.*, 404 So.2d 802, 803-04 (Fla. 1981) (stating that rule requiring a contemporaneous objection at trial is equally applicable in criminal and civil cases); *Cunningham v. Millers General Ins. Co.*, 591 N.E.2d 80, 83, 84 (Ill. App. 1992) (stating that the "rule is well established that the denial of a motion *in limine* does not preserve an objection to disputed evidence later introduced at trial" but noting that sometimes the trial court's ruling on motion *in limine* can be "so definite and unconditional that the parties may treat it as controlling"); *People v. Billip*, 883 N.Y.S.2d 528,

law of your jurisdiction on this point. Some jurisdictions treat *in limine* orders as final and appealable without subsequent objection. This means, if the judge denies your *in limine* motion, you do not need to object each time your opponent introduces the evidence you addressed in your motion. In both types of jurisdictions, it is best to ask the judge if you can have a *standing objection* to the evidence so you do not need to object at trial.

◆ When the judge grants a motion *in limine*, the other side may still attempt to offer evidence that the judge excluded. If your opponent does this, you need to object.[6]

---

529 (N.Y. App. 2009) (pretrial motion *in limine* seeking to exclude record in its entirety did not preserve hearsay objection, especially as judge denied the motion without prejudice). *But see* Fed. Evid. R. 103(b) (providing that once the court makes a definitive ruling on the record, either before or at trial, it is not necessary for a party to renew the objection or offer or proof to preserve the issue); *People v. Solomon*, 234 P.3d 501, 523–24 (Cal. 2010) ("A motion *in limine* can preserve an appellate claim, so long as the party objected to the specific evidence on the specific ground urged on appeal at a time when the court could determine the evidentiary question in the proper context" but if motion is not specific or court defers ruling, an objection at trial is required); *State v. Lujan*, 666 P.2d 71, 73 (Ariz. 1983) (Arizona courts have consistently held that where a party has properly made and the court has ruled upon a motion *in limine*, "the objection raised in the motion is preserved for purposes of appeal without the need for a specific objection at trial"); *State v. Sullivan*, 847 P.2d 953, 955 (Wash. 1993) ("Unless the trial court indicates further objections are required when making its ruling [denying motion *in limine*], its decision is final, and the party losing the motion *in limine* has a standing objection.").

[6] *Compton v. Ubilluz*, 819 N.E.2d 767 (Ill. App. 2004); *State v. Sullivan*, 847 P.2d 953, 955 (Wash. 1993). *But see Liberatore v. Thompson*, 760 P.2d 612, 619 (Ariz. App. 1988) (refusing to hold that a party has insufficiently preserved an objection to improper argument when the party made a successful motion *in limine* in advance of argument on the subject); *compare*, however, *State v. Lichon*, 786 P.2d 1037, 1040 (Ariz. App. 1989) (defendant did not preserve issue that prosecutor's argument violated pretrial order on motion *in limine* when he did not object to argument and judge other than the trial judge had granted order).

♦ It is improper to use an *in limine* motion as a summary judgment motion in disguise.[7] If an *in limine* motion will have the effect of dismissing an entire cause of action or claim, the judge may regard it as a disguised summary judgment motion.

Implementation

Check the pretrial order and the local rules to determine whether your jurisdiction has requirements for trial briefs and motions *in limine*. There are likely deadline, formatting, page-length, and substance requirements.

Write your briefs to the trial court in a way that is simple, direct, and as short as possible. Trial judges are extremely busy and often feel like they are drowning in paper. If you want to impress them, get to the point quickly and clearly. Most evidentiary issues are fairly simple. A brief in support of a motion *in limine* could begin like this:

> The defendant has three prior convictions for domestic violence. Because these convictions have no relevance to the present charges of Theft by Deception and would be unduly prejudicial to the defense, the

---

[7] *Amtower v. Photon Dynamics, Inc.*, 71 Cal. Rptr. 3d 361, 372–73 (Cal. App. 2008) (criticizing the use of *in limine* motions as substitutes for summary adjudication motions, motions for judgment on the pleadings, or other dispositive motions, but noting that trial courts could allow such practices, despite many disadvantages and the risk of error); *Brock v. G.D. Searle & Co.*, 530 So.2d 428, 431 (Fla. App. 1988) ("[T]rial courts should not allow motions *in limine* to be used as unwritten and unnoticed motions for pretrial summary judgment or motions to dismiss."); *Cannon v. William Chevrolet/Geo, Inc.*, 794 N.E.2d 843, 849 (Ill. App. 2003) ("Motions *in limine* are not designed to obtain rulings on dispositive matters but, rather, are designed to obtain rulings on evidentiary matters outside the presence of the jury."); *Rondout Elec., Inc. v. Dover Union Free School Dist.*, 758 N.Y.S.2d 394, 397 (N.Y. App. Div. 2003) (motion *in limine* is an inappropriate substitute for summary judgment); *Haves v. C.D. Plastics*, 876 P.2d 435, 445 (Wash. 1994) (treating order on motion *in limine* as if it were granted on summary judgment for purposes of appeal).

court should exclude evidence of them from trial pursuant to Evidence Rules 403 and 404.

In some instances, this could be the entire brief. In others, you might want to follow up with case citations. But to address an issue like this, your brief does not need to be more than three or four pages. I have heard trial judges joke that they usually only need one paragraph in an *in limine* brief to understand the issue and decide it. While this may be an overstatement, it conveys the attitude most trial judges have toward *in limine* motions. *They want you to get to the point!*

Even with more complex evidentiary issues, work hard to keep the brief short and clear. It truly will be more effective than a long brief laden with numerous citations and arguments.

Don't abuse the right to file an *in limine* motion asking to preadmit evidence. Generally, judges don't like to preadmit evidence over objection. Only file this kind of motion when the outcome will dramatically affect the conduct or fairness of the trial.

Finally, remember that the judge can change an *in limine* ruling at any time before she enters final judgment.[8] This means you may approach the judge at any time before the evidence has closed and ask her to reverse her ruling. You must do this outside the presence of the jury—no judge will take kindly to you asking her to reverse herself while the jury is watching. You will have a better outcome if you can point to changed circumstances to justify your request that the judge reconsider. You might begin, "Your Honor, now that the court has had the chance to hear Mr. Smith testify, I would like to ask that you reconsider your ruling on . . ."

QUESTIONS TO ASK

Ask court personnel or the judge:

- Is there a standing order or local rule on trial briefs?
- Would the judge like a trial brief?

---

[8] *See* note 4, above.

- When would she like it filed?
- What issues would she like addressed?
- Does she have any other specific requirements?
- Is there a standing order or a local rule on motions *in limine*?
- Is there a deadline for motions *in limine*?
- Can you have a standing objection? If the judge rules against you on a motion *in limine,* ask if, to avoid wasting time, you can have a standing objection to any evidence related to the motion. You can say, "I don't want to interrupt counsel by objecting to material you have already ruled on." This should be adequate to preserve your objections for appellate purposes and also help avoid drawing the jurors' attention to the harmful evidence.

Suggested Reading

Friedman, Rick, and Patrick Malone. "Motions and the Rules of the Road." In *Rules of the Road: A Plaintiff Lawyer's Guide to Proving Liability.* 2nd ed., 127–136. Portland, OR: Trial Guides, 2010.

7

The Pretrial Hearing

Before almost every trial, the court will conduct some sort of hearing. The hearing's purpose is to address remaining legal matters that need to be resolved before trial begins, and to make sure the court and the lawyers understand the procedures that will apply to the conduct of the trial. This hearing may be called a *pretrial hearing, status conference, trial readiness conference, oral argument on motions* in limine, or something similar.

The hearing may last a few minutes, hours, or even days. The court may hold it weeks before the trial begins, or in the few minutes before the prospective jurors file into the courtroom. The hearing may be off the record in chambers or on the record in the courtroom.

Here are the types of things the judge may address at the pretrial hearing:

- Marking and/or exchanging exhibits
- Voir dire procedure
- Motions *in limine* or other remaining legal issues
- Trial schedule
- Amount of time permitted for opening statements

How do you know what the judge will address at your pretrial hearing? *You ask.* Paradoxically, the more questions you ask, the more knowledgeable and experienced you appear.

Review the local rules and the court's pretrial orders. If these do not tell you what subjects the judge will cover during the pretrial hearing—or even if they do—contact the court personnel. Call the judge's bailiff or clerk and ask what the judge usually addresses at the pretrial hearing. Or walk over to the courthouse and ask in person.

Must it be said that you should always treat all court personnel with courtesy and respect, even deference? If so, becoming an effective trial lawyer is going to be tough going for you. If good manners and your common humanity are not reasons enough, think about your own self-interest. These are the people who make things work (or not work) for you in the court system. They can help you, or they can make your life miserable. They are in constant contact with the judge. They know more about how the judge will handle your case in this particular court system than you ever will. They have seen more trials than you ever will. And there is a good chance they are smarter than you.

So contact the court personnel and politely ask questions.

If you can, it is also a good idea to go to the courthouse and sit in on a trial or hearings that your judge conducts. This will give you a feel for her personality and the way she handles her courtroom. You will be much more comfortable at the pretrial hearing for having done that.

Once you are in the pretrial conference, *ask the judge questions.* Wait until she has finished going through her own agenda. It is now time to ask questions that she has not answered yet. Here are some questions you may want to ask:

- Can you explain the voir dire process?

- Are there any limits on the time you allow for any parts of the trial?

- When do you like to begin and end the trial day?

- When do you like to take lunch and for how long?
- Does the court require that documents intended for impeachment be marked and exchanged?[1]
- If we need to hand something to the jury, how would you prefer we handle that?
- Where do you want us to put up easels, screens, or TVs?
- How does the court like objections to be handled?

This last question deserves some discussion.

It seems as though every judge is convinced there is only one proper way to handle objections, but in fact, there are three distinctly different approaches. Many judges will be very unhappy if you try to employ an approach different from the one they prefer.

Speaking Objections

In a speaking objection, the lawyer stands to object. He states the basis for the objection and then argues to the court, with the jury listening, why he believes his objection should be upheld. A speaking objection might go like this:

Lawyer One: Objection, Your Honor. This is irrelevant. Whether my client had an abortion three years before the accident has nothing to do with any issue in this case. The defense is raising this issue simply to prejudice my client. These questions violate evidence rules 403 and 404.

Or the objection might go like this:

Lawyer One: Objection. The court excluded this evidence in its pretrial rulings.

---

[1] Many jurisdictions have specific rules or case law addressing this issue. For example, Federal Rule of Civil Procedure 26(a) excludes from disclosure requirements information and documents intended to be used solely for impeachment. Some state law versions of the rule differ on this issue.

LAWYER TWO: That's true, Your Honor, but Mr. Smith implied in direct examination that his client is an honest man; that opened the door to his thirteen felony convictions.

LAWYER ONE: Objection. He's just told the jury what this court specifically excluded.

As you can see, the speaking objection has great potential to work mischief. In the process of arguing about evidence, either side may end up with an unfair advantage. The jurors may hear about things they should not hear, or be left with a false impression due to inference or innuendos in the lawyers' arguments. For these reasons, the speaking objection has generally fallen out of favor.

Yet a minority of judges still insists on speaking objections. They believe it is faster than the other methods of dealing with objections, and that the jurors either won't understand what the lawyers are talking about or can be trusted to follow the court's instructions to disregard it.

THE ONE-PHRASE/ONE-RULE OBJECTION

In the one-phrase/one-rule (or one-phrase/one-word) objection, the judge wants counsel to object in front of the jury and state the basis for the objection in a single word, phrase, or rule. With this method, an exchange on an objection might sound like this:

LAWYER ONE: Objection, hearsay.

LAWYER TWO: It's not offered for the truth of the matter asserted, but for state of mind.

LAWYER ONE: This says nothing about any relevant state of mind.

In short, the lawyers are talking in tight, cryptic code.

Some judges will ask that you cite only the evidence rule you are relying upon. Then the objection might simply be: "Objection, Rule 802."

The judges who employ the one-word or one-phrase approach like the fact that they can quickly hear the objection and response, and most of the time, quickly rule upon it without hearing extended argument. If the lawyers honor the spirit of this approach, the jury is not exposed to prejudicial material and the judge can keep the trial moving. If the judge has questions or needs more explanation, she can ask the lawyers to approach the bench to argue.

APPROACHING THE BENCH, OR BENCH CONFERENCES

While most judges prefer the one-phrase/one-rule approach, some will ask you to approach the bench for any objection. This is sometimes called a *bench conference*. This is what happens:

LAWYER ONE: Objection, Rule 403.

COURT: Please approach the bench.

The lawyers then walk to the bench, or sometimes into the hallway behind the bench, and argue the issue.

Some judges will at the outset tell the lawyers they do not want to hear any objections in front of the jury. They will say you must ask to approach the bench if you want to argue an objection or a ruling. The lawyers and the judge then hold the legal argument in whispers, in front or to the side of the judge's bench. Sometimes, if the argument drags on, the judge will take the lawyers into the hallway, or send the jury out on a break.

Ask how the judge prefers handling objections or risk her ire. The truth is, however, that no judge adheres rigidly to any of these approaches. A judge who likes speaking objections may cut you off in midsentence, and a judge who prefers approaching the bench may on occasion ask for your argument from counsel table. The judge has discretion to handle objections any way she likes, and to change her approach from objection to objection. Learn the judge's preference, and be prepared to be flexible. (See chapter 12 for more on objections.)

When to Move Exhibits into Evidence

Technically, a jury should not see an exhibit until it is "in evidence." Most often, exhibits are "moved" into evidence. That is, one side makes what amounts to a motion, asking the judge to take action. The action is to take an exhibit and "admit" it, so that it becomes part of the record. The motion to move an exhibit into evidence is simple: "Your Honor, I move to have Exhibit 44 admitted into evidence," or "I'd ask to admit Exhibit 44."

Some judges will try to get the lawyers to stipulate to preadmitting exhibits there is no dispute about. Some judges prefer that disputed exhibits be moved into evidence while the witness who laid the foundation for the exhibit (established that it is what it purports to be) is still on the witness stand. This is probably the most common procedure. But other judges prefer that all exhibits be moved into evidence during breaks or at the end of the trial. You know what to do about this . . . *ask*. The pretrial conference is an excellent time to ask your judge how she prefers you to handle this.

Signal any Unusual Issues

Judges don't like surprises. If you see an unusual legal issue coming, let the judge know. "Judge, this case is against State Farm Insurance Company. I just wanted to let you know that during voir dire, we are going to ask that all State Farm policyholders be excused for cause. We have filed a brief on this, but you may not have had a chance to see it."

The same is true for scheduling or procedural issues. If you are worried that you might not have enough witnesses scheduled to fill the third day of trial, tell that to the judge now. She will treat you much better this way than if you tell the judge at 1:30 on a Wednesday afternoon that you have run out of witnesses for the day.

Suggested Reading

Markowitz, David B. *Mastering the Art of Persuading the Trial Judge* (CD/DVD set). Portland, OR: Trial Guides, 2012.

8

Jury Selection (Voir Dire)

Purpose

The purpose of the jury selection process, still referred to as voir dire, is to select competent, fair, impartial jurors to decide the case.[1] To further this goal, the court gives each side an

---

[1] *Press–Enterprise Co. v. Superior Court of Cal.,* 464 U.S. 501, 510, fn. 9 (1984) ("The process is to ensure a fair impartial jury, not a favorable one."); *Mu'Min v. Virginia,* 500 U.S. 415, 431 (1991) ("Voir dire examination serves the dual purposes of enabling the court to select an impartial jury and assisting counsel in exercising peremptory challenges."); *Hoskins v. State,* 965 So.2d 1, 13 (Fla. 2007) ("The purpose of voir dire is to 'obtain a fair and impartial jury, whose minds are free of all interest, bias, or prejudice,' not to . . . obtain a preview of their opinions of the evidence.") (citations omitted); *People v. Rinehart,* 962 N.E.2d 444, 450 (Ill. 2012) (stating the purpose of voir dire is "the selection of a jury free from bias or prejudice"); *Lopez-Stayer v. Pitts,* 93 P.3d 904, 908 (Wash. App. 2004) ("The primary purpose of voir dire is to give a litigant an opportunity to explore the potential jurors' attitudes in order to determine whether the jury should be challenged."). *See also* Ariz. R. Crim. P. 18.5(e) (specifying that voir dire is to gather information for challenges for cause or peremptory challenges).

opportunity to challenge jurors either *for cause* or with peremptory challenge.

In a for-cause challenge, a lawyer articulates a reason for removing the prospective juror from the panel. Depending on the jurisdiction, this can be called *a challenge for cause, a for-cause motion, a motion to strike for cause,* or something similar. By contrast, *peremptory challenges* allow a party to remove a juror from the panel without stating any reason at all. The thought is that if we remove all prospective jurors who appear unable to be competent or fair (for-cause challenges) and allow each side to remove some jurors they just don't feel right about (peremptory challenges), what is left is a truly fair and competent jury.

For-Cause Challenges

In a for-cause challenge, the lawyer asks the judge to remove the prospective juror from the panel because it appears he is not physically or mentally able to serve, may not be able to be fair and unbiased, or that he would be unwilling or unable to follow the instructions given by the judge. For example, the for-cause standard in New York for a criminal trial is found at New York Criminal Procedure Law § 270.20, which provides:

> A challenge for cause is an objection to a prospective juror and may be made only on the ground that:
>
> A. He does not have the qualifications required by the judiciary law[2]; or
>
> B. He has a state of mind that is likely to preclude him from rendering an impartial verdict based upon the evidence adduced at the trial; or

---

[2] New York law separately sets forth the basic requirements to be a juror: "1. Be a citizen of the United States, and a resident of the county. 2. Be not less than eighteen years of age. 3. Not have been convicted of a felony. 4. Be able to understand and communicate in the English language." N.Y. Judiciary Law § 510. Similar requirements can be found in every state. *See, e.g.,* Ariz. R.S. § 21–201; Cal. C.C.P. § 203; Fla. Stat. § 40.01; 705 ILCS 305/2; Wash. St. 2.36.070.

C. He is related within the sixth degree by consanguinity or affinity to the defendant, or to the person allegedly injured by the crime charged, or to a prospective witness at the trial, or to counsel for the people or for the defendant; or that he is or was a party adverse to any such person in a civil action; or that he has complained against or been accused by any such person in a criminal action; or that he bears some other relationship to any such person of such nature that it is likely to preclude him from rendering an impartial verdict; or

D. He was a witness at the preliminary examination or before the grand jury or is to be a witness at the trial; or

E. He served on the grand jury which found the indictment in issue or served on a trial jury in a prior civil or criminal action involving the same incident charged in such indictment; or

F. The crime charged may be punishable by death and the prospective juror entertains such conscientious opinions either against or in favor of such punishment as to preclude such juror from rendering an impartial verdict or from properly exercising the discretion conferred upon such juror by law in the determination of a sentence pursuant to section 400.27.

The standards for what constitutes a valid challenge for cause vary from jurisdiction to jurisdiction, as do the basic qualification requirements for all jurors. You can find these standards in court rules, statutes, or both. There will also be case law that explains and expands upon the court rule or statutory standards. Before your first trial, set aside an hour or two to research the challenge for cause standards in your jurisdiction. Keep the key sections of the statutes, rules, or cases in your trial notebook.

Your jurisdiction's statutes or court rules will specify the number of peremptory challenges each side is allowed. Using a peremptory challenge, you can excuse a prospective juror from the panel without stating a reason, but you can get into trouble if you excuse a juror for an unconstitutional reason.[3]

Advocacy Goals

- Identify and remove from the panel jurors who may be difficult to persuade to your view of the case. Ideally, this would leave only jurors predisposed to find in your favor. (This never happens.)

- Avoid alienating neutral jurors or those initially positively disposed to your case.

- Reveal—through your behavior—that you are a reliable source of information and a trustworthy participant in the trial process.

Applicable Law

The law applicable to jury selection varies greatly between jurisdictions. How judges conduct voir dire also varies greatly from judge to judge. Some judges do all the questioning of prospective jurors and do not allow the lawyers to ask a single question. Other judges say very little and give the lawyers a great deal of latitude in their questioning. There are even jurisdictions where the judge is not present when the lawyers question the jurors. The cases and principles listed below are designed to orient you to the legal issues that can arise in voir dire.

---

[3] Peremptory challenges cannot be exercised on the basis of race, ethnicity, or sex. See the discussion of *Batson v. Kentucky,* 476 U.S. 79 (1986) and its progeny below.

Voir Dire Conducted by the Judge

If the judge conducts voir dire, she has considerable discretion in the exact questions to ask.[4] Generally, the court abuses its discretion only if "its failure to ask questions renders the defendant's trial 'fundamentally unfair' or 'if the questioning is not reasonably sufficient to test the jury for bias or partiality.'"[5] And it is error for a judge not to allow or engage in questioning regarding racial prejudice in a case in which such prejudice may impact the verdict.[6]

Voir Dire Conducted by the Attorneys

Where the attorneys conduct all or a substantial portion of voir dire, the trial court still has considerable discretion to limit the examination of potential jurors, such as by imposing time constraints on questioning. Still, the court must allow the attorneys a meaningful opportunity to ascertain bias.[7]

Specific Requirements

Some states have rules or court decisions that require examination on certain subjects. For example, in Illinois, Supreme Court Rule 431(b) requires the trial court in a criminal case to ask each

---

[4] *See, e.g., People v. Taylor*, 229 P.3d 12, 44 (2010); *People v. Rinehart*, 962 N.E.2d 444, 450 (Ill. 2012).

[5] *People v. Taylor*, 229 P.3d 12, 44 (2010) (quoting *People v. Cleveland*, 86 P.3d 302 (2004)); *see also State v. Skaggs*, 586 P.2d 1279, 1281–82 (Ariz. 1978) ("Due process would require an examination by the trial judge on an issue if there was a nexus shown between the prejudice feared and the issues of the case.").

[6] *Aldridge v. U.S.*, 283 U.S. 308, 311, 51. S.Ct. 470, 472 (1931).

[7] *Mendez v. State*, 898 So.2d 1141, 1143 (Fla. App. 2005). In Florida, "even though trial judges may question prospective jurors, their role in jury selection must not impair counsel's right and duty to question the venire." *Sanders v. State*, 707 So.2d 664, 668 (Fla. 1998). *See also State v. Melendez*, 588 P.2d 294, 296 (Ariz. 1978) (scope of voir dire examination is left to the discretion of the trial court); *State v. Brady*, 64 P.3d 1258, 1261 (Wash. App. 2003) ("The trial court has broad discretion in determining the scope and extent of voir dire . . . limited only by the need to assure a fair trial by an impartial jury.").

potential juror whether that juror "understands and accepts" four basic principles:

> (1) that the defendant is presumed innocent of the charge(s) against him or her; (2) that before a defendant can be convicted the State must prove the defendant guilty beyond a reasonable doubt; (3) that the defendant is not required to offer any evidence on his or her own behalf; and (4) that the defendant's failure to testify cannot be held against him or her.

Be aware of any similar requirements in your jurisdiction.

Improper Purposes

Voir dire questions aimed at indoctrinating the jury or impaneling a jury predisposed to a particular result are improper, but there is often no clear demarcation between permissible and impermissible questions.[8] Therefore, review the cases in your jurisdiction to find out what has been allowed or disallowed. Again, the trial court has considerable discretion in drawing the line in each case.

Challenges for Cause

Because each case and voir dire is different, the rules for challenges for cause must be applied on a case-by-case basis.[9]

Sometimes, after a prospective juror makes a statement that indicates bias or an inability to be fair, one side may wish to rehabilitate the juror so that the juror cannot be successfully challenged for cause. This normally involves soliciting some promise from the juror about her ability to be fair. This can be a fact-intensive inquiry, focusing on the juror's exact words and whether the rehabilitation eliminated any ambiguity. Generally, attempts

---

[8] *People v. Rinehart*, 962 N.E.2d 444, 450–51 (Ill. 2012); *People v. Williams*, 628 P.2d 869, 877 (Cal. 1981) (superseded by statute on other grounds); *State v. Frederiksen*, 700 P.2d 369, 371–72 (Wash. 1985).

[9] *People v. Sims*, 736 N.E.2d 1048, 1069 (Ill. 2000).

to rehabilitate a potential juror are allowed,[10] although there is certainly authority to the contrary.[11]

Discriminatory Peremptory Challenges

As mentioned above, you may use peremptory challenges for almost any reason. You may strike a potential juror based on his nice clothes, his love of the Yankees, or his astrological sign—anything that gives you a gut feeling that this juror is not right for you and that, if you preempt him, a better juror will take his place. Your opponent will rely on her own gut instinct to try to do the same. Neither you nor your opponent, however, may preempt a juror because of race, sex, or ethnicity. The United States Supreme Court first announced a rule against a prosecutor exercising peremptory challenges based on race in *Batson v. Kentucky*.[12] Challenges to the other side's use of peremptory challenges in an apparently discriminatory way are often referred to as Batson *challenges*. The rule against discriminatory peremptory challenges has subsequently been extended to

---

[10] *State v. Anderson*, 4 P.3d 369 (Ariz. 2000) (holding that it was error not to allow defense counsel in capital murder case opportunity to rehabilitate prospective juror who indicated opposition to the death penalty); *People v. Mattson*, 789 P.2d 983, 996 (Cal. 1990) (stating that opposing counsel may seek to rehabilitate an apparently biased juror, subject to reasonable limitations); *Sanders v. State*, 707 So.2d 664, 668 (Fla. 1998) (stating that court had repeatedly held that it violated due process to refuse to allow defense counsel the opportunity to rehabilitate jurors with concerns about imposing death penalty); *but see Bell v. Greissman*, 902 So.2d 846 (Fla. App. 2005) (stating that if there is reasonable doubt about a prospective juror's impartiality, juror should be dismissed, close questions should be resolved in favor of dismissal, and it was error not to dismiss juror whose answers taken as a whole indicated bias); *People v. Reinhold*, 617 N.E.2d 436, 441 (Ill. App. 1993) (recognizing attempts to rehabilitate juror); *People v. Knight*, 813 N.Y.S.2d 431, 431–32 (N.Y. App. 2006) (describing rehabilitation of juror); *State v. Gonzales*, 45 P.3d 205, 207–08 (Wash. App. 2002) (recognizing that jurors can be rehabilitated after providing answers that indicate bias).

[11] *McGill v. Commonwealth*, 391 S.E.2d 597, 600 (Va. App. 1990); *Scott v. Commonwealth*, 708 S.E.2d 440, 443–44 (Va. App. 2011).

[12] *Batson v. Kentucky*, 476 U.S. 79 (1986).

criminal defendants,[13] civil parties,[14] gender discrimination,[15] and ethnicity discrimination.[16] A party may object to the other side's apparent discriminatory exclusion of jurors, regardless of either party's race, sex, or ethnicity.[17]

When one side suspects that the other side has made a peremptory challenge for discriminatory reasons, the court follows a three-step process to evaluate the claim.

1. First, the side that objects to the peremptory challenge must make a *prima facie* showing that the peremptory challenge is discriminatory. (For example, the lawyer could point out that all of the opponent's peremptory challenges have been exercised against Asian Americans.)

2. Second, if the judge agrees that *prima facie* showing of discrimination has been made, then the side that dismissed the juror must offer a nondiscriminatory basis for striking the juror (that is, a reason that is race-neutral, sex-neutral, and ethnicity-neutral, such as "all of these challenges were directed at people working in the restaurant business").

3. Finally, the court must determine whether the side that objected has shown purposeful discrimination.[18] The trial

---

[13] *Georgia v. McCollum*, 505 U.S. 42 (1992) (criminal defendant is not allowed to exercise peremptory challenges in a discriminatory manner).

[14] *Edmonson v. Leesville Concrete Co.*, 500 U.S. 614 (1991) (private litigants in civil cases may not use peremptory challenges in discriminatory manner, as it violates equal protection rights of the challenged jurors).

[15] *J.E.B. v. Alabama*, 511 U.S. 127 (1993) (intentional discrimination by government in exercise of peremptory challenges based on gender violates equal protection clause); *see also United States v. Martinez*, 621 F.3d 101 (2d Cir. 2010) (holding that criminal defendant also could not exercise peremptory challenges based on gender).

[16] *Hernandez v. New York*, 500 U.S. 352 (1991) (prohibiting discrimination based on ethnic origin).

[17] *See Powers v. Ohio*, 499 U.S. 400 (1991) (white defendant could challenge peremptory challenges to African American jurors).

[18] *See, e.g., Snyder v. Louisiana*, 552 U.S. 472, 476–77 (2008).

court's ruling is entitled to deference and will only be reversed if clearly erroneous.[19]

Parties May Have to Share Peremptory Challenges

If more than one party to the case is on the same "side," the court may require them to share challenges or may give parties on the same side extra challenges if they in fact have adverse interests. If multiple parties on one side collectively have more challenges than a single party on the other, the court may grant the single party additional challenges.[20]

---

[19] *Id.*

[20] *See, e.g.,* Ariz. R. Crim. Pro. 18.4(c)(2) (providing that where there is more than one criminal defendant, each shall get one-half the number of challenges as a single defendant would receive, but not allowing additional peremptory challenges to the prosecutor); Ariz. R. Civ. Pro. 47(e) (specifying number of challenges per side, but allowing court to increase number if two or more parties on same side are adverse; rule also requires that each side have equal number of peremptory challenges); Cal. Code of Civil Procedure, § 231 (setting forth number of peremptory challenges in criminal and civil cases, how such challenges must be shared, and providing for additional challenges to both sides where there are multiple parties on one side); Fla. St. § 913.08(2) (providing in criminal cases where there are multiple defendants for each defendant to receive same number of challenges as in one-defendant case, and prosecution to receive as many challenges as allowed all of the defendants); *see also* Fla. R. Crim. P. 3.350(b) (same); Fla. R. Civ. Pro. 1.431(d) (allowing three challenges to each party, except that if there are more parties on one side, the other side receives the same aggregate number as the first side); Ill. S.Ct R. 434 (setting forth number of challenges in criminal cases depending on type of case and number of defendants, and also providing that the state shall receive same number as all of the defendants); 735 ILCS 5/2-1106 (each side shall receive equal number of challenges; if there is more than one party on one side, court may allow additional challenges, but must allow each side the same amount; if parties on one side cannot agree on how to allocate challenges, court may do so); N.Y. CPL § 270.25(3) (providing that number of challenges is not increased when there are multiple criminal defendants, who must instead share challenges; challenges are disallowed if not joined by majority of defendants); N.Y. CPLR § 4109 (each side shall receive equal number of challenges which court may allocate among parties); RCWA 4.44.130 (providing that when there is more than one party on one side of a case, they must ordinarily

IMPLEMENTATION

The procedure for jury selection varies widely. Ideally, find the time to watch your judge select a jury before you go into court on your own case. Generally, the steps of jury selection go something like this:

1. Court employees (such as a bailiff) bring prospective jurors into court and the judge gives them a short description of the jury selection process. The prospective jurors swear to tell the truth.

2. The judge asks the group of prospects if they meet the statutory requirements for jury service. Generally, these are: U.S. citizens, at least eighteen years old, no felony convictions, and so on.

3. The court puts some number of prospects in the jury box (and in close proximity to it). This usually includes the total number of jurors needed to decide the case (usually six, eight, or twelve), plus the number of alternates (usually one to four), plus the total number of peremptory challenges allowed to the parties. For example, if the court needs twelve jurors to decide the case, and the court wants two alternates, and each side is allowed three peremptory challenges, the total number of prospects in the box would be twenty.

4. The judge tells the prospects the length of trial and length of trial days; the judge asks if the jurors have any reason they cannot serve. The judge excuses those with hardships preventing service. The court replaces the excused jurors with other potential jurors.

5. The judge asks the prospects in the box, one at a time, to answer certain basic questions: name, marital status, number of children, employment, and things of that kind.

6. The judge asks the prospects case-specific questions: "Do any of you have a close family member with a brain injury?"

---

join in a peremptory challenge before it can be made, but if there is a conflict between the parties, court may allow additional challenges).

if the case involves a brain injury, or "Has anyone been a victim of a burglary?" if the case involves a burglary. The judge may excuse some jurors for cause during this step because of strong feelings about the case's subject matter.

7. The plaintiff's lawyer or prosecutor is allowed to question jurors. Sometimes the judge will require that lawyers question jurors one at a time, asking all questions of juror number one first, and then moving on to juror number two. It is more common now for judges to allow the lawyers to question all jurors in the box in whatever order they like—usually with an overall time limit. The judge may require the questioning lawyer to state any challenges for cause when his questioning is done, or to alternatively state, "We pass the jurors for cause," indicating he won't make any cause challenges based on his questioning.

8. The defense lawyer is allowed to question the prospects. The judge may require the defense lawyer to state any challenges for cause.

9. Some judges will allow lawyers to wait until all lawyers have finished questioning before stating challenges for cause. This is the better practice, as only when lawyers have finished all their questioning will they know the full extent of any problems with a juror. At times during questioning, however, it will become apparent to everyone that a juror is biased or otherwise disqualified. The judge may interrupt and ask the lawyers if they wish to challenge for cause.

10. If it has not happened already, each side states their challenges for cause, they argue their challenges, and the judge decides them. If a prospect is excused, the court calls a new prospect from the back of the court to take the excused prospect's seat, and the process begins again at step four for that juror.

11. The judge allows the plaintiff's lawyer or prosecutor to exercise his first peremptory challenge. The defense lawyer then exercises his first peremptory challenge. Parties (or each

side) alternate until they have used all their challenges or all parties are satisfied with the panel.

12. The court swears the panel in and trial begins.

While these are important aspects of jury selection, they may not occur in exactly this order. Again, the exact procedures may differ widely from judge to judge. As you try more cases, you will become more familiar with the elements involved and more comfortable with variations in the procedure.

Two sets of variations are so common and fundamental they are worth noting here. First, in some jurisdictions, judges do not allow counsel to question *any* prospective jurors. In other jurisdictions, the judge is not involved in jury selection at all—she is not even in the room. Again, the best way to research this is to watch a jury being selected in your judge's courtroom.

Where to Sit?

Coming into a courtroom for the first time, it may not be clear to you which table is yours. Some courtrooms have small signs on the tables with "plaintiff" (which includes prosecutors) and "defendant" written on them. Others do not.

In some courtrooms, it is customary that the plaintiff or prosecutor sits closest to the jury; in others, it is not.

Some judges operate on the "first come, first choice" basis. Perhaps these judges like to watch the lawyers engage in unseemly gamesmanship as they walk in for the first time.

If there are no signs on the tables, the simplest thing is to just ask the court clerk or deputy if the judge prefers a particular side to sit at a particular table. If not, choose the table you prefer. Once you have a table, it will be yours for the entire trial. Rarely, if ever, will a judge permit lawyers to change tables during the trial.

How to Question Jurors

Many lawyers say jury selection is the most frightening part of the trial process. It is like going on a first date with fifty people at once, knowing that you will have to maintain a relationship with at least twelve of them. They are judging you; you are judging them. The consequences could be significant, even devastating.

Let's consider questioning jurors through the lenses of our three major advocacy goals:

- Identify and eliminate bad jurors.

- Don't alienate neutral or good jurors.

- Show you are reliable and trustworthy.

Identify and Eliminate Bad Jurors

Your biggest goal is to get jurors to talk. The more jurors talk, the more you will know about them, and the better chance you have of identifying and eliminating bad jurors. You are not questioning a witness. You are not trying to elicit particular opinions or observations. *You just want the prospects to talk to you.*

How do you get anyone to talk to you? For one thing, you have to be genuinely interested in what they have to say. You also have to *appear* genuinely interested in what they have to say. If you are strutting around the courtroom trying to impress everyone, not many prospects will believe you are interested in what they have to say. If your eyes are glued to your notepad, prospects will not be convinced you are interested in what they have to say.

If you have the time, ask some questions about the prospects' backgrounds. For example, "Can you tell me more about your job?" or "What exactly does a General Motors data processor do each day?" This will get you and the prospect more comfortable with each other. This background information may also be helpful as you decide how to exercise your peremptory challenges.

There was once a view among trial lawyers that a good lawyer would try to prevent prospective jurors from saying anything inflammatory, such as, "I think all plaintiffs' lawyers are liars and cheats." The thought was that such statements would "poison" the other jurors. Now it is generally accepted that such thoughts are not contagious, and it is better to bring them out into the open. The more negative a juror's attitude, the more you should want to hear it. It may give you the basis to challenge that juror for cause. It will also give you the chance to see if the other prospects agree or disagree.

Every cell in your body may cry out that you should browbeat the juror out of his opinion, or at least shut him up. But if you stand there, asking him, "Can you tell me more about that?" you are letting him build a record that may let you successfully challenge him for cause. You are also showing the other jurors:

- That your case is so strong, you have no need to be afraid of negative or critical opinions.

- That you will treat all of their thoughts and opinions with respect. This is important for getting the others to share their own thoughts and feelings, as it shows you are a safe person with whom to have a relationship.

Gerry Spence may have been the first lawyer to explicitly suggest making a list of everything about your case that makes you afraid, and then talking to the prospective jurors about the things on your list. This process does not need to be elegant or polished. Here are some examples to give you a sense of how it could go:

Mr. Smith, my client was convicted of burglary five years ago. Do you think that could make it harder for him to receive a fair trial? In what ways? Can you tell me more about that? Does anyone agree with Mr. Smith? Can you tell me about that? Does anyone disagree with Mr. Smith? Can you tell me about that?

Mr. Jones, my client has lived in this country for twenty years, but has never learned English. Do you think she should be treated differently by our legal system because of that? Can you tell me more about that? Does anyone agree with Mr. Jones?

Mr. Abbot, do you think it makes my clients look bad that they filed a lawsuit over the death of their son? Money isn't going to bring him back, is it? What's the point in a lawsuit then? Can you tell me more about that?

This type of questioning may draw out the bad jurors, and it will show the others you will be honest about the weaknesses or hard parts of your case. Stated another way, it shows they can trust you to treat them with respect and honesty.

If you get jurors to talk honestly with you about important issues in the case, you will be doing a better job than 90 percent of the lawyers who conduct jury selection.

Don't Alienate Neutral or Good Jurors, and Show You Are Reliable and Trustworthy

You can accomplish both of these goals with similar behavior; more to the point, you can defeat both with similar behavior.

Do Not Argue Your Case

Thirty years ago, the prevailing trial lawyer view was that jury selection was the first opportunity the lawyer had to convince jurors of the rightness of his cause. Lawyers would load their questions with facts from the case, using a level of finesse that ranged from heavy handed to argumentative. While a few gifted lawyers can do this effectively, most of us cannot. If you are not one of the gifted few, the result is that you will alienate the jurors. You are trying to get them to make up their minds before they have heard any evidence. They know this is wrong and unfair, both to the parties and to them. What does that say about you?

It is tempting to argue your case in jury selection, particularly if your opponent is doing so. Resist the temptation. If you want, ask the jurors questions about the points your opponent is arguing to them:

Mr. Abbot, defense counsel just told you that _____.
How do you think that might affect your verdict? Why?

Don't Patronize

Many lawyers loudly proclaim with their tone and manner, "I am a big shot lawyer and you are a common layman. I am smart, you . . . not so smart. I am clever, don't you agree?" Here is a painful secret. There will always be several jurors in the box who are smarter than you. In some cases, maybe all of them are. Patronize one of them, and you patronize them all. Patronize one of them, and you are on your way to losing your case.

Don't Waste Time

Famed Oregon trial lawyer Bill Barton tells of conducting a survey early in his career. He was not happy with his own voir dire or that of most of the lawyers he was watching. He asked the most respected judges and trial lawyers around the state whom they considered to be the best trial lawyers in the state. Then he obtained transcripts of these lawyers' voir dire examinations. He immediately noticed a huge difference between the average practitioners' voir dire examinations and those of the best practitioners: the best lawyers were taking about half the time in voir dire as the others.

The best lawyers know that voir dire is a tedious, often aggravating process for jurors. They spend hours, even days, waiting around for judges and lawyers to get the process moving. Then they listen to the lawyers ask the same questions over and over again of each prospective juror. The best way to alienate jurors is to appear to be dragging the process out even more. However long you take, some prospects will believe you took too long.

The best lawyers also know that there are limits to what you can accomplish in voir dire, and the best way to show you are reliable and trustworthy is to keep things moving—thereby showing respect for the jurors.

The best lawyers know that in voir dire, as in all other parts of trial, you can do more harm by going on too long than by stopping too soon.

Challenging for Cause

When you reach the point where the judge indicates she will hear challenges for cause, be ready to compare the prospects' answers with the legal standard for challenges for cause. You might say, "Your Honor, Mr. Smith, juror number six, rents an office from the hospital we are suing. Under _____, that qualifies as a landlord–tenant relationship, and we would like to challenge him for cause."

The most common challenges for cause are usually based not on bright-line bias rules—such as being the tenant of a party—but upon the more amorphous standards relating to the juror's expressed ability—or inability—to be fair. Spend the time to research the standards in your state on this subject, and have those standards readily at hand in the courtroom. When a juror gives an answer that indicates bias under your state's standards, you will know what to cite to the judge as the basis for your challenge.

Exercising Peremptory Challenges

To exercise a peremptory challenge, all you have to say is, "Your Honor, we thank and excuse juror number six." Some judges will not even ask you to say that. They will distribute a piece of paper with the jurors' names on it and ask you to indicate whom you would like excused. The tricky part, of course, is deciding whom to excuse, given your limited number of challenges.

Managing Chaos

Bring a friend. It is next to impossible to ask questions, listen to the answers, keep track of all the jurors' reactions to the questions and answers, and remember all of this information when it is time to exercise challenges. Bring another lawyer, a paralegal, a secretary, or a friend to help you keep track of all the information that will be pouring out into the courtroom during the relatively short period of jury selection.

Some judges will give you a seating chart, showing how the prospects are seated, and the number assigned to each seat. If the judge doesn't provide one, you can quickly sketch out your own seating chart. One simple way to organize is to write the name of each juror assigned to each seat, and then take notes in the box assigned to each juror. This method has simplicity to recommend it. The problem is that many of the jurors assigned to a box will be removed from their seats, and your box will now be filled with useless information. Some lawyers get around this problem by using Post-it Notes for each box, so when a juror is removed, a clean Post-it Note can be placed on the chart. With laptops now allowed in most courtrooms, the seating chart can be electronic—if someone else keeps it for you. Other lawyers use a simple list with numbers assigned to each juror, and plenty of space between each number to allow substitutions.

Each system has its strengths and weaknesses; none is ideal. Pick a system and use it for your first few trials, then modify it to account for your own strengths and weaknesses. If you feel your time selecting a jury is chaotic and uneven, welcome to the club.

Questions to Ask

Ask the judge how he conducts jury selection. Any method is likely to sound complicated when you first hear it described. Don't be afraid to ask follow-up questions like:

- Are there any factors you consider automatic excuses for hardship, like prepaid airline tickets or child care problems? (This will allow you to avoid spending time questioning jurors you know will be excused.)

- When would you like challenges for cause made?

- Would you prefer challenges for cause to be made at the bench or from counsel table?

- How many alternate jurors will there be?

- Will the jurors know they are alternates, or will they be selected randomly at the end of the trial?

- When and how would you like peremptory challenges made?

- Where will juror number one be seated, juror number two, and so on?

At this point, it is probably wise to also ask the judge where he prefers you to sit or stand when questioning jurors. Most judges require that lawyers stand when questioning prospective jurors or witnesses, or when addressing the court or jury. Some require that you sit when doing these things. Some judges are proud of the fact that they let lawyers wander around the courtroom at will while speaking. Others are equally proud of their ability to keep lawyers chained to a lectern or glued to their seats. So ask:

- Do you have a preference on where we stand while questioning the prospective jurors?

SUGGESTED READING

Ball, David. *David Ball on Damages.* 3rd ed. Portland, OR: Trial Guides, 2012.

Bettinger, Carl. *Twelve Heroes, One Voice: Guiding Jurors to Courageous Verdicts.* Portland, OR: Trial Guides, 2011.

Blue, Lisa, and Robert Hirschhorn. *Conducting Voir Dire.* The Little Blue Books. Portland, OR: Trial Guides, 2014.

———. *Preparing for Voir Dire.* The Little Blue Books. Portland, OR: Trial Guides, 2014.

Rowley, Nicholas. *Connecting with the Jury* (CD/DVD set). Portland, OR: Trial Guides, 2013.

9

OPENING STATEMENT

PURPOSE

The purpose of opening statement is to orient the fact-finder to the evidence that will be presented during the trial.[1] Over the course of a trial, evidence is often presented in a disjointed manner or out of logical order. Ideally, an opening statement gives the fact-finder a coherent overview of the evidence so he or she can make sense of it as it is presented.

ADVOCACY GOALS

This is your first chance to explain to the jury what the case is about and why your client deserves to win. Ideally, your opening will:

- Be interesting
- Discuss any facts or concepts the jurors might find unfamiliar

---

[1] *State v. Eisenlord*, 670 P.2d 1209, 1214 (Ariz. App. 1983); *People v. Farnam*, 47 P.3d 988, 1032 (Cal. 2002); *Occhicone v. State*, 570 So.2d 902, 904 (Fla. 1990); *People v. Kliner*, 705 N.E.2d 850, 874 (Ill. 1998); *De Vito v. Katsch*, 556 N.Y.S.2d 649 (N.Y. App. 1990); *State v. Kroll*, 558 P.2d 173 (Wash. 1976).

- Start to establish your credibility
- Place your client in the best (reasonably possible) light
- Undermine your opponent's case
- Explain why your client should win

Don't confuse this last point with arguing your case or stating your personal belief that your client should win. The court will not permit the first in opening statement, and it will not permit the second at any point in the trial. Still, ideally, you will tell the story, state the facts, and present the admissible evidence in such a way that at the end of your opening, the jurors will believe there is a high likelihood that the right verdict is for your client.

APPLICABLE LAW

May Not Argue or Be Argumentative

It is improper to argue your case in opening statements.[2] There is no doubt that argument occurs in many opening statements, often without objection. This is because "argument" is in the eye of the beholder. Generally speaking, stating what a witness or document will say is *not* argumentative. If you state what conclusions the jurors should draw from testimony or documents, the judge may consider this argumentative.

Your judge decides whether a statement is argumentative. Here are some cautionary points to help you avoid stepping over your judge's line.

---

[2] *See, e.g., State v. King,* 883 P.2d 1024, 1034 (Ariz. 1994) (cautioning lawyers not to argue a case through characterization of evidence in opening statements); *People v. McManus,* 4 Cal. Rptr. 642, 650 (Cal. App. 1960); *Juhasz v. Barton,* 1 So.2d 476 (Fla. 1941) ("Argumentative and imaginative creations have no proper place in an opening statement."); *State v. Kroll,* 558 P.2d 173, 179 (Wash. 1976) ("Argument and inflammatory remarks have no place in the opening statement.").

Avoid Expressing Conclusions about Matters in Dispute

Saying, "John Smith is a vicious rapist" will get you into trouble. You have not proven this yet; it is a conclusion you want the jury to draw. In addition, this is not effective advocacy. Why should the jury take *your* word that Smith is a rapist? On the other hand, suppose you said:

> On the evening of April 3rd of this year, two witnesses saw Sally Jones pushed out the passenger door of a red Ford Bronco while the Bronco was traveling about thirty miles per hour. These witnesses will tell you that they ran up to Ms. Jones, who was naked, with bruises about her face and neck... One of the witnesses took down the license number; the Bronco he saw was registered to John Smith...

As you add admissible fact to admissible fact, the jurors should be able to reach their own conclusions about whether Smith is the rapist. The jurors will always value their own conclusions more than yours.

You *are* allowed to state the opinions of lay witnesses ("Mr. Gonzalez will tell you the car was going very fast") and of experts ("the medical examiner will tell you the bruises on her throat were consistent with being strangled or tied by a rope around her neck").

Avoid Expressing Personal Opinion

This is unethical and poor advocacy.[3] New lawyers are particularly prone to this mistake: "I have never seen anything worse than the photos of Ms. Smith, taken that night." Do your best to

---

[3] ABA Model Rule of Professional Conduct 3.4(e) provides, "A lawyer shall not ... in trial, allude to any matter that the lawyer does not reasonably believe is relevant or that will not be supported by admissible evidence, assert personal knowledge of facts in issue except when testifying as a witness, *or state a personal opinion* as to the justness of a cause, the credibility of a witness, the culpability of a civil litigant or the guilt or innocence of an accused." (Emphasis added.)

leave the words "I" and "me" out of your opening statement, and you will be well on your way to avoiding this mistake.

"The Evidence Will Show" Is a Safe Harbor

Judges want you to restrict your comments to what the evidence will show. Accordingly, you could say, "On April 3rd of this year, Sally Jones was brutally raped. [Not in dispute.] *The evidence will show* John Smith committed this rape." Prefacing any statement with "the evidence will show" greatly reduces the chances of a sustained "argumentative" objection. With this preface, some judges will let you say (argue) almost anything: "The evidence will show John Smith is a vicious rapist." That doesn't mean you should abuse the privilege; use the phrase sparingly. If you want some variety, you can also use the phrases "We will prove" or "I will prove" to accomplish the same objective.

While these phrases can help you overcome objections, they are almost never the best way to present your case. Again, it is better to give the jurors the facts without your conclusions.

The Judge May Allow an Early Conclusory Statement

Most judges consider it appropriate for a lawyer to state his side's contentions in opening statement. The judge may well allow "We intend to prove to you that John Smith is a brutal rapist" in your opening, particularly if you say this early on. Or in a different case, you might say, "This is a case about one of the greediest corporations in America." If you say it in the first few minutes of your opening, it is unlikely the judge will sustain an objection. Judges want to give you the opportunity to clearly stake out your position. If you go on in this vein for more than a few sentences, be prepared for the judge to cut you off.

Watch Your Tone

Judges are much more likely to allow statements that could be construed as arguments if you deliver them in a calm, matter-of-fact tone. Conversely, if you use a strident, histrionic tone, the judge will often sustain an "argumentative" objection, even if your words aren't.

Don't Dwell on the Law

The judge will probably allow you to talk about the elements of the plaintiff's or prosecutor's case, or elements of affirmative defenses. This can be a valuable part of your opening. If you do so, do your best to use the actual language from the jury instructions. If the other side challenges you, you can show you are using language approved in pattern instructions. Spending too much time explaining why the evidence does or does not meet these elements may result in the judge sustaining an objection—it sounds like argument.

Avoiding Argument Does Not Require Avoiding a Compelling Presentation

As the California Supreme Court has recognized, "Nothing prevents the statement from being presented in a story-like manner that holds the attention of lay jurors and ties the facts and governing law together in an understandable way."[4]

Don't Worry Too Much about Objections

Every judge is different. If you are doing your job of trying to be convincing, your opponent may object—or he may not. The judge may sustain the objection—or she may not. *This is not a big deal.* Just move on. Perhaps begin your next sentence with, "The evidence will show . . ."

Limit Opening to Anticipated Evidence

Obviously, at the start of the trial, you may not necessarily know exactly what evidence the other side will present or what evidence will be admitted. But you cannot refer to matters that you do not reasonably expect to be shown by admissible evidence.[5]

---

[4] *People v. Farnam*, 47 P.3d 988, 1032 (Cal. 2002), quoting *People v. Millwee*, 954 P.2d 990, 1014 (Cal. 1998).

[5] *People v. Kliner*, 705 N.E.2d 850, 874 (Ill. 1998).

Stated a different way, any party may refer to admissible evidence it expects in good faith to be presented at trial.[6]

As an example, if the defense made a motion to exclude presentation of the defendant's two prior DUIs, but the judge has not ruled on the motion by the time of opening, *don't mention the DUIs*. If the admission of any piece or type of evidence is controversial, don't speak of it in opening without first clearing it with the judge.

Most Judges Allow the Showing of Admissible Exhibits

A related question is whether you can show or refer to exhibits during opening. Judges generally allow you to show the jury exhibits that all parties have agreed to admit before trial, exhibits that the court has ruled admissible through pretrial motions, and exhibits you expect to be admitted at trial,[7] although it is a good idea to check your judge's practice. Your ability to use demonstrative exhibits[8] in opening depends on the exhibits' content. Just as the judge won't allow an opening statement that is argumentative, she also won't allow demonstrative exhibits that are argumentative or contain argument.

---

[6] *See State v. Whelchel,* 801 P.2d 948 (Wash. 1990) ("It is well settled that any party may, in opening statement, refer to admissible evidence expected to be presented at trial.").

[7] *See State v. Sucharew,* 66 P.3d 59 (Ariz. App. 2003) (approving electronic presentation during opening of photographs and map later introduced at trial); *People v. Wash,* 861 P.2d 1107, 1133 (Cal. 1993) ("The purpose of the opening statement 'is to prepare the minds of the jury to follow the evidence and to more readily discern its materiality, force and effect' and the use of matters which are admissible in evidence, and which are subsequently in fact received in evidence, may aid this purpose."), quoting *People v. Green,* 47 Cal.2d 209, 215, 302 P.2d 307 (1956); *Decker v. St. Mary's Hosp.,* 619 N.E.2d 537, 545 (Ill. App. 1993) ("Clearly, a party is allowed to show exhibits, which will later be admitted into evidence, to the jury during the opening statement.").

[8] "Demonstrative exhibits" are things you show the jury that are not designed to be admitted into evidence. A large timeline on a poster board (or projected slide) could be a demonstrative exhibit, as could a small toy truck and car, used to show how an accident happened.

Describe Facts Establishing All Elements

At one time, in some jurisdictions, if the prosecutor or plaintiff's lawyer failed to describe facts supporting an element of the crime or cause of action in her opening statement, the judge could dismiss the case at the end of the opening statement. This view is becoming rarer.[9] If your opponent moves to dismiss your case because you failed to discuss an element of your case, simply ask to reopen your presentation to correct or repair the problem.[10]

IMPLEMENTATION

Remember, you have been working on the case for days, months, or years. And you are a lawyer. Much about the case may seem obvious to you. The jurors are starting in total and complete ignorance. You must educate them about the simplest parts of your case without patronizing.

---

[9] *See, e.g., People v. Baltes,* 904 N.Y.S.2d 554 (N.Y. App. 2010) (stating that trial court should have dismissed two counts based on prosecutor's failure to address them adequately in opening, but also noting that judge should have addressed issue before defendant's opening, in order to allow the prosecution the opportunity to supplement its statement); *De Vito v. Katsch,* 556 N.Y.S.2d 649, 653 (N.Y. App. 1990) ("[T]he prospect of a dismissal on opening exists only when, from all available indications, the case is doomed to defeat. . . . [T]he trial court has the power to dismiss upon the opening, but that power should be exercised 'with great caution.'"). The dismissal of a case based on opening is disfavored, and should be done only after a number of safeguards are followed. *Id.; State v. Gallagher,* 549 P.2d 499, 502 (Wash. 1976) (if civil plaintiff or prosecutor chooses to make opening statement and it eliminates material issues of fact and makes clear that the plaintiff has no claim, the case may be dismissed); *Scott v. Rainbow Ambulance Serv., Inc.,* 452 P.2d 220 (Wash. 1969) ("The authority of the trial court to summarily dismiss an action on the opening statement is recognized in our state. . . . [T]he trial judge, as a matter of justice, must be slow to grant such a motion.").

[10] *De Vito v. Katsch,* 556 N.Y.S.2d 649, 655 (N.Y. App. 1990) (explaining that in both civil and criminal cases, the party facing dismissal should be afforded the opportunity to correct inadequacies in the opening statement, if possible).

Be Interesting

Generally speaking, the best way to construct an opening statement is to tell the story of the case in chronological order. As you get more experienced, you can try fancier, more creative methods, but chances are, most of the really good opening statements you hear, read, or deliver yourself will be in story form, in chronological order.

This is not the time to go into great detail about all the facts the jury will hear about in the course of the trial. There is a limit to how much the jurors can absorb in their first exposure to the facts. You need to give them enough information to hook their interest in the drama that is about to unfold in front of them, without diluting the drama with too much detail. If you can save details for later, do so.

Discuss Facts or Concepts Unfamiliar to the Jurors

Often, you will need to educate jurors about some technical matter they have never before encountered. If your defense is that a police officer improperly administered a Breathalyzer test, the jurors need to understand what you claim he did wrong. If you claim your client suffered from post-traumatic stress disorder as a result of an accident, you need to explain what this is. Again, you do not want to deliver so much detail that your story bogs down. Still, part of your job is to educate the jurors so they can understand your position and contentions.

In opening, many lawyers make one of two mistakes when it comes to educating jurors. Some fail to mention or explain crucial technical information: "You say your client has PTSD, but what *is* that?" Others make the opposite mistake. They go on and on explaining technical details that the jurors will never need to understand. If your position is that the Breathalyzer was improperly cleaned, you do not have to explain who invented it or where the parts are manufactured.

To avoid these mistakes, ask yourself: What *must* the jurors understand to decide this case properly? Give them that level of technical information and no more.

Start to Establish Your Credibility

Many trial lawyers refer to a trial as a battle for credibility or a race for credibility. They recognize an indisputable truth: the lawyer with greater credibility with the jury has a huge advantage.

You don't begin trial with credibility; you have to earn it. You earn it by:

- Being prepared, organized, and knowledgeable

- Being respectful toward everyone in the courtroom, especially jurors

- Not wasting time

- Being as accurate and truthful as possible in your presentation to the jury

As an advocate, it is easy to fall in love with your own position, arguments, and facts, and to overlook or dismiss your opponent's. You may want to win so badly that you imply something is true when it isn't. You cannot and should not recite every fact in opening. But if you leave out something important, or you imply something is true when it isn't, you are killing your credibility.

Never, Ever

Never, ever, say or imply you will prove something you cannot.[11]

Never, ever do anything that jurors can construe as an attempt to mislead them.

Remember, there is a smart, educated, experienced advocate on the other side, just waiting for you to overstate your case or to say something he can prove is inaccurate or incorrect. He knows that if he can hurt your credibility, he can hurt your case.

As with all good advice, you can carry this last admonition too far. Some trial lawyers are so concerned with maintaining their credibility that they are afraid to take a stand in the courtroom,

---

[11] If you have doubts about whether evidence you will be relying on will be admissible, either seek a pretrial ruling that it is or leave it out of your opening.

afraid to vigorously advocate a position for fear that their opponent will undercut them in some way. The jurors *expect* you to advocate for your client. They will applaud you for fighting for your client; they will reject you for trying to mislead them. You know the difference; so do they.

Place Your Client in the Best (Reasonably Possible) Light

Often, though not always, your client is the protagonist in the story you must tell. With luck, you will have facts about your client that neither side disputes, and that place him in a favorable light. Is she a military veteran or a Little League coach? Is he a self-made, rags-to-riches businessman? What can you tell the jury about your client that is consistent with the verdict you want? If your client is a father of three and a Little League coach, the jury will be less inclined to convict him of burglary.

Simply stated, people or organizations that jurors perceive as having admirable qualities have a better chance at a favorable verdict. And all litigants, from the largest impersonal corporation to the lowest level street criminal, have some admirable qualities. As a well-known criminal defense saying goes, "everyone is innocent of something."

But as with every point you make in trial, you have to consider the counterpoint. If you talk about what a great work ethic your client has, that may allow your opponent to talk about the three jobs he was fired from—evidence that the judge might not have admitted if you hadn't *opened the door* to that subject.

Undermine Your Opponent's Case

In a very real sense, you are telling two stories in opening. The first is why your client deserves a favorable verdict; the second is why your opposition deserves an unfavorable verdict. If you structure your opening chronologically, you can tell both stories at once.

Often, one of these stories is much stronger than the other. An obvious example is the criminal case where the defendant does not take the stand or present evidence. As the defense lawyer, you can probably bring out some positive facts about your client, but your main story might be how the police bungled the crime investigation and now have inadequate evidence to convict.

No matter how strong your story of why your client deserves to win, you almost always want to integrate the story of why the other side deserves to lose. Do that by giving the jury facts that tell that story as well.

Explain Why Your Client Should Win

At a minimum, after hearing both openings, the jurors should understand why you think you should win. Hopefully, they will now believe you have the stronger case. Ideally, they will now *want* you to win. You usually can't achieve all of this in opening, but you can try.

To have any hope of the jurors wanting you to win after the openings are done, it is important to understand that you are in essence explaining two separate, but related things to the jurors. First, you are explaining why your client is legally entitled to the verdict you are asking for, and second, you are explaining why that is a fair and morally right result.

For example, in a medical malpractice case, the plaintiff's lawyer might explain how the defendant fell below the standard of care, causing his client injury. Legally, that might entitle the plaintiff to relief, but it will not be enough to get the jurors to *want* the plaintiff to win. If the jurors also hear that the doctor was arrogant, rude, and rushing out the door to play golf at the time he committed malpractice, then they may want the plaintiff to win.

Sometimes you can explain both the legal and moral basis for a favorable verdict in opening; other times, the moral basis must wait for closing. For example, in a criminal case where the defense presents no evidence, the defense lawyer may need to explain the reason why the reasonable doubt standard is morally fair and correct. But the defense lawyer must wait until closing—the judge would consider such an explanation argumentative in opening statement.

From the beginning to the end of trial, your job is to show the jury why a verdict in your favor is not only legally correct, but morally right.

Should You Reserve Opening?

Most jurisdictions allow a defendant to *reserve opening*. That means the defense does not follow the prosecution's or plaintiff's opening with one of its own. Instead, the defense waits until the prosecution or plaintiff has presented all their evidence. Then, before presenting their own evidence, the defense makes an opening statement.

From the earliest common law trials until the mid-1970s, reserving opening was quite common. The idea was for the defense to keep their evidence, strategy, and arguments a secret from the other side until that side had presented its entire case. Then, the defense would pounce, hopefully surprising the prosecution or plaintiff with an unexpected witness, document, or argument that would prove fatal to their case.

With the adoption of more expansive discovery in both civil and criminal cases, reserving opening has less chance of delivering a knockout surprise. In addition, reserved openings have numerous strategic disadvantages. If you reserve your opening, you give up the chance to counter the favorable impression your opponent makes in her opening, you give up the chance to tell a story that can compete with your opponent's story, and you risk the jurors having made up their minds against you before you do your own opening. For all these reasons, a reserved opening is now almost unheard of. Still, in the right case, this high-risk strategy might be the best chance for a favorable verdict.

Practical Considerations

Should you object to the other side's opening? Usually not. It won't get you anywhere unless the other lawyer is violating an *in limine* ruling. Otherwise, the judge will just tell your opponent to move on, and you look defensive even before the evidence starts coming in.

Should you stay at the lectern or walk around? Should you use notes or memorize your opening? Should you use PowerPoint or other demonstrative aids to tell your story? You can find excellent lawyers who answer each of these questions differently. How you answer them will depend on your level of experience, what your judge will allow, your personality, and the characteristics of your case. To the extent you are allowed, do what feels most natural to you as you tell your story to the jury.

Questions to Ask

- Does the court have time limits for opening statements? (Be prepared to tell the judge how much time you would like.)

- May I show these exhibits to the jury during opening? (Be prepared with copies to show the court and opposing counsel.)

- Where should I place the easel or screen during opening?

- May I show demonstrative exhibits to the jury during opening?

- Are there any restrictions on where I can stand during opening?

- I would like to mention _____ [piece or type of evidence] in opening, but wanted to make sure the court does not have a problem with that.

Suggested Reading

Bailey, William S., and Robert W. Bailey. *Show the Story: The Power of Visual Advocacy.* Portland, OR: Trial Guides, 2011.

Julien, Al. *Opening Statements.* Callaghan, 1980.

Klonoff, Robert, and Paul Colby. *Winning Jury Trials: Trial Tactics and Sponsorship Strategy.* 3rd ed. New York: LexisNexis, 2007.

Perdue, Jim. *Winning with Stories: Using the Narrative to Persuade in Trials, Speeches and Lectures.* Austin, TX: Texas Bar Books, 2006.

10

PRESENTING YOUR CASE-IN-CHIEF: DIRECT EXAMINATION

PURPOSE

Case-in-chief refers to the part of the trial when it is a party's turn to present evidence. This is primarily done by calling witnesses to the stand and asking them questions—*direct examination*—and by admitting exhibits. The opposition may also introduce evidence, through cross-examination or admitting exhibits during cross-examination.

After the prosecution or plaintiff presents their case-in-chief, the defendant may then present their own case-in-chief. When the defense presents their case, the opposition may present additional evidence through cross-examining the defense witnesses.

When the defendant's case-in-chief is over, the prosecution or plaintiff may be allowed to present rebuttal evidence.

The purpose of a plaintiff or prosecution case-in-chief is to introduce evidence to support the legal elements that must be proven to secure a favorable verdict. The purpose of the defense case-in-chief is to introduce evidence to disprove or undermine those elements or to establish an affirmative defense.

ADVOCACY GOALS

◆ Establish the legal elements you must prove to obtain a favorable verdict.

◆ Tell your story, through witnesses and exhibits, in a smooth, coherent, easy-to-follow manner.

◆ Undermine the opposition's claims or positions.

◆ Have the jurors like or identify with your client, your witnesses, and you.

◆ Have the jurors *want* to decide in your favor.

APPLICABLE LAW

No Leading Questions

You may not ask leading questions of a witness you have called to testify unless that witness is somehow adverse or hostile to your case.[1] A leading question is a question that suggests the answer.[2] It is "leading" the witness to give a particular answer. For example:

---

[1] Ariz. Evid. R. 611(c) (prohibiting leading questions on direct examination "except as necessary to develop the witness's testimony" or where the witness is hostile, an adverse party, or identified with an adverse party); Cal. Evid. Code § 767(a)(1) (prohibiting leading questions except under special circumstances); *People v. Spain,* 201 Cal. Rptr. 555, 560 (Cal. App. 1984) (noting that being faced with a hostile witness has long been considered "special circumstances"); Fla. Stat. Ann. § 90.612(3) (essentially the same as Ariz. Evid. R. 611(c)); Ill. Evid. R. 611(c) (essentially the same as Ariz. Evid. R. 611(c)); *Ferri v. Ferri,* 878 N.Y.S.2d 67, 68–69 (N.Y. App. 2009) (whether to permit leading questions on direct of adverse or hostile witness is within the sound discretion of trial court); Wash. Evid. R. 611(c) (essentially the same as Ariz. Evid. R. 611(c)).

[2] *State v. Agnew,* 647 P.2d 1165, 1175 (Ariz. App. 1982); Cal. Evid. Code § 764; *Porter v. State,* 386 So.2d 1209, 1211 (Fla. App. 1980); *Launius v. Board of Fire and Police Commissioners,* 603 N.E.2d 477, 482 (Ill. 1992); *People v. Mather,* 4 Wend. 229, 247 (N.Y. Sup. Ct. 1830); *State v. Scott,* 149 P.2d 152 (Wash. 1944) ("The principal test of a leading question is: Does it suggest the answer desired?").

"On December 1st of last year, you were on the corner of Elm and Stuart streets at 10:00 a.m.?" The witness—and everyone else in the courtroom—knows what answer you want and expect. By contrast, "Where were you at 10:00 a.m. on December 1st of last year?" is not leading because the question does not provide information for the answer.

As with many evidentiary issues, the boundaries of propriety are drawn differently from courtroom to courtroom. "Did you see the color of the traffic light?" is arguably a leading question because it suggests there *was* a traffic light *and* that the witness was able to see it. "What is your name?" suggests the witness has a name. Ridiculous examples like these can tie you into mental knots and cause unnecessary labor and anxiety.

You will hear lawyers and judges argue extensively about whether a particular question is leading. The truth is, there is a lot of grey area here. Whether a question is leading also depends on context. Rather than attempting to apply some rigid formula to the issue of whether a question is leading, it is better to remember the purpose behind the rule: we do not want lawyers coaching witnesses on the stand, or effectively telling witnesses what to say.

On the other hand, we do not want to laboriously walk through uncontested material in a non-leading manner: "Do you have a name?" "Do you have a house?" "Did you leave your house at some time last year?" "On what date?" "At what time?"

All judges allow what are arguably leading questions when, as a practical matter, the leading is unimportant and helps move things along. Leading can be unimportant either because the fact you are suggesting is itself unimportant or because the fact you are suggesting is uncontested. If both sides agree the witness was on the corner of Elm and Stuart on December 1st of last year, there is no harm in suggesting that in the question.

This is not to say you want to ask leading questions just because the judge will allow them. As a matter of style, tactics, or presentation, leading your own witness is often not as effective as letting her offer up the facts in her own words.

Generally speaking, the closer you are to the important, disputed issues in your case, the more care you must take *not* to lead.

The further you are from important, disputed issues, the more leading the judge (and your opponent) will allow.

If you are unsure of yourself, or the judge or opposing counsel are tormenting you over leading questions, remember the journalistic device: *who, what, when, where, why, and how.* It is almost impossible to ask a leading question that begins with one of these words. *Did, do,* and *could* are also good words to start non-leading questions:

- *Where* were you on December 1st of last year at 10:00 a.m.?
- *Did* you see anything unusual?
- *What* did you see?
- *Could* you see the color of the traffic light?

Of course, it is still possible to begin a question with one of these words and have it be leading: "Did you see the red Corvette race through the intersection?" But if you are trying to avoid leading questions, these words are a good start.

Implementation

Preparing Your Case-in-Chief

Go through the jury instructions—both yours and those you expect or have received from your opponent. What are the elements you must prove to receive a favorable verdict?

The instructions are your starting point for thinking about this issue, but you must go further. For example, if a car hit your client while she was crossing the street, the jury instruction will tell you that you must prove the defendant driver was negligent. But what does that mean, in practical terms?

If your claim is that the defendant was negligent because he ran a red light, then the fact that the light was red is one of the essential facts you must prove to receive a favorable verdict. You may also want to prove that your client was clearly visible to an alert driver, and that may also be a fact you will seek to prove to support a negligence verdict.

Conversely, representing the defendant driver, attempting to defeat a negligence claim, you may want to prove lack of negligence by showing:

- The light was green.
- The plaintiff was wearing dark clothing at night.
- The plaintiff unexpectedly ran across the road.
- The defendant was driving at or below the speed limit.

Yes, you may want to prove these things, but how will you do it? Which witness(es) will establish each point? On the plaintiff's side, you may have a witness walking alongside the plaintiff who can say the light had changed before they started across the street. Perhaps that witness helps with the color of the light, but can say nothing about how fast the defendant's car was going. You may be lucky enough to have a passenger in the defendant's car who never saw the traffic light, but can testify she was concerned about the speed of the car. Maybe you did your homework and obtained the defendant's cell phone records, which show he was talking on his phone at the time of the accident. Your case-in-chief outline might look something like this:

Negligence
Red light
Mrs. Jones
Car speeding
Mr. Smith
Defendant inattentive
Police officer [to establish time of accident from 911 call]
Phone company records custodian [to introduce phone records showing defendant on phone at time of call]

Damages
Nature of injuries
Dr. Wise [treating doctor]

Wage loss
> Mr. Bell [boss, to show wage loss and that plaintiff is a good worker]

Past medical expenses
> Mr. Green [to introduce medical bills]

Future medical expenses
> Dr. Wise [treating doctor]

Noneconomic damages
> Dr. Wise [pain of procedures employed]
> Wife [can't sleep; can't mow lawn or play with kids]
> Hunting friends [can't hunt; used to love it]
> Coworker [used to be happy at work; now very uncomfortable and unhappy]

Note that a single witness, like Dr. Wise in the outline above, may establish more than one point or element. And it may take a number of witnesses for you to prove a single point.

You may also annotate your outline with the exhibit numbers of the documents that help establish each case element. This is especially important in a document-intensive case.

Once you have figured out which witnesses and documents support each element of your case, it is time to prepare each witness outline.

Preparing Your Witness Outlines

You should not call a witness unless he can help you establish (or refute) at least one important fact or element of the case. But each witness may also have things to say that you believe are helpful to your case, although not essential. For example, Mrs. Jones, who crossed the street with the plaintiff when he got hit, may walk with him every Saturday morning to the YMCA where they both volunteer to work with disadvantaged children. Must you prove this to win your case? No. Does it help you win? You bet.

As you prepare your witness outline, it may be helpful to think of each witness as having at least one story to tell. You don't have to get fancy or complicated here. Just think of each story as having a beginning, a middle, and an end.

Beginning: Who Is the Witness and Why Does She Have Anything Important to Say?

Q: *Where* do you live?[3]

A: 1734 Elm Street.

Q: *How* long have you lived there?

A: Forty-two years.

Q: *Do* you know Mr. Taylor [the plaintiff]?

A: Yes, we've been neighbors for about twenty years.

Q: *Were* you with him on December 1st of last year at about 10:00 in the morning?

A: Yes, that was a Saturday. We are together almost every Saturday morning.

Q: *Why* is that?

A: We volunteer together at the YMCA every Saturday from 10:30 a.m. to 3:00 p.m.

Q: *Did* you see the accident?

A: Yes I did.

Middle: What Does She Have to Say?

Q: *Can* you tell us what happened?

A: John met me at the corner like he always does. We waited for the light to turn, and when the "walk" sign lit up, we started across the street.

---

[3] Certain words are italicized in this example to illustrate the non-leading nature of the questions. You would not want to audibly emphasize the words as shown here.

Q: *Can* you show us on this diagram where you were when you started across the street?

A: Yes. We were standing right here; then when the light turned, we started across Elm like this.

Q: *Did* you see any cars as you started across the road?

A: I didn't really look; I just saw the light change and we both started across.

The witness would go on, in response to your questioning, to describe the accident.

End: Addressing Your Opponent's Points, Summing Up, and Editorializing

The end of the story is where the meaning becomes clear, you and the witness deliver the moral, and you put the opponent's points to rest, if you haven't done this already. You may also need or want to address some points you know your opponent will raise in cross:

Q: *Were* you wearing your regular glasses that day?

A: No, my regular glasses were broken, and I was wearing an older pair.

Q: So *how* can you be sure the light changed?

A: I had no trouble seeing the sign. The glasses I was wearing aren't that old.

You might sum up like this:

Q: *Is* there any question in your mind that the "walk" light went on before you started across the street?

Q: *How* can you be so sure?

Or, you could insert some commentary:

Q: *Why* do you remember this so clearly?

A: It was one of the most frightening and horrible experiences of my life.

Think of Each Point Separately

Each witness may have more than one important point to make. Again, it is helpful to think of each important point as its own story: beginning (why does this witness know what she is about to tell us?), middle (what can she tell us?), end (address opposition points, sum up, and commentary).

Mrs. Jones may have another story to tell about calling 911 and going to the hospital with your client. The main point of this story might be how much your client suffered—or how brave and stoic he was. She may have yet another story about the impact of the injuries on your client in the years since the accident. Each of these stories has its own beginning, middle, and end. For example:

Beginning

Q: You told us earlier you volunteered at the YMCA with Mr. Taylor?[4]

A: Yes.

Q: *How* long have you been doing that with him?

A: I don't know how long he was doing it, but he got me involved about five years ago. We've been doing it almost every Saturday since then.

Q: *What* do the two of you actually do there?

A: John coaches basketball and baseball—for all ages. He teaches them really more than coaches. He'll take a few kids aside and work with them on their skills. I usually supervise to make sure the kids are all behaving themselves.

Q: On most Saturdays, *would* you be in a position to see John working with the kids?

A: Oh yes, we are almost always within sight of each other.

---

[4] Technically, this is leading, but she has already told the jury about this. In the unlikely event of an objection, you tell the judge you are just transitioning to a new topic and laying the foundation.

Middle

You could then ask question to elicit information about what John did with the kids before the accident and how active, energetic, and happy he was. This would be followed by questions eliciting observations about the problems he has had since the accident. Maybe he must frequently sit down to rest, she sees him wince in pain, or he has had to go back to the doctor after a Saturday session at the Y.

End

Q: Given all these problems, *are* you surprised that John keeps going to the Y?

A: No, he loves working with those kids.

Q: Does he ever talk about quitting?

A: I tell him sometimes he should stop or shorten his hours, but he won't hear of it.

You can string story after story together—beginning, middle, end. When all your stories are strung together, you have your direct exam outline.

This example shows you questions so you can see the end result. But in preparing your outline, there is no need to write out questions at all. The outline for this exam might just contain the facts, like this:

Has lived at 1734 Elm St. for 42 years.

Known Mr. Taylor for 20 yrs.

Was with him 12/1 at 10:00 a.m. They volunteer at the YMCA together . . .

Every lawyer finds her own way to structure witness outlines. Do what is most comfortable for you.

A note of caution: You may have multiple witnesses who can testify to the same factual issues. That does not mean that they all *should* testify to those issues. For one thing, having several witnesses cover the same ground is usually boring. Moreover, there is a serious risk that they will contradict each other on some points. (See chapter 5's discussion on overtrying your case.) Decide who your best witness is to establish a particular fact, and think long and hard about presenting another witness on that same issue. Weigh the risks of boredom and contradiction against any benefit you think you might gain.

Listen to the Answers

Every advocacy book makes this point and virtually every CLE speaker addressing witness examination makes it too: get your eyes and ears off your outline and listen to what the witness is actually saying in real time. With the witness on the stand, the examination is no longer an abstract construct in your head—it should be a real conversation with the witness. If you don't listen, it won't be; and it won't be interesting, compelling, or persuasive.

Preparing Your Witness

If you have followed the advice in chapter 3, you have met with every witness who will testify at trial, except those you are legally prohibited from meeting.[5] This includes witnesses whom the other side may call.

---

[5] For example, you are not permitted to meet with the adverse party or, if it is a corporation, its managing agents or decision makers. *E.g.* Fla. R. Prof. Conduct 4–4.2 (barring communications "with a person the lawyer knows to be represented by another lawyer in the matter" without consent or under other certain limited circumstances). States vary in their formulation of how this general rule applies to the employees of a corporation, and such nuances are beyond the scope of this book. You are also not permitted to communicate with the other side's expert witnesses. *County of Los Angeles v. Superior Court,* 271 Cal. Rptr. 698 (Cal. App. 1990) (attorney who contacted opposing party's expert was disqualified from case); *Kenneth C. v. Delonda R.,* 814 N.Y.S.2d 562 (N.Y. Family Ct. 2006) (discussing ABA and New York ethic opinions that held that while contacting opponent's expert may not be strictly prohibited by ethics rules, such contact is likely to violate court rules); *In re Firestorm 1991,* 916 P.2d 411 (Wash. 1998) (holding that Wash. Civil Rule 26(b)(5) prohibits ex parte contact with an expert retained by an opposing party). See generally Fed. R. Civ. P. 26(b)(4) (providing significant work product protection to expert preparation).

Now it is time to meet with your witnesses and tell them what to expect at trial. By now, you have completed your outline. Go over the basic facts of each story your witnesses have to tell. Let them know that you are not asking them to memorize a script, but are simply trying to ensure you understand their story well enough to ask the right questions. Be alert. As you go over your outline with a witness, he may tell you things you haven't heard before. It is not too late to change your outline.

Remind your witnesses of the context of their testimony—how they fit into the case. Tell them about the judge's and opposing counsel's style and personalities. If you have time, bring them by the courtroom to show them the physical layout.

You are the witness's guide to appropriate behavior in the courtroom. You might want to cover the following issues with your client and your witnesses:

- Dress as if you are going to church or a business meeting.

- If you run into jurors anywhere outside the courtroom, you may smile and nod at them, but don't speak with them at all until the case is over.

- The jury is judging your nonverbal communication as well as the substance of what you say. They are always watching you, inside and outside of the courtroom.

- There is nothing wrong with having met with an attorney (you) before the trial. The attorney wanted to understand what you saw, heard, or did.

- If you don't understand a question, ask the lawyer or judge to repeat it or explain it.

- If a lawyer refers to a document or deposition, ask to see the portion he is referring to before you answer the question.

- There is nothing wrong with pausing to think about an answer. Silence can feel scary, but it actually gives you more power.

- When the opposing lawyer is asking you questions, do not look over at me—*ever*.

◆ Be polite at all times. Leave the sarcasm and wisecracks at home.

Order of Proof

Which witness do you call first? Most lawyers like to start with a strong witness whom the other side cannot impeach. But others will call the adverse party as their first witness. There is no "right" witness to call first, and no "right" order of proof. Put yourself in the jurors' shoes. They know nothing about your case. Which witness's testimony best sets the stage for your case and will be easy to assimilate?

Admitting Exhibits

When an exhibit is admitted into evidence, it becomes a part of the record that the jury or judge can consider in arriving at a decision. It can also later be designated as part of the appellate record.

The law of evidence controls whether an exhibit is admissible. Is it relevant? Is it overly prejudicial? Does it contain hearsay?

The admissibility of evidence is beyond the scope of this book. But before you can ask a judge to admit an exhibit, you must first *introduce* the exhibit and *lay a foundation* for the judge to admit it. While the law of evidence also governs this, it is also an important practical part of a trying a case, and many evidence teachers do not do a very good job of explaining how to do this.

Introducing an exhibit is just what the term implies: either you or a witness announce what the exhibit is:

Q: Can you tell us what Exhibit 43 is?

Or

Q: I am handing you a letter from Mr. Smith to Mr. Jones dated March 18th, 2013, which we have marked as Exhibit 43; have you seen that before?

In the first example, the witness is asked to introduce the exhibit. In the second example, the lawyer is introducing it. It ordinarily makes no difference who introduces the exhibit; this is almost never a point of contention.

Laying a foundation is another matter. Many lawyers and judges are hypertechnical about laying a proper foundation—often without fully understanding the concept themselves.

To lay a proper foundation, you must present enough information to the judge[6] for her to decide that a reasonable juror could conclude the exhibit is authentic—that is, that it is what you say it is.[7] Stated in plain English: could a reasonable person conclude this is authentic, not a fake?

Note that this does not mean you must prove beyond doubt that the exhibit is authentic, or even that you need to *prove* it at all. Rather, you only need to offer evidence sufficient to support a finding in your favor, in the absence of contrary evidence.[8]

Particularly if your opponent has no evidence of fraud or fabrication, it is enough if direct or circumstantial evidence is presented to the judge from which it reasonably could be concluded that the evidence is what you say it is.[9]

Let's try a few examples:

---

[6] *See* Fed. R. Evid. 104 (preliminary questions of admissibility of evidence are determined by the judge). This basic foundational principle, expressed in Fed. R. Evid. 104, is similar in all American jurisdictions.

[7] *See* Fed. R. Evid. 901(a) ("The requirement of authentication or identification as a condition precedent to admissibility is satisfied by evidence sufficient to support a finding that the matter in question is what the proponent claims."). *See also* Fed. R. Evid. 104(b).

[8] *See State v. Lavers*, 814 P.2d 333, 343 (Ariz. 1991) ("The judge does not determine whether the evidence is authentic, but only whether evidence exists from which the jury could reasonably conclude that it is authentic.") (citations omitted); *ITT Real Estate Equities, Inc. v. Chandler Ins. Agency, Inc.*, 617 So.2d 750, 750 (Fla. App. 1993) ("Evidence is authenticated when *prima facie* evidence is introduced to prove that the proffered evidence is authentic."); *Rice v. Offshore Systems, Inc.*, 272 P.3d 865, 870 (Wash. 2012) (stating that proponent of evidence must make a *prima facie* showing of authenticity and that, in evaluating issue, court considers only evidence in favor of admissibility); *see also* Fed. R. Evid. 901(b) (listing illustrations of authentication and identification methods that comply with the rule).

[9] *See, e.g.*, Fed. R. Evid. 901(b)(4).

Q: I am handing you a letter from Mr. Smith to Mr. Jones dated March 18th, 2013; have you seen that before?

A: Yes, I am the Mr. Jones the letter is addressed to; I received this letter in late March of 2013.

Foundation laid.

Q: I am handing you a letter from Mr. Smith to Mr. Jones dated March 18th, 2013, which we have marked as Exhibit 43; have you seen that before?

A: No. I stopped being Mr. Smith's secretary earlier that year.

Q: How long had you been his secretary?

A: Fifteen years.

Q: How many letters did you send out for him?

A: Thousands, maybe more.

Q: Are you familiar with the letterhead he would use?

A: Yes, that is it.

Q: Are you familiar with his signature?

A: Yes, that is it.

Foundation laid.

The foundation of business documents is often not contested. When it is contested, different judges require different levels of detail to establish foundation. Most are extremely impatient with foundation objections and foundation testimony when there is really no legitimate question as to a document's authenticity. But you always want to be thinking about how you will lay a foundation if necessary.

Whenever you hear a foundation objection—whether to an exhibit or testimony by a witness—the real question you need to answer is: "How does this witness know what he is trying to tell us?" or "How does this witness know this document is what he says it is?"

Some exhibits are designed to re-create an event. A computer animation of an accident or surgery would be an example. In the case of such exhibits, laying a foundation may take more time and involve more detailed questioning. The exact requirements vary between jurisdictions, and vary again depending on whether disputed scientific principles are incorporated in the exhibit, the purpose for which you are introducing the exhibit, and whether you are seeking to admit the exhibit into evidence or just show it to the jury to illustrate a point. In any event, research the law in your jurisdiction ahead of time, and at a minimum, be prepared to show the judge that your exhibit is accurate, reliable, and not misleading.

Once you have introduced the exhibit and laid its foundation, you still need to ask to have it admitted. To admit an exhibit, you must first:

Identify the Exhibit

Q: I am handing you a letter from Mr. Smith to Mr. Jones dated March 18th, 2013, which we have marked as Exhibit 43; have you seen that before?

Lay a Foundation for the Exhibit

Q: Did you receive that letter from Mr. Smith sometime after March 18th?

A: Yes.

Q: Did you alter that letter in any way?

[This would usually be overkill.]

A: No.

Ask That the Exhibit Be Admitted into Evidence

You: Your Honor, I would ask that Exhibit 43 be admitted into evidence.

Court: Any objection?

Opponent: No, Your Honor.

Court: Exhibit 43 is admitted.

This is the basic pattern, and you won't go far wrong trying to follow it. But if you have time, go to the courtroom and watch your judge conduct a trial. You will quickly pick up on how he likes to handle exhibits.

Once the judge has admitted the exhibit, you can show it to the jury, read it to the jury, and question witnesses about it.

Once the exhibit is admitted, you should show it to the jury if you are going to continue asking questions about it. Lawyers commonly achieve admission of an exhibit and proceed to ask detailed questions about it without ever showing it to the jury. It makes jurors feel excluded, disrespected, and, yes, annoyed. Let them see what you are talking about.

Objecting, Responding to Objections, and Bench Conferences

A good way to get a trial judge angry is to make or respond to objections in a way he dislikes. The three basic ways judges want objections handled were introduced in chapter 7: speaking objections, one-phrase/one-rule objections, and bench conferences.

The truth is that almost every judge uses all three of these approaches in almost every trial. But the exact mix is different for each judge, and even varies for individual judges from trial to trial—or from day to day in the same trial.

The best way to stay out of trouble is to simply ask the judge how he wants you to handle objections, and then follow his lead. Stay flexible, and recognize all three approaches are likely to be used to some degree in your trial. Also recognize that the easiest way to get the judge angry is to start arguing your case in front of the jury when the judge is trying to deal with an evidentiary issue.

Offers of Proof

If your opponent is blocking an important piece of evidence with an objection, be prepared to make an offer of proof. Offers of proof (also called *proffers*) occur when an attorney tells the judge what he will prove if permitted. You can make offers of proof orally or in writing. Chapter 12 discusses the law and strategy behind offers of proof in more detail. For now, it is enough to note that the offer of proof is an important tool in your arsenal for responding to objections. Let's look at an example.

Example: Drunk Driving Case

You are the plaintiff's lawyer. Your client was injured by a drunk driver who ran a red light at ninety miles per hour. The defendant had two prior DUIs. Your state does not allow punitive damages.

The defendant admits liability and then makes a motion *in limine* to exclude evidence of the prior DUIs or the facts of the accident. The defense argues these facts are not relevant and are prejudicial.

A judge's first instinct is to grant this motion. If you simply argue in your brief that this evidence is relevant to damages because the facts of the accident have exacerbated your client's injuries, you will probably lose. It is time for an offer of proof. This can be in the form of a sworn or unsworn statement from you, or a sworn statement from a witness. If from you, the statement could look like this:

> **Offer of Proof Regarding Defense MIL #5**
> David Smith, PhD, is the plaintiff's psychologist. He has been treating the plaintiff almost weekly since approximately two months after the accident.
> Dr. Smith has diagnosed the plaintiff with post-traumatic stress disorder (PTSD). If allowed to so testify, Dr. Smith will testify that the plaintiff's PTSD has been particularly difficult to treat, and has a guarded prognosis, in part, because of the facts of the accident. In particular, Dr. Smith will testify that . . .

You would then outline, in as much detail as possible, the basis for Dr. Smith's opinion that the plaintiff's PTSD has been made worse due to the plaintiff's knowledge of the facts of the accident and the defendant's prior DUIs. Alternatively, you could submit an affidavit from Dr. Smith, or even his deposition testimony if it is compelling.

Judges pay attention to offers of proof. They are used to lawyers bluffing and posturing. If you take the trouble to cite the detailed evidentiary basis for your position, they are much more likely to listen to you. They also have more information—your information—to evaluate. Most judges are cautious by nature. By submitting an offer of proof, you are essentially saying, "This is what I am going to show the court of appeals; wouldn't you like to take a closer look first?"

Questions to Ask

- Where would you like the lawyers to stand when they examine witnesses?
- How do you like to handle objections?

Suggested Reading

Bailey, William S., and Robert W. Bailey. *Show the Story: The Power of Visual Advocacy.* Portland, OR: Trial Guides, 2011.

Ball, David. "Your Cast Rehearsals: The Ten Commandments of Witness Preparation." In *Theater Tips and Strategies for Jury Trials.* 3rd ed. Boulder, CO: National Institute for Trial Advocacy, 2003.

Barton, William A. *Recovering for Psychological Injuries.* 3rd ed. Portland, OR: Trial Guides and the American Association for Justice Press, 2010.

Friedman, Rick. *Polarizing the Case: Exposing and Defeating the Malingering Myth.* Portland, OR: Trial Guides, 2007. See especially chapter 3, "Screening and Preparing the Case," and chapter 15, "Case-in-Chief."

———. *Rick Friedman on Becoming a Trial Lawyer.* Portland, OR: Trial Guides, 2008. See especially chapter 18, "Don't Gorge on Experts and Starve for Lay Witnesses," and chapter 19, "Spend More Time with Witnesses and Clients."

Spence, Gerry. *Win Your Case: How to Present, Persuade, and Prevail—Every Place, Every Time.* New York: St. Martin's Griffin, 2006.

11

Cross-Examination

Purpose

It seems there is a law written somewhere that requires anyone writing about cross-examination to quote Professor Wigmore, who called cross-examination the "greatest legal engine ever invented for the discovery of truth."[1]

He may be right, but that quote suggests too limited an approach to cross-examination. In fact, "discovering" truth in cross is relatively rare. More often, the cross-examiner is pointing out additional facts or issues, which both sides already know, that support her position in the case. One reason cross-examination exists is so each side can elicit helpful facts for the jury from each particular witness. The side that calls a witness can be expected to obtain those facts on direct examination, with non-leading questions. Because the witness may be hostile or unwilling to prepare with the other side, leading questions are allowed on cross-examination.

---

[1] John Henry Wigmore, *Wigmore on Evidence,* sec. 1367, 3rd ed. (New York: Little, Brown and Co., 1940). Currently 4th edition, Aspen Publishing, 2012.

While facts that help both sides often come from a single witness, sometimes the witness has nothing helpful to say about your case. Still, you are allowed to test (and hopefully hurt) the witness's credibility by asking questions related to motive, bias, or interest.

Sometimes, in the process of filling in facts not presented by your adversary's questions, or by asking questions that raise doubts about an adverse witness's credibility, a "truth" you hadn't previously discovered emerges.

In criminal cases, the defense is constitutionally entitled to use cross-examination as an exploratory tool in testing the witness's general credibility, motive, bias, interest, or direct testimony.[2] Improper preclusion or curtailment of defense cross-examination violates the Confrontation Clause.[3]

The Sixth Amendment confrontation right does not apply to civil litigants. Nevertheless, courts recognize cross-examination as an essential trial right.[4] The right to cross-examination is not

---

[2] *See, e.g., Alford v. United States,* 282 U.S. 687, 691 (1931); *Davis v. Alaska,* 415 U.S. 308, 315–16 (1974); *State v. Dunlap,* 608 P.2d 41 (Ariz. 1980); *Alvarado v. Superior Court,* 5 P.3d 203 (Cal. 2000); *Steinhorst v. State,* 412 So.2d 332, 337 (Fla. 1982); *People v. Triplett,* 485 N.E.2d 9 (Ill. 1985) *People v. Stanard,* 365 N.E.2d 857 (N.Y. 1977); *In re Restraint of Benn,* 952 P.2d 116, 154 (Wash. 1998).

[3] *Delaware v. Van Arsdall,* 475 U.S. 673, 678–79 (1986), quoting *Davis v. Alaska,* 415 U.S. 308, 316–17 (1974) ("exposure of a witness's motivation in testifying is a proper and important function of the constitutionally protected right of cross-examination").

[4] *Alford v. United States,* 282 U.S. 687, 691 (1931); *Fremont Indemnity Co. v. Workers' Comp. Appeals Bd.,* 200 Cal. Rptr. 762 (Cal. App. 1984) (holding that workers' compensation appeal board required to afford claimant fundamental due process, including right to cross-examine witnesses); *Matter of Click,* 554 N.E.2d 494 (Ill. App. 1990) ("While there may be no constitutional right to cross-examine witnesses as in criminal cases, cross-examination is generally a matter of right in all cases."); *Friedel v. Board of Regents of University of New York,* 73 N.E.2d 545, 547 (N.Y. 1947) ("Cross-examination of adverse witnesses is a matter of right in any trial of a disputed issue of fact."); *Baxter v. Jones,* 658 P.2d 1274, 1276 (Wash. App. 1983) ("Although the process which is due varies according to the type of proceeding, cross-examination is an integral part of both criminal and civil judicial proceedings.").

unlimited, however, and is subject to reasonable control by the trial court.[5]

Advocacy Goals

Some lawyers forget that cross-examination can often accomplish much more than simply attacking the witness's credibility. Impeachment may be an important goal at times, but through cross-examination, you may also:

- Tell your own story, through witnesses and exhibits.

- Establish the legal elements you must prove to obtain a favorable verdict.

- Undermine the opposition's claims or positions.

- Have the jurors like or identify with your witnesses, including your client, or dislike the opposition witnesses or client.

- Encourage the jurors to *want* to decide in your favor.

Applicable Law

There are very few categorical restrictions on cross-examination. You can ask leading or non-leading questions. You can attack the reliability of the direct testimony directly—for example, by suggesting that the witness didn't see what he thinks he saw or is not

---

[5] *Cervantes v. Rijlaarsdam*, 949 P.2d 56, 59 (Ariz. 1997) (stating that the right to cross-examine is not unlimited and is subject to discretionary control of trial court); *People v. Smith*, 150 P.3d 1224. 1247 (Cal. 2007) (trial court retains "wide latitude" in restricting cross-examination even by criminal defendant); *King v. State*, 89 So.3d 209, 223 (Fla. 2012); *Kurrack v. American Dist. Telegraph Co.*, 625 N.E.2d 675, 686 (Ill. App. 1993) (citing E. Cleary & M. Graham, *Handbook of Illinois Evidence* § 611.11, at 418–21 (5th ed. 1990)); *Friedel v. Board of Regents of University of New York*, 73 N.E.2d 545, 548 (N.Y. 1947); *Baxter v. Jones*, 658 P.2d 1274, 1276 (Wash. App. 1983) (describing limits on cross-examination); *State v. Darden*, 41 P.3d 1189, 1193 (Wash. 2002) (right of cross-examination is not absolute and may be curtailed "if the evidence sought is vague, argumentative, or speculative").

remembering accurately. You can attack the witness's credibility—for example, by saying that the witness is lying.[6] Because impeachment is a proper goal of cross-examination, wide latitude is granted to the questioner.[7] However, impeachment on collateral matters may be limited.[8] Any fact that arguably casts doubt upon the witness's story is fair game. Similarly, because bias is never collateral[9] many subjects that would otherwise be off-limits are allowed.

[6] *Penn v. State,* 574 So.2d 1079, 1082 (Fla. 1991) (stating that cross-examination must relate to credibility or to the matters brought out on direct examination); *State v. Darden,* 41 P.3d 1189, 1193 (Wash. 2002) (purpose of cross-examination is "to test the perception, memory, and credibility of witnesses").

[7] *State v. Rothe,* 249 P.2d 946, 948 (Ariz. 1952) ("It is a well-known rule of law that a cross-examiner should be given great latitude in his questions which seek to impeach an adverse witness being examined."); *Jennings v. Superior Court,* 428 P.2d 304, 310 (Cal. 1967) (emphasizing need for wide latitude in cross-examination); *Geralds v. State,* 674 So.2d 96 (Fla. 1996) (stating that cross-examination may explore "all matters that may modify, supplement, contradict, rebut, or make clearer the facts testified to in chief.") (quoting *Coco v. State,* 62 So.2d 892, 895 (Fla. 1953) (additional citations omitted)); *People v. Kirkman,* 609 N.E.2d 827, 830 (Ill. App. 1993) ("Generally, any permissible kind of impeaching matter may be developed on cross-examination since one of the purposes of cross-examination is to test the credibility of the witnesses."); *People v. Lake,* 378 N.E.2d 364, 367 (Ill. App. 1978) ("Although the scope of cross-examination is generally left to the trial court's discretion, the accused must be given wide latitude to establish bias or motive."); *State v. Spencer,* 45 P.3d 209, 214 (Wash. App. 2002) (criminal defendant should be given great latitude in cross-examining prosecution witness to show motive or credibility).

[8] *See People v. Griffin,* 599 N.Y.S.2d 825, 826 (N.Y. App. 1993) (trial court has discretion to limit cross-examination designed to impeach witness on collateral matter).

[9] *Davis v. Alaska,* 415 U.S. 308, 316 (1974) ("The partiality of a witness is subject to exploration at trial, and is 'always relevant as discrediting the witness and affecting the weight of his testimony.'") (quoting 3A J. Wigmore, *Evidences* 940, p. 775 (Chadbourn rev. 1970)); *State v. Rothe,* 249 P.2d 946, 948 (Ariz. 1952) ("It is always proper to inquire as to the motive of the adverse witness in testifying, and to show any matter which bears on the credibility of that witness."); *Kelley v. Bailey,* 11 Cal. Rptr. 448, 453–54 (Cal. App. 1961); *State v. Basiliere,* 353 So.2d 820, 824 (Fla. 1977); *People v. Gonzalez,* 472 N.E.2d 417, 419–20 (Ill. 1984); *People v. Chin,* 490 N.E.2d 505, 510 (N.Y. 1986); *Moy Quon v. M. Furuya Co.,* 143 P. 99 (Wash. 1914).

For example, if a witness is under indictment or in custody, but not convicted, that would normally not be admissible as impeachment, but is admissible to show why the witness might be lying to obtain favor with the prosecutor.[10] A witness's racial prejudices might not otherwise be relevant, but are a proper subject of cross-examination to show favoritism toward or bias against the defendant's race or ethnicity.[11] Similarly, gang affiliation is a reasonable subject of cross-examination to show bias.[12] An expert witness's financial interest in the present case and future work is also fair game.[13] Essentially, if you can identify some factual reason a witness may be more favorably inclined toward the other side or against your client, you should be able to explore it in cross.

Courts may, however, limit cross-examination that is irrelevant, unfairly prejudicial, confusing, a waste of time, or needlessly cumulative, even in criminal cases.[14]

---

[10] *See Alford v. United States,* 282 U.S. 687, 693 (1931) (defendant should have been able to explore fact that witness was in federal custody, not "to discredit the witness by showing that he was charged with crime, but to show by such facts as proper cross-examination might develop, that his testimony was biased because given under promise or expectation of immunity, or under the coercive effect of his detention by officers of the United States, which was conducting the present prosecution").

[11] *See, e.g., In re Anthony P.,* 213 Cal. Rptr. 424, 428–30 (Cal. App. 1985) (appropriate to allow cross-examination to explore bias against the defendant's racial group, but also noting that as a practical matter, such questioning might be risky for examiner) (citing cases from numerous jurisdictions); *People v. Krug,* 51 P.2d 445, 447 (Cal. 1935) (holding that questioning regarding nationality was permissible on theory that witnesses might testify more favorably toward countrymen).

[12] *People v. Gonzalez,* 472 N.E.2d 417, 419–20 (Ill. 1984); *see also United States v. Abel,* 469 U.S. 45, 52 (1984) ("A witness's and a party's common membership in an organization . . . is certainly probative of bias.").

[13] *See Flores v. Miami-Dade County,* 787 So.2d 955, 957–58 (Fla. App. 2001); *Trower v. Jones,* 520 N.E.2d 297, 300 (Ill. 1988); *Brown v. Spokane County Fire Protection Dist. No. 1,* 668 P.2d 571, 580 (Wash. 1983).

[14] *Delaware v. Van Arsdall,* 475 U.S. 673, 679 (1986) ("[T]rial judges retain wide latitude insofar as the Confrontation Clause is concerned to impose

Two more legal principles you should know:

You may not ask argumentative questions.[15] Argumentative questions are questions that make statements about the case rather than pose a question,[16] seek to engage the witness in argument,[17] or that require the witness to agree to inferences that you have drawn from prior testimony.[18]

You may not ask a question that suggests facts you do not have a good faith basis to believe are true.[19] For example, you cannot ask a witness, "You are a child molester, aren't you?" unless you have a reason to believe that is actually true.

---

reasonable limits on such cross-examination based on concerns about, among other things, harassment, prejudice, confusion of the issues, the witness's safety, or interrogation that is repetitive or only marginally relevant."); *see also* cases cited in footnote 5, above.

[15] *Pool v. Superior Court*, 677 P.2d 261, 266 (Ariz. 1984); *People v. Mayfield*, 928 P.2d 485, 535 (Cal. 1997); *People v. Clay*, 187 N.E.2d 719, 721 (Ill. 1963); *People v. Jodhan*, 831 N.Y.S.2d 53, 54 (N.Y. App. 2007); *State v. Roberts*, 611 P.2d 1297, 1300 (Wash. 1980).

[16] *People v. Chatman*, 133 P.3d 534, 563 (Cal. 2006).

[17] *People v. Mayfield*, 928 P.2d 485, 535 (Cal. 1997).

[18] Kenneth Broun, 1 *McCormick on Evidence* § 7 (6th ed. 2009).

[19] *See People v. Ramos*, 938 P.2d 950, 977 (Cal. 1997) ("Counsel must not be permitted to take random shots at a reputation imprudently exposed, or to ask groundless questions 'to waft an unwarranted innuendo into the jury box' . . . There is also a responsibility on trial courts to scrupulously prevent cross-examination based upon mere fantasy.") (quoting *People v. Eli*, 424 P.2d 356, 367 (Cal. 1967)); *People v. Duffy*, 326 N.E.2d 804, 806 (N.Y. 1975); *State v. Briscoe*, 474 P.2d 267, 269 (Wash. 1970) ("If it develops that the questions asked on cross-examination are not made in good faith and are without foundation in fact, then upon proper motion a mistrial should be ordered."). Asking questions that imply that a matter is true without a good faith belief in its truth may also raise ethical concerns, as it implicates a lawyer's duty of candor to the tribunal. *See, e.g.*, Fla. R. Prof. Conduct 4–3.3.

IMPLEMENTATION

To Cross or Not?

The first question is always whether to cross-examine the witness at all. The two most common types of witnesses *not* to cross are:

1. Those who have not hurt your case at all
2. Those from whom you cannot hope to get any helpful testimony

A records custodian from the phone company who testifies that a certain exhibit contains your client's phone records for the month of March might fall into the first category. What can you gain by cross-examining this employee? Maybe nothing. In that case, don't cross-examine.

It is rare to find a witness who falls within the second category, although our records custodian might again fall there. Even if he has hurt your case, there may be no point in cross-examining him because there is nothing helpful to get out of him. But almost every witness, no matter how narrow his testimony, no matter how skilled and biased, will have to admit some facts favorable to your case. This raises the next question.

To Attack or Not?

Far too many lawyers think the purpose of cross-examination is always to attack the opposing witness's credibility. In fact, many witnesses the opposition offers against you will be credible. Attacking their credibility may only hurt your own. These witnesses may also have testimony they can give that supports parts of your story. *Many of the best cross-examinations do not attack the witness's credibility, but elicit—from the "hostile" witness—facts favorable to your case.*

Even if you have material to attack the witness's credibility, your better course may be to leave credibility alone and bring out favorable testimony. This is true even if the witness is genuinely hostile to your case. Make a list of all the facts that support your case that the witness:

- Has admitted in prior statements

- Must admit because they are common sense

- Must admit because they naturally follow from admitted facts

Often, you can construct a powerful cross-examination by just walking through this list and getting the witness to admit these facts. If he does that, do you still need to attack his credibility?

It is in cross-examination where jurors often decide whether they like you as a person. They see you under stress or tension, encountering a witness who stands in your way. They are judging you, as much as they are judging the witness. They will draw conclusions about who you are as a person—and also about your case—based on how you treat the witness you are cross-examining. Are you respectful or rude; sneaky or fair; aggressive or calm? Judges often remark that during cross-examination, they can watch jurors get hostile to a lawyer—and his case—that the jurors were previously open to.

Collect and Organize

Unless you are a genius, the key to good cross-examination is preparation—and even a genius will greatly improve with painstaking preparation. The first step is to organize all available information by topic. Keep an electronic or hard copy file on each witness, and a subfile on each topic the witness might possibly testify on—whether helpful to you or the other side. Everyone develops their own way of doing this, but you might want to start by referring to our journalistic device from chapter 10: *who, what, when, where, why, and how.*

Who

- Who is the witness?

- What is her background?

- What evidence of bias do you have?

- Is she an ex-wife?

- What did she say about your client during divorce proceedings? Alternatively, maybe this witness has previously said many good things about your client.

All material, good and bad, about the witness's background should be in your file.

What

- What is she going to say about the issues in the case?
- Do you have police reports, depositions, or letters from the witness?

All statements from the witness on issues possibly relevant to the case should be in your file.

When

- When did the witness make the statements she made?
- When does she claim to have witnessed key events?

Make sure the dates of these events and the dates the witness made these statements are in your timeline. Remember the timeline from chapter 4? A good timeline is crucial to most cross-examinations. When you put key events (and even events you think are not key) in sequential order, flaws in the other side's case can jump out at you.

Where

- Where was the witness when she observed key events or made important statements?

Why

- Why would the witness testify in this way?

Jurors are particularly attuned to issues of motivation. Motivation means more than just a reason to dislike or hurt your client. A witness may have made a mistake in doing his job, and not want to admit it. Or maybe he is too proud to admit he needs glasses. The evidence may even point to mixed or contradictory motives. For now, you are just collecting evidence of possible motives; you can decide what to do with this evidence later.

How

- How did this person come to be a witness for the other side?
- How can she know what she claims to know?
- How can her story be true?
- How does her story fit with the other evidence in the case?

However you decide to organize your information, you want to end up with easy access to everything potentially relevant to a direct and cross-examination of the witness. Then, make an outline addressing each topic or area you *might* want to question the witness about. If a police officer will testify against your client, you might have a topic outline that looks like this:

Bias/credibility

Personnel file, p. 4 [Where officer disciplined for making racial remarks; your client is African American]

Competence

State v. Davis, p. 3 [Order from judge in prior case rebuking officer for mishandling evidence]

Police report, p. 3 [Admission in this case by officer that some evidence was lost or mishandled]

Gun?

Police report, p. 7—says saw something "metallic" in client's hand

Grand jury testimony, p. 56—says saw "gun" in client's hand

Incriminating statements

Police report—no mention of statements on way to police station

Grand jury, p. 68—says on ride to police station, client refers to having a gun

Favorable facts
> Never saw client with drugs—grand jury testimony, p. 89
>
> Looked where he says client threw "gun" and found nothing—grand jury, p. 93
>
> Client never ran or resisted—grand jury, p. 58
>
> Not client's house—police report, p. 17, grand jury, p. 63

A topic outline like this can take up less than a page, or, in the case of an important witness in a complex case, thirty or more pages. For an expert witness, the citations may include prior testimony in other cases, medical or scientific articles or texts, or even television interviews. Include anything you might possibly want to question the witness about on this outline. Note that even potentially inadmissible material should be in the outline. The reason is that the witness may give an answer while testifying that suddenly opens the door to this evidence. You want to be able to respond quickly. (A good deal of trial practice is preparing for things that never happen.)

If you do this right, all of the source material for your citations will be in a trial notebook, in a tab behind the witness's name. (See chapter 4.) While preparing or conducting your cross, you will immediately be able to find any document or transcript you need.

Planning and Writing Your Cross

Once you have all of your material organized, and a comprehensive outline created, you can plan and write your cross. Note that outlining all matters is not enough. You still need to decide what you will actually ask, and the order of your questioning.

You have two big advantages over the witness you're about to cross-examine:

1. You know the details of the entire case better than any single witness.
2. You decide what subjects to address with the witness and what subjects to avoid.

If, in the example above, another officer found a gun with your client's fingerprints on it in the general location the first officer said your client threw something, there is a good chance you do not want to cross on the subject of inconsistency between his police report and grand jury testimony.

Much of cross-examination is an exercise in judgment. To properly exercise that judgment, you must know every detail of the case. Once you are prepared, no one can teach you how to exercise that judgment. But most good cross-examiners are constantly asking themselves the questions:

- Who is this witness?

- What motivates him?

- What will he say if I ask this question?

- What do I do if he answers that way?

- What do I do if he answers differently?

Often, there will be good facts about your client or your case that you can be pretty sure the witness will not fight you on. It is usually better to ask questions about these subjects before moving on to areas where you know there will be a fight. In our example above, you might start out:

Q: When you entered the room, you noticed there was a back door?

Q: Mr. Smith could have turned and run through the door?

Q: He made no attempt to do so?

Q: He didn't resist you in any way?

Q: You noticed he had a college history book in his hand?

The purpose of eliciting these facts might be to suggest they are inconsistent with your client having a guilty mental state. The college history book also suggests to the jurors that your client does not fit their image of a drug dealer.

If your client is being charged with possession of drugs found in the room, you might move on to other favorable, indisputable facts:

Q: After taking Mr. Smith to the police station, you looked at city property records?

Q: Mr. Smith's driver's license?

Q: Jimmy Jones's driver's license?

Q: Documents found in the house?

Q: You concluded this was Jimmy Jones's house?

Q: You learned that Jimmy Jones was Mr. Smith's cousin?

Q: You found no documents in the house addressed to Mr. Smith?

Q: No property of any kind belonging to him?

Q: Mr. Smith told you he was at the house to bring Jimmy a history book?

Q: You did find the history book?

These examples illustrate the point made earlier in this chapter. Much of good cross-examination is not so much attacking a witness or his story as bringing out undisputed facts that favor your version of events.

Decide what order you want to address the various topics in your outline, and then draft questions to bring out the facts in the order you wish the jury to hear them. After each question, write in your outline any source material that supports your position regarding that question. If the witness gives an unexpected answer, you can quickly direct him to the document that supports your position.

To Lead or Not to Lead?

You may ask leading questions in cross. A leading question is one that suggests the answer. For example, "You found no documents in the house addressed to Mr. Smith?" tells the witness and everyone else the answer you are looking for. A witness can answer most leading questions with a simple yes or no.

"Can you tell us what documents you found in the house with Mr. Smith's name on them?" is a non-leading question. You are not necessarily suggesting that there were or weren't such documents in the house.

In the mid-1970s, Professor Irving Younger began lecturing on the rules he thought should govern good cross-examination. He went so far as to call these rules "commandments." His third commandment was, "Always ask leading questions." His fourth commandment was, "Don't ask a question to which you do not know the answer." His commandments caught on and became articles of faith for many trial lawyers. They became tools for scrutinizing and critiquing the performance of lawyers who lost a case—as in, "She broke the third and eighth commandments."

There is a lot of wisdom in Younger's commandments, and it is worth studying them and thinking about the reasons he wrote them the way he did.[20] However, most good trial lawyers violate many of these commandments in *every* trial. It is also true that all good trial lawyers know how to ask good, crisp, leading questions. Sometimes good, crisp, leading questions can get the job done; sometimes they won't. Sometimes you must ask questions without knowing what answers you will receive.

---

[20] The commandments are:
1. Be brief.
2. Short questions, plain words.
3. Always ask leading questions.
4. Don't ask a question to which you do not know the answer.
5. Listen to the witness's answers.
6. Don't quarrel with the witness.
7. Don't allow the witness to repeat his direct testimony.
8. Don't permit the witness to explain his answers.
9. Don't ask the "one question too many."
10. Save the ultimate point of your cross for summation.

See Irving Younger, *The Art of Cross-Examination,* The Section of Litigation Monograph Series, no. 1, published by the American Bar Association Section on Litigation, from a speech by Irving Younger at the ABA Annual Meeting in Montreal, August 1975.

Trying cases is not for the fainthearted.

As you decide whether to lead or not, you should know that it is extraordinarily rare to lose a case on cross-examination. If you think about this for a minute, you will understand why. If a witness has bad things to say about your case, your adversary will know them and bring them out on direct examination. If you ask some poor cross-examination questions, the witness will repeat the bad things he said on direct, but the jury has heard them already—hearing them again may be unpleasant, but not likely to kill your case. So exploring areas your opponent already covered in direct may not get you anywhere, but is unlikely to lead to catastrophe.

Perhaps you will want to ask non-leading questions about the direct testimony to see if the witness's story makes sense. Does it hold together? Are there pieces the witness has skipped over—intentionally or not?

Then there are areas the witness didn't cover in direct. Maybe there are issues of bias or motive. Maybe you will ask questions related to damages to a witness called to testify about liability. Again, chances are, if there was material there to hurt you, your opponent would have brought it up in direct. But maybe not. Ask yourself: What do you really need from this witness? How much risk are you willing to take? If you have thoroughly prepared, you are in a position to evaluate risk, but are never guaranteed safety. There is no one right way to cross-examine a witness. One lawyer might use nothing but leading questions and achieve what he needs; another might use nothing but non-leading questions and achieve just as much or more.

Again, you are very unlikely to lose a case on cross-examination. However, there are two notable exceptions to this pronouncement.

First, you can lose a case on cross-examination if you go exploring in an area where there is highly prejudicial information available about your client that the judge excluded from evidence. If your client has a conviction for child molestation that the judge excluded in response to your motion *in limine,* you better not ask a hostile witness about your client's character. Always have the rulings on your motions *in limine* in mind when you cross-examine, and don't ask questions that might give the witness the opportunity to answer with prejudicial material. The judge may rule that you have opened the door to that evidence by asking the question.

Second, you can lose a case on cross-examination if you are rude and obnoxious toward the witness. If you work hard enough at this, you can get the jury to dislike you enough to rule against your client. But you are not going to do that, are you?

If you realize you are unlikely to lose a case on cross-examination, it can free you up to relax a little and explore the witness's story. The world will not come to an end if you don't do this perfectly.

But what if you want to *win* the case on cross? This most often happens when the fact-finder must believe one or more witnesses in order for the other side to prevail. Ask yourself the following:

- What are the weaknesses in these witnesses' stories?

- What are they saying that doesn't make sense?

- Why are these witnesses unworthy of belief?

When you have identified the weak points, construct questions to reveal them. You know how to do this. You have been doing it all your life.

- "If Sally broke the cookie jar, why are you, Johnny, the one with crumbs on your shirt?"

- "You told the police five minutes after the accident that the light was red?" [Implication: Why should anyone believe you now when you say it was green?]

A technically beautiful cross is thrilling to watch, but you do not need technical excellence to win a case on cross. Ask commonsense questions about the other side's weak points and watch what happens.

The previous few paragraphs are meant to counter the fear-based teachings that have paralyzed many trial lawyers over the last few decades. They are not meant to encourage lazy preparation or undisciplined questioning. You have to know your case inside out and carefully plan your lines of attack. This takes time—lots of it. And not just time, but time actively, thoughtfully thinking about the issues in your case and the issues the witness presents. Once you have done that though, let yourself relax and enjoy the process of asking the hard questions. You know how to do that.

Implementation—A Summary

The one thing all great trial lawyers agree on is that preparation—mind-numbing, eye-blurring preparation—is essential for success. And in no area of trial is this truer than in cross-examination.

No lawyer should try a case without first having read Pozner and Dodd's *Cross-Examination: Science and Techniques*. This book does a superb job of teaching you how to organize and prepare a cross-examination. Then read *Dynamic Cross-Examination* by James McComas to learn how to get to the next level.

QUESTIONS TO ASK

♦ Does the court allow re-cross-examination?

The ordinary sequence of questioning is direct, cross-, and redirect examination. Some judges will allow the cross-examining party to conduct *re-cross-examination* as a matter of course; others will allow it if one side raised a new matter in redirect; still others will not allow it no matter what. Find out who will ordinarily have the last word with the witness: the party sponsoring him or the party cross-examining him.

SUGGESTED READING

McComas, James. *Dynamic Cross-Examination: A Whole New Way to Create Opportunities to Win*. Portland, OR: Trial Guides, 2011.

Pozner, Larry, and Roger Dodd. *Cross-Examination: Science and Techniques.* 2nd ed. New York: LexisNexis, 2004.

Spence, Gerry. *Win Your Case: How to Present, Persuade, and Prevail—Every Place, Every Time.* New York: St. Martin's Griffin, 2006.

Wellman, Francis L. *The Art of Cross-Examination.* New York: Touchstone Books, 1997. First published 1903 by the Macmillan Company.

12

Making a Record
Objections, Offers of Proof, and Midtrial Jury Instructions

Purpose

The major tasks of an appellate court are to decide whether the lower court made a mistake, and if so, whether the mistake was serious enough to send the case back to the lower court for further proceedings.

Not being present at the trial, the appellate judges rely on the *record of proceedings* in the lower court. Any pleading filed in court becomes part of the record, but pleadings rarely reflect what goes on in the courtroom. The courtroom record can be as sparse as a few notes scribbled by a court clerk, to a full, line-by-line transcript of everything that everyone said in court. Some courts also keep an official audio or audiovisual recording of what goes on in court and consider this part of the record.

Part of your job is to make sure you have clearly stated your position to the judge, and that it is preserved *on the record*,[1] so that if the judge rules against you, the appellate court will understand the mistake the judge made. From an appellate perspective, if an argument or ruling is not on the record, it didn't happen.[2]

An *objection* is a way of stating on the record that you believe what might happen, or is happening, is contrary to law and prejudicial to your client.[3] It states your position so the trial judge and the appellate court may understand it and rule on it. Federal Rule of Civil Procedure 46 provides, for example,

---

[1] The phrase "*on* the record" is usually used to signify that what took place orally in court has been somehow recorded for appellate review. "*In* the record" is usually used to indicate that written materials—pleadings or exhibits—have become part of the official court record, available for appellate review.

[2] *See, e.g., State v. Jessen*, 633 P.2d 410, 417 (Ariz. 1981) (rejecting claim regarding refusal to give instruction because the proffered instruction was not in the record); *Gutierrez v. Casiar Min. Corp.*, 75 Cal. Rptr. 2d 132 (Cal. App. 1982) (stating that because party failed to make offer of proof, there was no basis for concluding that exclusion of evidence caused prejudice); *Saka v. Saka*, 831 So.2d 709, 711 (Fla. App. 2002) (discussing requirements for preserving issues for appeal); *Foutch v. O'Bryant*, 459 N.E.2d 958, 959 (Ill. 1984) (appellant's burden to present a sufficiently complete record to allow for review of claimed error); *Saratoga Spa & Bath, Inc. v. Beeche Systems Corp.*, 656 N.Y.S.2d 787 (N.Y. App. 1997) (objection allegedly made off the record was not sufficient to preserve issue for appeal); *In re Detention of Morgan*, 253 P.3d 394, 403 (Wash. App. 2011) (stating that insufficient appellate record precludes review of alleged errors).

[3] Rules of evidence typically require objections and offers of proof to preserve issues for appeal. *See, e.g.,* Fed. R. Evid. 103(a) (stating that on appeal, error may not be predicated on a ruling admitting or excluding evidence unless a substantial right is affected and the party either made a timely objection to the admission of evidence, or the substance of the excluded evidence was made known to the court through an offer of proof or was otherwise apparent). Arizona, Illinois, and Washington have similar rules with the same numbering. *See also* Cal. Evid. Code § 353 (requiring objection to preserve error as to admission of evidence); Cal. Code Evid. § 354 (stating that if error is claimed based on exclusion of evidence, nature of evidence must be made known by offer of proof or otherwise); Fla. S.A. 90.104 (essentially the same as Fed. R. Evid. 103(a)).

A formal exception to a ruling or order is unnecessary. When the ruling or order is requested or made, a party need only state the action that it wants the court to take or objects to, along with the grounds for the request or objection. Failing to object does not prejudice a party who had no opportunity to do so when the ruling or order was made.

Federal Rule of Criminal Procedure 51 is similar.[4]

An *offer of proof* (sometimes also called a *proffer*) is a way of making a record when you might be prevented from doing something you wish to do. Essentially, you give the judge more information about the evidence you want to present, hoping that information changes his mind. There are actually two purposes behind making an offer of proof. The first is to convince the judge to allow the presentation of certain evidence; the second is to make a record of what was excluded from the trial so the appellate court can evaluate whether the trial judge properly ruled.[5]

---

[4] *See also* Ariz. Civ. R. 46; Fla. R. Civ. P. 1.470; N.Y. CPL § 470.05 (requiring some form of protest to preserve position in criminal cases); N.Y. CPLR § 4017 (requiring civil party to make known what action it wants court to take or its objection to action taken); Wash. Civ. R. 46.

[5] *State v. Belcher*, 514 P.2d 472, 474 (Ariz. 1973) ("[A]n offer of proof is necessary in order to secure review of exclusion of evidence unless from the evidence it is obvious what the answer of the witness will be or what the proof will be . . . [and] can be of great assistance to the trial court in determining whether to ultimately admit the evidence tendered."); *Espinoza v. Calva*, 87 Cal. Rptr. 3d 492, 495–96 (2008) (An offer of proof "permits the trial court to evaluate whether the objection should be sustained. If the objection is sustained, it informs the appellate court whether the exclusion was improper and, if so, whether the exclusion resulted in a miscarriage of justice."); *Nienhouse v. Superior Court*, 49 Cal. Rptr. 2d 573 (1996) ("The function of an offer of proof is to lay an adequate record for appellate review."); *Jacobs v. Wainwright*, 450 So.2d 200, 201 (Fla. 1984) (stating that the purpose of offer of proof is making complete record on appeal); *People v. Thompkins*, 690 N.E.2d 984, 989 (Ill. 1998) ("The two primary functions of an offer of proof are to disclose to the trial judge and opposing counsel the nature of the offered evidence, enabling them to take appropriate action, and to provide the reviewing court with a record to determine whether exclusion of the evidence was erroneous

Midtrial jury instructions are primarily used to help jurors evaluate evidence as each side presents it or to understand a court procedure that might otherwise puzzle them. The most common midtrial instructions relate to an evidence rule that exists in every evidence code. The federal version states:

> When evidence which is admissible as to one party or for one purpose but not admissible as to another party or for another purpose is admitted, the court, upon request, shall restrict the evidence to its proper scope and instruct the jury accordingly.[6]

The trial judge may also give midtrial instructions when she believes the jury has improperly heard evidence. The judge may then instruct the jury to disregard the evidence. Other possible midtrial instructions include explanations of certain types of evidence, such as testimony from a deposition or the introduction of interrogatory responses.

Advocacy Goals

In a jury trial, you have at least three audiences. The first is the jury. The jury will determine the facts and deliver a verdict. Along the way, the judge—the second audience—will make rulings that will influence the verdict. On occasion, the judge may even take the case away from the jury and decide it himself.[7] The third

---

and harmful."); *People v. Pereyra*, 882 N.Y.S.2d 30, 32 (N.Y. App. Div. 2009) (failure to make offer of proof meant that issue was not preserved for appeal); *Walker v. Bangs*, 601 P.2d 1279, 1283 (Wash. 1979) ("The purpose of an offer of proof is to (1) inform the court of the legal theory under which offered evidence is admissible; (2) inform the trial judge of the specific nature of admissibility; and (3) create a record for review.").

[6] Fed. R. Evid. 105; *see also* Ariz. Evid. R. 105; Cal. Evid. Code § 355; Fla. St. § 90.107; Ill. Evid R. 105; *People v. Kass*, 874 N.Y.S.2d 475, 481 (N.Y. App. 2008) (error not to give limiting instruction when evidence admitted for limited purpose); Wash. Evid. R. 105.

[7] See chapter 13, *infra*.

audience is the potential appellate court. Your job is to influence all three audiences.

You want jurors to see and hear your good evidence. You want to keep them from hearing and seeing evidence that unfairly hurts your case. At the end of the trial, you want the judge to give legally correct jury instructions, consistent with your theory of the case. In all of these situations, you must state your position clearly, at a time when the court reporter is on the record, taking down your statements, or when the court's official recording device is on.

But that is not enough, because the goal of influencing one audience may conflict with your goal of influencing another. This means you must engage in a constant cost-benefit analysis, balancing your interests in persuading each audience against your interests in persuading the others. While you must sometimes make hard choices, this is not as complicated as it sounds.

Suppose your opponent asks a question that calls for a hearsay response. Do you object? To answer this question, you must evaluate:

- The chance of winning the objection

- The chance that the jury will get the information in some other way, even if you win the objection

- Whether your objection will alienate the jurors, causing them to think you are trying to hide important evidence from them

- Whether the objection will alienate the judge because she thinks the objection is hypertechnical or unnecessarily slowing down the proceedings

- Whether, even if the objection is improperly overruled, an appellate court will find the issue important enough to act upon

This is a simple example, but it illustrates the type of competing considerations that you must evaluate anytime you are objecting or making a record. There is no formula for how to conduct this risk-benefit analysis. The point is that the advocacy goals involved in making a record may conflict. In a trial that is going well, for example, your primary goals may be to maintain credibility with the jury and not create appeal points for your adversary. So you may choose not to object, even where you have a solid legal position. In a case where the judge is against you and things are going badly, your primary goal may be to make a record for the appellate court. In that case, you may be more likely to object or ask for clarifying instructions. The important point here is that you must always be conscious of your goals with respect to each of your three audiences.

Applicable Law

Objections

If something is going on in the courtroom and you do not object, you have *waived* your objection.[8] That means the appellate court will ordinarily not consider your argument that what went on was improper or contrary to law. There is an exception for what is called *plain error*—something so obviously prejudicial and contrary to law that, in effect, the appellate court says, "The trial court should have known better and prevented this."[9] It is not a good idea to rely upon plain error to save you in the appellate court. If you believe something improper is going on in the courtroom that you want to correct or possibly address on appeal, raise an objection.

---

[8] *See* Fed. Evid. R. 103(a) and related state rules cited above. The rule that you must preserve your position also applies to jury instructions and other potentially prejudicial events in the courtroom. *See, e.g.,* Fed. R. Civ. P. 51(c) (discussing how and when to make objections to instructions) and 51(d) (stating that a party may assign error to an instruction actually given only if the party properly objected to it and to the failure to give an instruction only if it was proposed and the court either definitively rejected it on the record or the party properly objected to the failure).

[9] *See* Fed. R. Civ. P. 51(d)(2) (stating when court may consider plain error in jury instructions); Fed. Evid. R. 103(d) (stating that the federal rules of evidence do not preclude courts from "taking notice of plain errors affecting substantial rights although they were not brought to the attention of the court.").

Offers of Proof

Offers of proof should specifically explain what evidence you seek to admit and why it is relevant.[10] It is your duty, as the party seeking to admit the evidence, to make a sufficient offer of proof, showing the content of the evidence and its purpose.[11] A trial court's refusal to allow an offer of proof is error.[12]

Midtrial Jury Instructions

Similarly, other midtrial instructions may be appropriate where there is some reason to believe that the jury will benefit from

---

[10] An offer of proof should consist of admissible evidence and specifically explain the purpose of the testimony, the name of the witness, and the content of the testimony to be elicited. *Semsch v. Henry Mayo Newhalll Memorial Hosp.*, 216 Cal. Rptr. 913, 916 (Cal. App. 1985); *see also Phillips v. State*, 351 So.2d 738, 740 (Fla. App. 1977); *Mad River Orchard, Inc. v. Krack Corp.*, 573 P.2d 796, 797 (Wash. 1978) (holding that an offer of proof must be specific and disclose the theory of admissibility).

[11] *See Warfel v. Cheney*, 758 P.2d 1326 (Ariz. App. 1988) ("Rule 103, Arizona Rules of Evidence, provides that error may not be predicated on a ruling excluding evidence unless the substance of the evidence was made known to the trial court. An offer of proof thus is a prerequisite to an appellate argument of admissibility of excluded evidence.") *McCleery v. City of Bakersfield*, 216 Cal. Rptr. 852, 862 (Cal. App. 1985) ("The responsibility for providing the court with the requisite offer of proof rests on the proponent of the proffered evidence and the obvious teaching of Evidence Code section 354 is that failure to meet that responsibility is fatal to an appeal based on exclusion of the evidence."); *G.A. v. State*, 549 So.2d 1203, 1204 (Fla. App. 1989) (stating that ordinarily "the adversely affected party must make a proffer of excluded testimony"); *People v. Armstrong*, 700 N.E.2d 960. 971 (Ill. 1998) (stating that defendant waived argument regarding excluded evidence by failing to make offer of proof); *Naclerio v. Naclerio*, 216 N.Y.S.2d 413, 414–15 (N.Y. App. 1961) (finding that party failed to specify content of proposed testimony sufficiently to show that it was admissible); *Tomlinson v. Bean*, 173 P.2d 972, 976 (Wash. 1946) ("[I]t is the duty of a party to make clear to the trial court what it is that he offers in proof, and the reason why he deems the offer admissible over the objections of his opponent, so that the court may make an informed ruling.").

[12] *State v. Belcher*, 514 P.2d 472, 474 (Ariz. 1973); *In re Candido B.*, 168 Cal. Rptr. 793, 794–95 (Cal. App. 1980); *Fehringer v. State*, 976 So.2d 1218, 1220 (Fla. App. 2008); *People v. Thompkins*, 690 N.E.2d 984, 988 (Ill. 1998).

contemporaneous legal explanation of the evidence or of events in the courtroom. For example, these instructions could explain the striking of evidence, the use of discovery responses, or the use of depositions.

A common reason for midtrial instruction is to explain that evidence is admissible for one purpose, but not another. For example:

- Testimony about an out-of-court statement may not be admissible for the truth because it is hearsay, but may be admissible to show its effect on the listener.

- An out-of-court statement may be admissible against the declarant as an admission, but inadmissible hearsay as to other parties.

If the judge doesn't explain the evidence's limited purpose to the jury immediately, there would be a substantial risk that a later instruction would be too late to prevent the jurors from considering the evidence for the improper purpose. This gives rise to the recognized need for midtrial instructions from the court, limiting the purpose for which certain evidence is considered.[13]

IMPLEMENTATION

Objections

As discussed in chapter 6, if you suspect in advance that your opponent or the court will do something prejudicial or contrary to law, you can file a motion *in limine*. However, issues you can't anticipate frequently come up in trial. In addition, as discussed in chapter 6, you may need to object at trial to preserve an issue for appeal that you raised in a motion *in limine*.

As discussed in chapters 7 and 10, there are three main styles of making objections: speaking objections, one-phrase/one-rule objections, and bench conferences. In almost any jury trial, you will see each of these styles employed.

---

[13] *See* footnote 6, above, for relevant evidence rules.

If you have followed the advice in chapter 7, you will have asked the judge before witness testimony began which style of objection she prefers. Whatever the judge says, be prepared to engage in all three types of objections.

There is a chaotic element to speaking objections. In the course of the arguments, the jurors usually hear much of what one side or the other doesn't want them to hear. Judges know that. They also know that speaking objections have a tendency to go on and on, back and forth, with each lawyer trying to get the last word. It takes a firm and nimble judge to control the speaking objection process. For all these reasons, most judges will tell you they do not allow speaking objections. And yet, you will see speaking objections in almost every judge's courtroom. How this happens, when a judge does "not allow speaking objections," goes something like this:

ATTORNEY 1: Objection. Hearsay and Evidence Rule 403.

JUDGE: Why is that prejudicial?

ATTORNEY 1: The question asks for information about my client's personal life that has no bearing on the case. [Notice the poor lawyer trying not to reveal the prejudicial nature of the evidence.] And it is clearly hearsay—asking this witness to report what someone said to him.

ATTORNEY 2: This is not hearsay. It is not offered for the truth that the defendant is a child molester, but to explain why my client did what she did—which is clearly relevant to the issues in this case.

Even in the strictest one-phrase/one-rule objection courtrooms, a judge or lawyer will occasionally succumb to the temptation to start discussing the merits of the objection in front of the jury. Your opponent may even believe that there will be no cost for intentionally violating the judge's pronouncement. Then you may hear something like this.

ATTORNEY 1: Objection, counsel is trying to get in hearsay statements of Mr. Smith, a known child molester, whom counsel is unwilling to call to the witness stand.

You may need to be ready to engage in self-help and respond in kind if your judge is not firm:

ATTORNEY 2: As the court knows, I am willing to call Mr. Smith, but counsel filed a motion asking the court to rule that I can't call him.

These are extreme examples to illustrate the point: you must be ready to argue your legal issue in front of the jury, even if you are in a one-word-objection courtroom. And remember your three audiences. When engaged in a speaking objection argument, be constantly aware of the argument's effect on your judge, your jurors, and the appellate court.

If you believe arguing in front of the jury will prejudice your client, ask the judge if you can approach the bench to argue the issue, or ask if the issue can be set aside and taken up during the next break.

Some judges also announce that they dislike having bench conferences. The thought is that they take too much time, and jurors feel disrespected by the process. This can be a problem if the judge announces that she does not permit bench conferences and insists on the one-word-objection style. Taken literally, this can result in a record that looks like this:

ATTORNEY 1: Objection. Hearsay and Rule 403.

COURT: Overruled.

How does the appellate court know the basis of your objection? Why are you citing Rule 403? Because you think this is a waste of time, or because something prejudicial is going on? If the context of the exchange does not indicate the basis for your objection, *and you believe the point could be dispositive on appeal,* then it is your job to make a record. Here are your main options for doing so:

- Ask the judge if you can approach the bench to make a record.
- At the next break, ask the judge if you can go on record without the jury to make a record as to the basis of your

objection. All but the most unfair judges will allow you to do that.

- If the judge won't allow the first two options, prepare a written objection to file at the next opportunity.

You will rarely need a written objection. If you think you need to write one, it can read something like this:

> During the afternoon of July 11, 2013, plaintiff objected to a question posed by defense counsel:
>
> Q: What did Mr. Smith tell you about the black rifle?
>
> Plaintiff objected on the grounds of hearsay and violation of Evidence Rule 403. Plaintiff's counsel asked permission to state the basis for his objection either at the bench or during a break, but the court denied her this opportunity. Accordingly, this pleading is filed to state in full the basis of the objection, and ensure that basis becomes part of the record.
>
> Plaintiff objected to this question because . . .

Offers of Proof

When the court is considering an objection to your evidence—or has sustained an objection to your evidence—consider making an offer of proof. Write offers of proof for two of your three audiences: the trial judge and the appellate court. An offer of proof informs both audiences about the substance and significance of the evidence you want the jury to hear.

Suppose you wish to call John Smith as a witness. Your adversary objects, correctly pointing out that you missed the deadline for placing Mr. Smith on your witness list. You may argue that this witness only came to your attention recently, after the deadline passed. You may argue you acted diligently and in good faith in preparing your witness list. You may cite cases in support of your right to call a witness in these circumstances. It is quite common for a judge to rule on such a motion without even knowing what Mr. Smith might say. This is because many lawyers fail to make offers of proof. As the proponent of Mr. Smith's testimony, you can strengthen (or weaken) your argument by making an offer of proof. Such an offer allows the trial and appellate courts to weigh the significance of the witness's testimony. Without an offer of proof, and unless the content of the excluded testimony is otherwise clear, it will be very difficult to establish that the trial court's decision was prejudicial to your client.

An offer of proof can be as short and informal as simply saying, "Judge, in response to this next series of questions, the witness will explain how he knew the decedent, and how he [the witness] found the rifle." Or you might need to expand on this by continuing: "This is relevant because . . ."

An offer of proof can also be more formal, either in oral presentation or in writing. As part of an offer of proof, a witness may testify in court, outside the presence of the jury. Hearing the testimony directly from the witness, the judge can ask questions and get an even better understanding of the evidence you are offering.

Documents or physical evidence can also raise an offer of proof type issue. Suppose you offer a letter into evidence and the court refuses to admit the letter. *You need to make sure the letter is part of the record.* Different courts have different procedures for ensuring that excluded documents and physical items are part of the record for appellate review. Perhaps a photo of the physical item is enough. Perhaps the clerk keeps custody of offered, but unadmitted documents. Courts differ on how they deal with this subject, so ask!

You can include offers of proof in your oppositions to motions *in limine* or in trial briefs. A separate written offer of proof can also be particularly valuable after the judge has ruled against you. Showing up the next day with a written offer of proof sends several messages to the judge:

- You think she has made a mistake.

- The issue is important.

- There is a chance an appellate court will reverse her on this issue.

Most times, the judge will take a second look.

Maybe you didn't even get a chance to argue—the judge just made a ruling that excluded critical evidence. He hurt you bad, but don't give up or get mad. At the end of the day, ask the judge if you may submit an offer of proof on the issue. Whether or not he says yes, get working on it. The purpose of asking is so he can start thinking, "Maybe I made a mistake . . ." You are also communicating that this is not a routine evidentiary issue, and it deserves his careful attention.

An offer of proof after an adverse ruling can begin like this:

> **Offer of Proof**
> On the morning of July 11, 2012, the court prohibited John Smith from testifying as to how he knew the decedent or how he came into possession of the rifle. If allowed to testify on these subjects, John Smith would have stated that:
> 1. . . .
> 2. . . .
> 3. . . .
>
> Such evidence is relevant because . . .

As an officer of the court, your offer of proof must be honest and accurate. But it need not be complete. In other words, the point is to communicate to the judge (and ultimately, the appellate court) the favorable testimony the witness could offer for your side of the case, and show how your client will be unfairly prejudiced if the judge does not admit that testimony. If you have time, you can also submit a brief arguing why the facts you have offered are relevant and admissible. When you appear in court the next morning, make sure you bring your pleadings to the judge's attention. Of course, do all this in a polite, respectful way. You would be surprised at how many lawyers act like the judge is an idiot when he rules against them. There is no better way to ensure such rulings will continue.

Judges pay attention to offers of proof. Use them when the issue is important and you truly believe the judge is wrong.

Midtrial Instructions

Most state pattern or model instruction books will have a section for midtrial instructions or evidence instructions. With some adjustment, judges can give these instructions either during trial or at the end of the case. These can range from cautioning jurors at each break not to talk about the case to explanations of what a deposition is. Flip through your own state's midtrial or evidence pattern instructions and you will have a good sense of the instructions that a judge might give midtrial.

In addition to these noncontroversial types of midtrial instructions, there is another type of midtrial instructions that is more relevant to advocacy. These are instructions that tell the jurors to disregard evidence they have just heard or to use the evidence in a limited way.

Many states have pattern instructions telling the jurors to consider evidence for only a limited purpose. For example, Florida's pattern civil jury instruction regarding evidence admitted for a limited purpose reads:

> The (describe item of evidence) has now been received into evidence. It has been admitted only [for the purpose of (describe purpose)] [as to (name party)]. You may consider it only [for that purpose] [as it might affect (name party)]. You may not consider that evidence [for any other purpose] [as to (any other party)] [(name other party(s))].[14]

As the bracketed material in this instruction illustrates, there are a variety of ways in which evidence may be admissible for only a limited purpose. A classic example of evidence properly used for one purpose but not another is when hearsay evidence is offered not for the truth of the matter asserted, but rather to show the witness's state of mind. Mrs. Jones might testify, "Dave Andrews told me his brother had a gun." This might not come

---

[14] Florida Standard Jury Instructions—Civil Cases, Instruction 301.5, Evidence Admitted for a Limited Purpose, available at http://www.floridasupremecourt.org/civ_jury_instructions/instructions.shtml#300.

into evidence to prove that Kent Andrews (the brother) had a gun, but instead to explain why Mrs. Jones did what she did next. The party who might be at a disadvantage because of evidence that Kent Andrews had a gun could ask for a *limiting instruction* when the jury hears this evidence. The instruction might look something like this:

> You may not use the evidence you just heard from Mrs. Jones to suggest that Kent Andrews actually had a gun at the time. That would not be fair, as neither Dave Andrews or Kent Andrews is on the witness stand and they cannot be questioned. I let you hear that evidence so you might evaluate Mrs. Jones's state of mind when she heard that statement—which might or might not be true—and what she did afterward. You may only use this evidence for this purpose.

There are many situations when a judge admits evidence for one purpose but won't allow the jury to use it for another purpose. Whether you ask the judge for a limiting instruction at the time is a judgment call and primarily depends on three factors:

1. How important is it that the jurors not use the evidence for an improper purpose?

2. How effective will a limiting instruction be with the jury?

3. Will a limiting instruction help with the appellate court?

If you want the judge to admit the evidence, write a limiting instruction and be ready to hand it to the court. Likewise, if the judge is admitting important evidence over your objection, be prepared to give the judge a limiting instruction for the jury. If you don't have a limiting instruction written out, you can still orally describe the instruction you would like the judge to give.

Some lawyers believe that limiting instructions make no difference and are a waste of time. Others believe they draw unnecessary attention to "bad" evidence, and so they prefer these instructions not be given. Another view is that generally, jurors will try to follow the law—particularly if they understand the reason behind it.

A similar issue is presented when trial judges must tell jurors to completely disregard something they have just seen or heard. Some state pattern instructions provide a preliminary instruction that anticipates this issue.[15] During trial, most judges will quickly explain that they have stricken the evidence and the jury should not consider it. You may wish to go beyond the pattern instruction and write an instruction that tells the jury *why* it is fair and right that they disregard this evidence. Jurors are more likely to follow the law when you explain the reason for it to them.

Questions to Ask

- How would you like to handle objections?
- How would you like to handle speaking objections?
- How would you like to handle bench conferences (approaching the bench)?
- How should we make a record of proposed exhibits that were excluded from evidence?

---

[15] *See, e.g.,* Arizona Preliminary Instruction 7, Evidence, Statements of Lawyers and Rulings, which tells jurors, among other things, "At times I may order some evidence to be stricken, or thrown out. Because it is no longer evidence, you must not consider it." Available at http://www.azbar.org/media/58448/preliminary.pdf.

13

DIRECTED VERDICT

Motion for Judgment as a Matter of Law and Motion for Judgment of Acquittal

---

When the opposing side has finished submitting their evidence, you may move the court for an order dismissing all or part of its case. Traditionally, this was called a *motion for directed verdict*.

- By rule, in both federal and in many state courts, this is now called a *motion for judgment as a matter of law (JMOL)* in civil cases.

- By rule, in both federal and many state courts, this is now called a *motion for judgment of acquittal* in criminal cases.

These terms will be used interchangeably with *directed verdict* in this book, except where a distinction is necessary. In many states, *directed verdict* is still the preferred term.

Purpose

Most jurisdictions have a rule similar to Federal Rule of Civil Procedure 50(a),[1] which provides:

(a) Judgment as a Matter of Law.
  (1) In General. If a party has been fully heard on an issue during a jury trial and the court finds that a reasonable jury would not have a legally sufficient evidentiary basis to find for the party on that issue, the court may:
    (A) resolve the issue against the party; and
    (B) grant a motion for judgment as a matter of law against the party on a claim or defense that, under the controlling law, can be maintained or defeated only with a favorable finding on that issue.
  (2) Motion. A motion for judgment as a matter of law may be made at any time before the case is submitted to the jury. The motion must specify the judgment sought and the law and facts that entitle the movant to the judgment.

Federal Rule of Criminal Procedure 29(a) similarly states:

(a) Before Submission to the Jury. After the government closes its evidence or after the close of all the evidence, the court on the defendant's motion must enter a judgment of acquittal of any offense for which the evidence is insufficient to sustain a conviction. The court may on its own consider whether the evidence is insufficient to sustain a conviction. If the court denies a motion for a judgment of acquittal at the close of the government's evidence, the defendant may offer evidence without having reserved the right to do so.

---

[1] *See* Ariz. R. Civ. P. 50(a); Cal. Code Civ. P. § 581c, subd. a; Fla. R. Civ. P. 1.480(a); 735 ILCS 5/2-1202; N.Y. CPLR § 4401; Wash. R. Civ. P. 50(a).

Most states have similar rules.[2]

The purpose of these rules is obvious: If the plaintiff, civil defendant, or prosecutor has not established all elements of his case, cause of action, defense, or charge, why continue with the trial on that case, cause of action, defense, or charge?

Advocacy Goals

Getting part or all of your opponent's case dismissed is usually a good thing. Other reasons to make a motion for directed verdict include:

- Causing the judge to reconsider evidentiary rulings
- Setting the stage for obtaining favorable jury instructions from the judge
- Preserving legal issues for posttrial motions
- Preserving appellate arguments that your opponent's case is factually or legally deficient

Judges are understandably reluctant to grant motions for judgment as a matter of law, although they will do so in obvious situations. If the judge lets the issue go to the jury, many times the jury will also reject the claim or defense and therefore eliminate a potential appeal point and the possible need for a new trial. And, if the jury does find in favor of a claim or defense that the judge determines was legally insufficient, the judge will still have the opportunity to grant the motion posttrial.[3] So in many situations, you may make a JMOL motion not because you expect

---

[2] *See, e.g.,* Ariz. Crim. R. 20(a); Cal. Penal Code § 1118.1; Fla. R. Crim P. 3.380; 725 ILCS 5/115-4(k); N.Y. CPL § 290.10. Washington only provides by rule for a motion to arrest the judgment after verdict, Wash. Crim. R. 7.3, but a criminal defendant "may challenge the sufficiency of the evidence (a) before trial, (b) at the end of the State's case-in-chief, (c) at the end of all the evidence, (d) after verdict, and (e) on appeal." *See State v. Jackson,* 918 P.2d 945, 953 (Wash. App. 1996).

[3] See chapter 18.

immediate success, but because it is necessary to preserve issues for posttrial motions and appeal.

Briefing and oral argument on a JMOL after the opponent has fully presented his case-in-chief also serves an educational purpose. Judges are busy people, and when they rule on pretrial motions, including motions for summary and motions *in limine,* they simply may not yet understand the case fully. But after sitting through at least the plaintiff's or prosecutor's case, they will have a greater understanding of the facts and will have had time to think more about the legal issues in the particular context of your case. Even an unsuccessful motion can sharpen the court's analysis and set up your position for future rulings.

APPLICABLE LAW

As FRCP 50(a) states, a federal court may grant a motion for judgment as a matter of law if "the court finds that a reasonable jury would not have a legally sufficient evidentiary basis to find for the party on that issue." This is similar to a summary judgment standard, although different courts may state the standard somewhat differently.[4]

---

[4] *Orme School v. Reeves,* 802 P.2d 1000, 1008 (Ariz. 1990) (JMOL motion, like motion for summary judgment, "should be granted if the facts produced in support of the claim or defense have so little probative value, given the quantum of evidence required, that reasonable people could not agree with the conclusion advanced by the proponent of the claim or defense"); *Nally v. Grace Community Church,* 763 P.2d 948, 955 (Cal. 1988) ("A defendant is entitled to a nonsuit if the trial court determines that, as a matter of law, the evidence presented by plaintiff is insufficient to permit a jury to find in his favor."); *Collins v. School Board of Broward County,* 471 So.2d 560, 563 (Fla. App. 1985) ("Only where there is no evidence upon which a jury could properly rely, in finding for the plaintiff, should a directed verdict be granted."); *Krywin v. Chicago Transit Authority,* 938 N.E.2d 440, 446 (Ill. 2010) ("A motion for directed verdict will not be granted unless all of the evidence so overwhelmingly favors the movant that no contrary verdict based on that evidence could ever stand."); *Szczerbiak v. Pilat,* 686 N.E.2d 1346, 1348 (N.Y. 1997) (appropriate to grant motion "where the trial court finds that, upon the evidence presented, there is no rational process by which the fact trier could base a finding

Similarly, in criminal trials, judgment of acquittal is appropriate only when "the evidence is insufficient to sustain a conviction."[5] If there is substantial evidence that could support a conviction, and reasonable minds may differ on the inferences to be drawn from the evidence, the judge should not grant a motion for judgment of acquittal.[6] In criminal cases, *sufficient evidence* is evidence that reasonable people could accept as sufficient to support a conclusion of the defendant's guilt beyond a reasonable doubt.[7]

As the federal rule states, the motion must specify the law and facts upon which it is based.[8] Evidence is considered in the

---

in favor of the nonmoving party"); *Faust v. Albertson*, 222 P.3d 1208, 1212 (Wash. 2009) ("Judgment as a matter of law under CR 50 is appropriate only when no competent and substantial evidence exists to support a verdict.").

[5] Fed. R. Crim. P. 29(a).

[6] *State v. Mosley*, 581 P.2d 238, 247 (Ariz. 1978); *People v. Lake*, 67 Cal. Rptr. 3d 452, 455 (Cal. App. 2007) (trial court must determine whether there is "substantial evidence of the existence of each element of the offense charged") (citations omitted); *Williams v. State*, 967 So.2d 735, 755 (Fla. 2007); *People v. Withers*, 429 N.E.2d 853, 856 (Ill. 1981); *People v. Barnes*, 577 N.Y.S.2d 630, 630–31 (N.Y. App. 1991) (motion for dismissal should be denied if evidence, if accepted as true, would establish every element of offense without reference to the quality or weight of the evidence).

[7] *State v. Spears*, 908 P.2d 1062, 1075 (Ariz. 1996); *People v. Cuevas*, 906 P.2d 1290, 1295 (Cal. 1995); *Pagan v. State*, 830 So.2d 792, 803 (Fla. 2002); *State v. Green*, 616 P.2d 628, 632 (Wash. 1980) (stating that "the proper test is whether there was sufficient evidence to justify a rational trier of fact to find guilt beyond a reasonable doubt").

[8] *See La Bonne v. First Nat. Bank of Arizona*, 254 P.2d 435 (Ariz. 1953) (stating that while technical precision is not required, motion must state specific grounds "sufficiently to apprise the court fairly as to movant's position"); *Consolidated World Investments, Inc. v. Lido Preferred Ltd.*, 11 Cal. Rptr. 2d 524, 526 (Cal. App. 1992) (defects not specifically pointed out by moving party cannot be considered); *Nunez v. Motor Vehicle Acc. Indemnification Corp.*, 947 N.Y.S.2d 150, 152 (N.Y. App. 2012); *Allen v. Blyth*, 23 P.2d 567 (Wash. 1933).

light most favorable to the nonmoving party in civil[9] and criminal cases.[10]

In states where the rule is similar to the federal rule, if you don't make a timely motion for judgment as a matter of law, you waive your right to make a renewed motion after the jury's verdict is entered.[11] Such posttrial motions are still sometimes

---

[9] *Salica v. Tucson Heart Hosp.-Carondelet, LLC,* 231 P.3d 946, 949 (Ariz. App. 2010); *Nally v. Grace Community Church,* 763 P.2d 948, 955 (Cal. 1988); *Brewer v. Better Business Brokers & Consultants, Inc.,* 727 So.2d 1081, 1082 (Fla. App. 1999); *Krywin v. Chicago Transit Authority,* 938 N.E.2d 440, 446 (Ill. 2010); *Szczerbiak v. Pilat,* 686 N.E.2d 1346, 1348 (N.Y. 1997); *Davis v. Early Const. Co.,* 386 P.2d 958, 960 (Wash. 1963); *Faust v. Albertson,* 222 P.3d 1208, 1212 (Wash. 2009).

[10] *State v. West,* 250 P.3d 1188, 1191 (Ariz. 2011), citing *State v. Mathers,* 796 P.2d 866, 869 (Ariz. 1990); *People v. Johnson,* 606 P.2d 738 (Cal. 1980) ("[T]he relevant question is whether, after viewing the evidence in the light most favorable to the prosecution, any rational trier of fact could have found the essential elements of the crime beyond a reasonable doubt.") (quoting *Jackson v. Virginia,* 443 U.S. 307, 319 (1979)); *Pagan v. State,* 830 So.2d 792, 803 (Fla. 2002) ("If, after viewing the evidence in the light most favorable to the State, a rational trier of fact could find the existence of the elements of the crime beyond a reasonable doubt, sufficient evidence exists to sustain a conviction."); *People v. McCord,* 361 N.E.2d 13, 16 (Ill. App. 1977) ("[A] directed finding of not guilty is proper when the evidence adduced by the State, when viewed in a manner most favorable to the State, fails to establish defendant's guilt beyond a reasonable doubt."); *People v. Contes,* 454 N.E.2d 932, 932–33 (N.Y. 1983); *State v. Gentry,* 888 P.2d 1105, 1123 (Wash. 1995).

[11] *County of La Paz v. Yakima Compost Co.,* 233 P.3d 1169, 1186 (Ariz. App. 2010) (failure to raise evidence-based arguments in motion for judgment as a matter of law waived the arguments); *Allstate Ins. Co. v. Gonzalez,* 619 So.2d 318 (Fla. App. 1993) (reversing JNOV because party failed to move for a directed verdict at trial); *Hanks v. Grace,* 273 P.3d 1029 (Wash. App. 2012) (party must move for judgment as a matter of law prior to submission of the case to jury in order to make posttrial motion); *see also* Wash. Civ. R. 50, drafter comments, as described in 14A Wash. Prac., Civil Procedure § 24:18 (2d ed. 2012). *But see* Cal. Code Civ. P. § 629 (stating that judgment should be entered pursuant to motion for judgment notwithstanding the verdict "whenever a motion for a directed verdict for the aggrieved party should have been granted had a previous motion been made"); 735 ILCS 5/2-1202(b) (stating that judgment may be entered on posttrial motion "even though no motion

called *motions for judgment notwithstanding the verdict*, or *JNOV motions*, or judgment *non obstante veredicto*. Where this is the rule, the motion for judgment as a matter of law only preserves those issues it raises.[12] Arizona has made an exception from this waiver rule for pure issues of law that have previously been raised.[13]

Until 2006, the federal civil rule required parties to make a motion at the close of all evidence in order to renew it after the verdict, even if a motion had already been made at the close of the plaintiff's case.[14] Some state rules may still impose a similar restriction, so it is important to be familiar with your local rule. But as many states have modified their rules to conform to the federal rule, it is also important to be careful of older precedents that may no longer be valid in light of the rule change.[15]

Renewed motions for judgment as a matter of law are discussed along with other posttrial motions in chapter 18.

---

for directed verdict was made"); N.Y. CPLR 4404 (not requiring prior motion as prerequisite for posttrial motion).

[12] *Standard Chartered PLC v. Price Waterhouse*, 945 P.2d 317, 338 (Ariz. App. 1996) (explaining that "because a motion for directed verdict must state the specific grounds on which relief is sought, Ariz. R. Civ. P. 50(a), and because the motion for JNOV renews the motion for directed verdict, the scope of the former is generally limited by the scope of the latter"); *City of Hollywood v. Hogan*, 986 So.2d 634 (Fla. App. 2008).

[13] *Standard Chartered PLC v. Price Waterhouse*, 945 P.2d 317, 338–39 (Ariz. App. 1996).

[14] *See* former Rule 50(b) and Advisory Committee Notes to 2006 changes to the Rule.

[15] *See* Ariz. R. Civ. P 50, State Bar Committee Note, 2010 Amendment ("This amendment eliminates the need to make a motion for judgment as a matter of law at the close of all the evidence as a prerequisite to renewing a motion made earlier during trial, as the former rule had been interpreted by cases such as *Ash v. Flieger*, 118 Ariz. 547, 578 P. 2d 628 (App. 1978)."); Fla. R. Civ. P 1.480, 2010 Committee Notes (noting that change to subdivision (b) to conform to federal rules "eliminate[s] the requirement for renewing at the close of all the evidence a motion for directed verdict already made at the close of an adverse party's evidence").

If you are faced with a motion for judgment as a matter of law based on the absence of evidence in the record on a particular point and you have evidence on that point, you may move to reopen your case for purposes of presenting the evidence, but the trial court has discretion to deny such a motion.[16]

IMPLEMENTATION AND QUESTIONS TO ASK

By custom, if not rule, most judges hear motions for directed verdict outside the jury's presence. All judges recognize a party's right to make these motions. You may make the motion orally or in writing in most jurisdictions.[17] You must make the motion after the opposing party has completed her case (and of course, you would not want to alert your opponent to any failure to present evidence on a particular factual point before she rests).

Usually, these motions are argued shortly after the last witness for the prosecution or plaintiff has finished testifying. Some judges will send the jury out of the courtroom to allow the defense

---

[16] *See Chavez v. Tolleson Elementary School Dist.*, 595 P.2d 1017, 1021 (Ariz. App. 1979) (recognizing that one purpose of rule requiring any issue of insufficient evidence to be raised on a motion for directed verdict is that omission may be cured by a reopening of the plaintiff's case); *State v. Cota*, 408 P.2d 27 (Ariz. 1965) (in criminal case, trial court has discretion to reopen case to allow prosecutor to supply missing evidence); *People v. Riley*, 110 Cal. Rptr. 3d 585 (Cal. App. 2010) (trial court in criminal case has discretion to allow prosecutor to reopen case after motion for acquittal to present omitted evidence, so long as earlier failure was not tactical); *Kay Foundation v. S & F Towing Serv. of Staten Island, Inc.*, 819 N.Y.S.2d 765, 767 (N.Y. App. 2006) (trial court has discretion to reopen case to correct defects, but such discretion should be used sparingly); *People v. Whipple*, 760 N.E.2d 337, (N.Y. 2001) (trial court has discretion to allow state to reopen case to present additional evidence in criminal case).

[17] *A Tumbling-T Ranches v. Flood Control Dist. of Maricopa County*, 217 P.3d 1220, 1229 n.8 (Ariz. App. 2009) (rejecting argument that motion at trial needed to be in writing); *Trillet v. Bachman*, 421 N.E.2d 580, 583 (Ill. App. 1981) (stating that while better practice is to put motions in writing, it is not required); *Berry v. Dumdai*, 496 P.2d 975, 976 (Wash. App. 1972) (stating that although written motion is "better practice," an oral motion is sufficient).

to make its motion. Others will ask that you reserve your motion until the next break or until the end of the day. During a break in the trial, when the jury is not present, say to the judge: "We anticipate filing a motion when the plaintiff finishes his last witness this afternoon. How would you like to handle that motion? Do you want to take it up at that time? Or would you prefer that we reserve our right to make the motion until the end of the day?"

You do not have to write and file a motion for directed verdict. An oral motion, citing your key arguments and cases, is enough to preserve your points on appeal. In a complex case or in dealing with a complex argument, you may want to write a motion and brief. It does not hurt to ask the judge which she prefers.

14

Rebuttal Case

Purpose

You are the plaintiff's lawyer or the prosecutor. The defense has just put on their case. They have presented evidence you wish to attack. Will the judge allow you to present opposing evidence of your own?

A judge admits rebuttal evidence to enable the plaintiff or prosecutor to answer new issues that the defense raised in their case.[1] It would not be fair for the defense to interject a new matter into the trial in its case-in-chief and not allow the opposition to respond with evidence of its own on the same point.

Advocacy Goals

The goal of rebuttal is to discredit all or part of your adversary's case.

---

[1] *State v. White*, 444 P.2d 661, 667 (Wash. 1968), quoting *W. E. Roche Fruit Co. v. Northern Pac. R.R. Co.*, 84 Wash. 695, 52 P.2d 325 (1935).

Applicable Law

Here is a good summary of the law on rebuttal evidence:

> Genuine rebuttal evidence is not simply a reiteration of evidence in chief but consists of evidence offered in reply to new matters. The plaintiff, therefore, is not allowed to withhold substantial evidence supporting any of the issues which it has the burden of proving in its case-in-chief merely in order to present this evidence cumulatively at the end of defendant's case. Ascertaining whether the rebuttal evidence is in reply to new matters established by the defense, however, is a difficult matter at times. Frequently true rebuttal evidence will, in some degree, overlap or coalesce with the evidence in chief. Therefore, the question of admissibility of evidence on rebuttal rests largely on the trial court's discretion, and error in denying or allowing it can be predicated only upon a manifest abuse of that discretion.[2]

Generally, the judge will not preclude testimony from your rebuttal presentation just because you could have introduced it in your case-in-chief.[3] But the judge will not allow evidence that is cumulative of evidence you presented in the case-in-chief.[4]

---

[2] *State v. White*, 444 P.2d 661, 667 (Wash. 1968).

[3] *Jansen v. Lichwa*, 474 P.2d 1020, 1023 (Ariz. App. 1970); *Zanoletti v. Norle Properties, Corp.*, 688 So.2d 952, 954 (Fla. App. 1997) ("[A] plaintiff has no obligation to anticipate the defendant's theory of the case and present evidence during the case-in-chief to disprove that theory.").

[4] *Edgar v. Workmen's Compensation Appeals Bd.*, 56 Cal. Rptr. 37, 40 (Cal. App. 1966) ("Rebuttal evidence is generally defined as evidence addressed to the evidence produced by the opposite party and does not include mere cumulative evidence of the plaintiff's case-in-chief."); *Naleway v. Agnich*, 897 N.E.2d 902, 917 (Ill. App. 2008) ("The purpose of rebuttal, of course, is not to provide a second opportunity to introduce evidence that could have been introduced in a plaintiff's case-in-chief. Rather, '[r]ebuttal evidence is admissible "if it tends to explain, repel, contradict or disprove the evidence of [the]

Trial courts have broad discretion in determining whether they will allow rebuttal evidence.[5] Despite that broad discretion, appellate courts can reverse for failure to allow rebuttal evidence.[6]

IMPLEMENTATION

As a prosecutor or plaintiff's lawyer planning your own case-in-chief, it is usually a bad tactic to try to answer every possible issue the defense might raise in their case. Why try to knock down an issue that the defense may never raise?

The best practice is to put on your case-in-chief and address the points you are confident the defense will raise. Don't hold back your good evidence on these points hoping the judge will allow rebuttal; that is a risky strategy.

If the defense surprises you and raises an unexpected issue, ask yourself three questions:

---

defendant.""""), quoting *Lagestee v. Days Inn Management Co.*, 303 Ill.App.3d 935, 942, 237 Ill.Dec. 284, 709 N.E.2d 270 (1999). See *Young-Chin v. City of Homestead,* 597 So.2d 879 (Fla. App. 1992) (a trial court abuses its discretion when it limits noncumulative rebuttal that goes to the heart of the principal defense).

[5] *Bahman v. Estes Homes,* 710 P.2d 1087, 1090 (Ariz. App. 1985) (trial court's discretion will not be disturbed "absent a showing of manifest abuse or prejudice"); *Tesoro Del Valle Master Homeowners Ass'n v. Griffin,* 133 Cal. Rptr. 3d 167, 185 (Cal. App. 2011); *See Dale v. Ford Motor Co.,* 409 So.2d 232 (Fla. App. 1982); *Chapman v. Hubbard Woods Motors, Inc.,* 812 N.E.2d 389, 396 (Ill. App. 2004); *Lane v. Lane,* 892 N.Y.S.2d 130, 133 (N.Y. App. 2009); *State v. White,* 444 P.2d 661, 667 (Wash. 1968).

[6] *Mendez v. John Caddell Const. Co.,* 700 So.2d 439, 440–41 (Fla. App. 1997) (reversing based on trial court's refusal to allow rebuttal expert testimony); *Probkevitz v. Velda Farms, LLC,* 22 So.3d 609, 616 (Fla. App. 2009) ("[A] trial court abuses its discretion when it forbids the presentation of rebuttal evidence that negates the theory of defense.") (quoting *Gerber v. Iyengar,* 725 So.2d 1181, 1185 (Fla. App. 1998)); see *Chapman v. Hubbard Woods Motors, Inc.,* 812 N.E.2d 389, 396 (Ill. App. 2004) ("[A]n abuse of discretion is likely to occur only when a party is prevented from impeaching witnesses, supporting the credibility of impeached witnesses, or responding to new points raised by the opponent.") (citations omitted).

1. Do I have any rebuttal evidence?

2. Will this evidence help me enough to justify any risks involved in presenting it?

3. Will the court allow me to present it?

The first question seems obvious; you either have rebuttal evidence or you don't. But two things can happen at trial to affect this question. First, having heard the defense case play out at trial, you can go out and investigate in a way you couldn't before. Witnesses or documents you ignored may now seem critical. Further investigation may give you evidence you didn't have at the beginning of the trial. Along the same lines, it is quite common for the trial itself to generate new evidence. For the first time, witnesses may read about the case or hear about it from acquaintances. These witnesses may contact you or your client and give you good rebuttal evidence.

As discussed in chapter 5, every time you present additional evidence, you are taking some risk. Often, the issue that the defense raised *feels* like it hurts your case more than it actually does. If you overreact and put on rebuttal evidence, that may give the defense more opportunities to showcase an issue that you do not want to emphasize. Think hard about that.

Finally, you must convince the court to allow you to present the evidence. There is one question in the judge's mind that you must answer: "Why didn't you present this evidence in your case-in-chief?" You need a good answer.

Good answers can be:

◆ We did not know for sure the defense would raise this issue.

◆ We didn't know about this witness until he contacted my office two days ago.

◆ We were unaware of how the court's rulings would affect this issue.

You will undoubtedly come up with other good answers; just make sure you have at least one.

QUESTIONS TO ASK

If you think there is a chance you will be interested in presenting a rebuttal case, before trial begins, ask the judge how she feels about rebuttal evidence. Some judges will tell you they are strict; others will tell you that if the evidence is "true rebuttal," they have no problem with it. *True rebuttal* is usually a euphemism for evidence that is countering an issue that appeared for the first time in the defense case. Whatever her stance, the judge will appreciate you raising the issue in advance so she can watch the evidence come in with an eye to whether rebuttal is proper.

15

THE CHARGING CONFERENCE
Finalizing Jury Instructions

PURPOSE

There is a time when counsel and the court meet to decide what instructions the judge will give the jury at the end of the case and how the verdict form will read. This is usually called the *charging conference* or *jury instruction conference*. Judges handle this process in various ways, but the law is clear that the parties should be allowed to argue their positions on the law before the jury is instructed.[1] This hopefully allows the judge to avoid mistakes, and it allows the parties to make a record of any mistakes they think she is making.

---

[1] *See, e.g.,* Fed. R. Civ. P. 51(b) (providing that court must inform the parties of proposed instructions and give the parties an opportunity to object on the record before giving the instructions and before closing argument); Fed. R. Crim. P. 30(b) & (d) (requiring court to inform parties of proposed instructions and provide opportunity to object on the record). *See also* Ariz. R. Civ. Pro. 51(a); Ariz. R. Crim. P. 21.3; Cal. Code Civ. P. § 607a; Cal. Penal Code § 1127; Fla. R. Civ. P. 1.470(b); Fla. R. Cri. P. 3.390(d); 735 ILCS 5/2-1107(c); ILCS S. Ct. R. 451(c); N.Y. CPLR § 4110-b; N.Y. CPL § 300.10; Wash. Civ. R. 51(f); Wash. Crim. R. 6.15.

Advocacy Goals

It is common to hear lawyers and even judges say that jurors ignore instructions. That may happen on occasion, but usually, jurors pay close attention to the instructions and do their best to follow them. In most jurisdictions, the jury instructions are written, and go with the jury to the jury room for deliberations. Why would you not want to influence the words in those instructions? The charging conference is your last chance to argue for the instructions you want.

The verdict form lists the questions the jury must answer. Again, why would you *not* want to influence those questions?

Applicable Law

- If a jury instruction is not submitted on an issue or no objection is made to an offered instruction, the issue is waived in most states.[2]

- An objection to an instruction should also specify the grounds of the objection; the objection is waived as to grounds not specified.[3]

Implementation

The judge almost always holds the charging conference toward the end of a trial, though a few judges will hold one before the trial starts. Some judges insist that the conference not be held until both sides have presented all the evidence; others prefer to get a jump on the job by holding the conference before all the evidence is in.

---

[2] *See* footnote 3 in chapter 2.

[3] *Duran v. Safeway Stores, Inc.*, 726 P.2d 1102, 1103 (Ariz. App. 1986); *Feliciano v. School Bd. of Palm Beach County*, 776 So.2d 306, 307–08 (Fla. App. 2000); *Studt v. Sherman Health Systems*, 951 N.E.2d 1131, 1136 (Ill. 2011); *Hamilton v. Raftopoulos*, 575 N.Y.S.2d 531, 532 (N.Y. App. 1991); *Goehle v. Fred Hutchinson Cancer Research Center*, 1 P.3d 579, 582–83 (Wash. App. 2000).

Sometimes the judge will set aside a morning or afternoon to hold the conference. Others hold it over the noon hour.

Whether or not the judge requires it, it is a good idea to present a pleading to the judge that outlines how you disagree with the other side's proposed instructions, and that advocates for your own. Have this in the judge's hands as early as possible—even before the trial starts, if you can. The simpler, shorter, and more direct you make this pleading, the better. Judges are busy, and the last thing they need in the middle of trial is a long law review-style brief on jury instructions. Get to the point and show the key authorities supporting your positions.

Here are a few of the common ways judges handle the charging conference:

- Some will have formal oral argument on instructions, allowing each side to support and attack the proposed instructions in turn.

- Some will give you a set of instructions they are considering and then meet informally, off the record, with both sides to discuss these instructions. There is a give-and-take, more like a discussion than an oral argument, as the judge hears both sides' arguments and decides which instructions to give. After the judge decides, she will go on the record and allow each side to state their position as to each instruction she will give the jury.

- Some will simply hand you a set of instructions, tell you these are the instructions that she will give, and allow you an opportunity to put your objections on the record.

One way or another, make sure you object *on the record* to the judge's failure to give any instructions you want, and to the giving of any instructions you believe are improper.[4] Similarly, make sure to object *on the record* to any deficiencies you perceive in the verdict form.

---

[4] *See, e.g., Romero v. Cooper*, 325 P.2d 412, 413 (Ariz. 1958) (any error in form of instruction not preserved where charging conference was off the record and plaintiff did not put objections on the record).

Questions to Ask

Before the trial starts, or at least midway through the trial, simply ask: "How do you prefer to handle decisions on jury instructions?"

Suggested Reading

All the annotations to the pattern or model instructions that you cite or your opponent cites.

16

Closing Argument

Purpose

The purpose of closing argument, or summation, is to provide each side an opportunity to show the judge or jury how the law applies to the evidence and requires a favorable verdict.[1] The value of closing argument is universally recognized.[2]

Advocacy Goals

Your ultimate goal is to win the trial. What should a closing do to maximize your chances of winning? There are two ways of thinking about this, both of which are correct.

First, you can think about closing as a chance to persuade two types of jurors: those undecided, and those who are leaning against you. Closing argument is your last chance to persuade both types of jurors that your side deserves to win.

---

[1] *Murphy v. International Robotic Systems, Inc.*, 786 So.2d 1010, 1028 (Fla. 2000).

[2] See Rick Friedman, *Rick Friedman on Becoming a Trial Lawyer* (Portland, OR: Trial Guides, 2008).

The second way to look at closing argument is that when the jurors leave to deliberate, the process of persuasion will continue among the jurors themselves. The jurors who support your side will try to convince the undecided jurors and the ones who support your opponent to come over to your side. You can look at closing as your last chance to arm your juror allies with arguments and evidence to fight for your cause. With what do you arm them?

- Jury instructions supporting your positions
- Reminders of the strongest testimony supporting your positions
- Arguments about why the law and the facts support your positions
- Counterarguments against the best arguments you think your opponent will make

Regardless of how you think about your job here, remember that the presentation of evidence at trial can be disjointed, and the evidence's significance may be unclear to or completely lost on the jurors. Closing argument is your chance to explain. If you don't explain, the jury may get off track and do the wrong thing.

If you represent the defendant, it may be the *absence* of evidence that is most significant and that you need to explain.

You almost always need to explain the law and how it fits with the facts.

APPLICABLE LAW

Generally, closing argument is allowed in all cases,[3] although sometimes, in judge-tried civil cases, the judge will request or the parties will agree to provide written closings. In criminal cases, there is a constitutional right in both jury and nonjury trials for

---

[3] *But see Fuentes v. Fuentes*, 97 P.3d 876, 882–83 (Ariz. 2004) (stating that there is no absolute right to presentation of closing argument, especially in judge-tried civil case).

the defense to give a closing argument.[4] Trial judges do have the power to set reasonable limitations on closings, such as reasonable time limits.[5] Generally, judges give broad latitude to argue the case, if the argument is based on evidence presented and reasonable inferences from that evidence.[6]

Within these general rules, the law related to closing argument varies greatly across jurisdictions. Arguments that one state regards as so improper as to deserve sanction, another state's appellate courts might endorse. The legal culture also varies widely across jurisdictions. In practical application, virtually anything goes in some states; as long as you don't step over a few clearly stated boundaries, you are safe. The appellate courts in some other states seem intent on declaring improper any argument that appears effective. In those states, you must be particularly careful to read all of the improper argument case law, do your best to understand the principles behind that case law, and then stay clear of any argument that could be construed as violating those principles. Whatever state you are in, it is a good idea to make a closing cheat sheet to remind you of the key holdings in your state and where the argument boundaries are.

---

[4] *Herring v. New York*, 422 U.S. 853, 862, 865 (1975).

[5] *State v. Davis*, 244 P.2d 97, 101–02 (Ariz. App. 2010); *People v. Harris*, 118 P.3d 545, 576 (Cal. 2005); *Stockton v. State*, 544 So.2d 1006, 1009 (Fla. 1989); *People v. Graves*, 965 N.E.2d 546, 559–60 (Ill. App. 2012); *People v. Gibian*, 907 N.Y.S.2d 226, 231 (N.Y. App. 2010); *State v. Frost*, 161 P.3d 361, 365–66 (Wash. 2007).

[6] *Hales v. Pittman*, 576 P.2d 493, 501 (Ariz. 1978); *People v. Ward*, 114 P.3d 717, 736 (Cal. 2005); *Cassim v. Allstate Ins. Co.*, 94 P.3d 513, 521 (Cal. 2004); *Murphy v. International Robotic Systems, Inc.*, 786 So.2d 1010, 1028 (Fla. 2000); *Brown v. Moawad*, 570 N.E.2d 490, 498 (Ill. App. 1991); *People v. Ashwal*, 347 N.E.2d 564, 566 (N.Y. 1976) ("[A]lthough counsel is to be afforded 'the widest latitude by way of comment, denunciation or appeal in advocating his cause' summation is not an unbridled debate in which the restraints imposed at trial are cast aside so that counsel may employ all the rhetorical devices at his command.") (quoting *Williams v. Brooklyn E.I. R.R. Co.*, 26 N.E. 1048, 1049 (N.Y. 1891)); *State v. Thorgerson*, 258 P.3d 43, 49 (Wash. 2011); *Jones v. Hogan*, 351 P.2d 153, 159 (Wash. 1960).

The following sections cover five groupings of improper arguments, including those that are improper for:

- Any lawyer
- Prosecutors
- Criminal defense lawyers
- Plaintiffs' lawyers
- Civil defense lawyers

Even if you practice in one of the six jurisdictions emphasized in this book, do not expect that every improper argument in your jurisdiction will be listed here, or that every nuance will be explored. The most common improper arguments are included to help you understand the types of issues involved, but this list does not include every possible improper argument.

Universally Improper Arguments

No matter what your role at trial, or what state you are in, you should *not* do the following in your closing arguments:

- Talk about facts not in evidence,[7] except matters of "common knowledge or [matters that] are illustrations drawn from common experience, history, or literature"[8]
- Express your personal belief [9]

---

[7] *Sisk v. Ball*, 371 P.2d 594, 598 (Ariz. 1962); *People v. Boyette*, 58 P.3d 391, 444 (Cal. 2002); *Ruiz v. State*, 743 So.2d 1, 4, 5 (Fla. 1999); *SDG Dadeland Associates, Inc. v. Anthony*, 979 So.2d 997, 1002 (Fla. App. 2008); *People v. Fort*, 153 N.E.2d 26, 31–32 (Ill. 1958); *People v. Smith*, 945 N.E.2d 477, 479 (N.Y. 2011); *State v. Clafflin*, 690 P.2d 1186, 1189 (Wash. App. 1984).

[8] *Standard Chartered PLC v. Price Waterhouse*, 945 P.2d 317, 359 (Ariz. 1996); *People v. Ward*, 114 P.3d 717, 736 (Cal. 2005); *Profit Management Development, Inc. v. Jacobsen, Brandvik & Anderson, Ltd.*, 721 N.E.2d 826, 839 (Ill. App. 1999); *People v. Ngo*, 904 N.E.2d 98, 105 (Ill. App. 2008); *State v. Clafflin*, 690 P.2d 1186, 1189–90 (Wash. App. 1984).

[9] *United States v. Young*, 470 U.S. 1, 8–9 (1985) (stating that both prosecutor and defense counsel have duty to "refrain from interjecting personal beliefs"

- Vouch for a witness[10] (stating your personal belief in the witness's credibility, character, or testimony)
- Play on jurors' sympathies, fears, biases, or prejudices, or otherwise inflame passions[11]
- Ask the jury to disregard the law (*jury nullification*)[12]

---

into case); *Hales v. Pittman,* 576 P.2d 493, 501 (Ariz. 1978); *People v. Adcox,* 763 P.2d 906, 920 (Cal. 1988); *Mayo v. Gazarosian,* 727 So.2d 1140, 1141 (Fla. App. 1999); R. Regulating Fla. Bar 4-3.4(e) (prohibiting expression of personal opinion by lawyer in trial); *Airport Rent-A-Car, Inc. v. Lewis,* 701 So.2d 893, 896 (Fla. App. 1997); *People v. Tiller,* 447 N.E.2d 174, 182 (Ill. 1982); *People v. Moye,* 907 N.E.2d 267 (N.Y. 2009); *State v. Sandoval,* 154 P.3d 271, 275 (Wash. App. 2007).

[10] *United States v. Young,* 470 U.S. 1, 18–19 (1985); *State v. Lee,* 917 P.2d 692, 697 (Ariz. 1996); *People v. Ward,* 114 P.3d 717, 736 (Cal. 2005); *Airport Rent-A-Car, Inc. v. Lewis,* 701 So.2d 893 (Fla. App. 1997); *People v. Emerson,* 522 N.E.2d 1109, 1118 (Ill. 1987); *People v. Moye,* 907 N.E.2d 267 (N.Y. 2009); *People v. Goldstein,* 763 N.Y.S.2d 390, 393 (N.Y. App. 2003); *State v. Brett,* 892 P.2d 29, 49 (Wash. 1995).

[11] *Standard Chartered PLC v. Price Waterhouse,* 945 P.2d 317, 358–59 (Ariz. 1996) (disapproving videotape shown during closing interspersing facts from the case with scenes from the movie *Titanic*); *but see State v. Gonzales,* 466 P.2d 388, 391 (Ariz. 1970) ("In the closing argument, excessive and emotional language is the bread and butter weapon of counsel's forensic arsenal, limited by the principle that attorneys are not permitted to introduce or comment upon evidence which has not previously been offered and placed before the jury."); *People v. Redd,* 229 P.3d 101, 144 (Cal. 2010); *Kiwanis Club of Little Havana, Inc. v. de Kalafe,* 723 So.2d 838, 842 (Fla. App. 1998); *Russell, Inc. v. Trento,* 445 So.2d 390, 391–92 (Fla. App. 1984) (attorney found to have made "shrewdly calculated" emotional breakdown in order to solicit sympathetic response); *People v. Tiller,* 447 N.E.2d 174, 182 (Ill. 1982) (prosecutor calling defendant an animal and referring to murders as a holocaust); *People v. Robinson,* 689 N.Y.S.2d 163, 164 (N.Y. App. 1999); *State v. Belgarde,* 755 P.2d 174, 175–76 (Wash. 1988); *State v. Prado,* 181 P.3d 901, 914 (Wash. App. 2008).

[12] *Urbin v. State,* 714 So.2d 411, 420 (Fla. 1998) (disapproving of prosecutor telling jury in capital phase that if defendant is sentenced to life, he could get out because the law could change); *Harding v. State,* 736 So.2d 1230, 1231 (Fla. App. 1999) (counsel cannot argue jury nullification); *Lioce v. Cohen,* 174 P.2d 970, 982–83 (Nev. 2008); *People v. Weinberg,* 631 N.E.2d 97, 100 (N.Y. 1994).

186   *The Elements of Trial*

♦ Disparage opposing counsel[13] or suggest that opposing counsel must be really good to make her case seem credible[14]

♦ State that evidence is fabricated or a witness lied unless you can support that accusation with record evidence[15]

Among our six states, Florida has the most comprehensive set of decisions on improper arguments. For example, the following types of arguments are restricted there but may be acceptable elsewhere:

♦ Denigrating another party or witness[16]

---

[13] *State v. Newell,* 132 P.3d 833, 847 (Ariz. 2006); *People v. Clark,* 261 P.3d 243, 328 (Cal. 2011) (prosecutor is not permitted to make unsubstantiated charges that defense counsel is fabricating defense or deceiving the jury, but can argue that defense selected experts with favorable opinions); *People v. Vance,* 116 Cal. Rptr. 3d 98 (Cal. App. 2010); *Wicklow v. State,* 43 So.3d 85, 87–88 (Fla. App. 2010); *Owens Corning Fiberglass Corp. v. Crane,* 683 So.2d 552, 555 (Fla. App. 1996) ("[I]t is never acceptable for one attorney to effectively impugn the integrity or credibility of opposing counsel before the jury."); *People v. Kirchner,* 743 N.E.2d 94, 119 (Ill. 2000); *People v. Calabria,* 727 N.E.2d 1245, 1247 (N.Y. 2000); *State v. Thorgerson,* 258 P.3d 43, 50–51 (Wash. 2011).

[14] *Hales v. Pittman,* 576 P.2d 493, 501 (Ariz. 1978) (disapproving argument that only lawyer of plaintiff's counsel's skill could make case seem plausible).

[15] *State v. Gonzales,* 466 P.2d 388, 390 (Ariz. 1970); *People v. Earp,* 978 P.2d 15, 38 (Cal. 1999); *Owens Corning Fiberglass Corp. v. Crane,* 683 So.2d 552, 554–55 (Fla. App. 1996); *SDG Dadeland Associates, Inc. v. Anthony,* 979 So.2d 997, 1001 (Fla. App. 2008); *People v. Weathers,* 338 N.E.2d 880, 883–84 (Ill. 1975); *People v. Tiller,* 447 N.E.2d 174, 182 (Ill. 1982); *People v. Goldstein,* 763 N.Y.S.2d 390, 393 (N.Y. App. 2003); *People v. Alston,* 431 N.Y.S.2d 82, 83 (N.Y. App. 1980); *State v. McKenzie,* 134 P.3d 221, 229 (Wash. 2006).

[16] *King v. Byrd,* 716 So.2d 831 (Fla. App 1998) (referring to expert witness as "hired gun" was improper); *George v. Mann,* 622 So.2d 151, 152 (Fla. App 1993) (claiming plaintiff suffered "lawsuit pain" and "set up" lawsuit); *Al-Site Corp v. Della Croce,* 647 So.2d 296, 297–98 (Fla. App. 1994) ("character attacks, name calling, and grossly inappropriate language" required reversal even in absence of objection); *McArdle v. Hurley,* 858 N.Y.S.2d 690, 692 (N.Y. App. 2008).

♦ Suggesting a claim or defense is frivolous or the judicial system is out of control[17]

Improper Arguments—Prosecutor

A prosecutor should not:

♦ Comment on the defendant's exercise of her constitutional rights, including the right to remain silent or asking for a lawyer[18]

♦ Express personal opinion on the defendant's guilt[19]

♦ Ask jurors to put themselves in the place of the victim[20]

♦ Tell jurors that to acquit, they must find that a prosecution witness lied[21]

---

[17] *Norman v. Gloria Farms, Inc.*, 668 So.2d 1016, 1022 (Fla. App. 1996); *Bellsouth Human Resources Admin., Inc. v. Colatarci*, 641 So.2d 427, 429–30 (Fla. App. 1994).

[18] *Griffin v. California*, 380 U.S. 609, 615 (1965); *United States v. Hale*, 422 U.S. 171 (1975); *Doyle v. Ohio*, 426 U.S. 610, 617–20 (1976); *State v. VanWinkle*, 273 P.3d 1148, 1150–52 (Ariz. 2012); *People v. Castaneda*, 254 P.3d 249, 282 (Cal. 2011); *State v. Smith*, 573 So.2d 306, 317 (Fla. 1990); *People v. Mulero*, 680 N.E.2d 1329, 1338 (Ill. 1997); *State v. Belgarde*, 755 P.2d 174, 177–78 (Wash. 1988).

[19] *State v. King*, 514 P.2d 1032, 1038 (Ariz. 1973); *People v. Thomas*, 247 P.3d 886, 914 (Cal. 2011); *Ruiz v. State*, 743 So.2d 1, 4, 5 (Fla. 1999); *People v. Cabellero*, 533 N.E.2d 1089, 1097 (Ill. 1989); *People v. Bailey*, 447 N.E.2d 1273, 1275 (N.Y. 1983); *State v. Dhaliwal*, 79 P.3d 432, 442 (Wash. 2003).

[20] *State v. Morris*, 160 P.3d 203, 216 (Ariz. 2007); *People v. Arias*, 913 P.2d 980, 1023 (Cal. 1996); *People v. Vance*, 116 Cal. Rptr. 3d 98, 105–07 (Cal. App. 2010) (referring to this type of argument as a "golden rule" argument); *Wicklow v. State*, 43 So.3d 85, 87 (Fla. App. 2010); *People v. Spreitzer*, 525 N.E.2d 30, 45 (Ill. 1988); *People v. Spruill*, 775 N.Y.S.2d 249, 251 (N.Y. App. 2004); *State v. Pierce*, 280 P.3d 1158, 1170–71 (Wash. App. 2012).

[21] *Atkins v. State*, 878 So.2d 460, 461 (Fla. App. 2004); *People v. Banks*, 934 N.E.2d 435, 451–52 (Ill. 2010) (distinguishing between proper argument that to believe defendant you have to disbelieve prosecution witnesses, and improper argument that to acquit defendant, prosecution witnesses must be

- Tell jurors they must "fill in the blank" with a reason for acquittal, or otherwise shift the burden of proof by stating or implying that the defendant must establish a reason for a not-guilty verdict[22]

Improper Arguments—Criminal Defense

Because the Fifth Amendment prohibits double jeopardy, appellate courts generally do not review criminal cases in which the jury acquitted the defendant. When the defendant appeals, the prosecution rarely cross-appeals defense conduct. As a result, there are few cases anywhere on improper argument by criminal defense counsel. Criminal defense lawyers must still refrain from improper argument, such as:

- Jury nullification
- Vouching for their client or witnesses
- Asking jurors to consider their own self-interest
- Stating facts not in evidence
- Expressing personal opinions
- Appealing to jury bias, passion, or prejudice

Improper Arguments—Plaintiff

One of the primary limitations on the plaintiff's summation is the *golden rule*. A golden rule argument asks the jurors "to place themselves in the plaintiffs' position and urge[s] them to award an amount of money they would desire if they had been the victims,"[23]

---

shown to be lying); *People v. Baum*, 863 N.Y.S.2d 672, 674 (N.Y. App. 2008); *State v. Fleming*, 921 P.2d 1076, 1078 (Wash. App. 1996).

[22] *People v. Woods*, 53 Cal. Rptr. 3d 7, 11–12 (Cal. App. 2006); *Gore v. State*, 719 So.2d 1197, 1200–01 (Fla. 1998); *People v. Clarke*, 915 N.E.2d 1, 19 (Ill. App. 2009); *People v. Collins*, 784 N.Y.S.2d 489, 493 (N.Y. App. 2004); *State v. Anderson*, 220 P.3d 1273, 1279–80, 1281 (Wash. App. 2009); *State v. Emery*, 278 P.3d 653, 663–64 (Wash. 2012).

[23] *Coral Gables Hosp., Inc. v. Zabala*, 520 So.2d 653, 653 (Fla. App. 1988).

or the amount they would "charge" for undergoing a similar disability.[24] Courts generally consider a golden rule argument improper[25] because it is an attempt to inflame the jury's passions.[26]

Other arguments that the plaintiff's counsel cannot make in some or all states include:

---

[24] *Nishihama v. City and County of San Francisco,* 112 Cal. Rptr. 2d 861 (Cal. App. 2001).

[25] *Taylor v. DiRico,* 606 P.2d 3, 8 (Ariz. 1980) (describing plea for juries to imagine they or their loved ones treated like the plaintiff was treated as improper golden rule argument); *Cassim v. Allstate Ins. Co.,* 94 P.3d 513 (Cal. 2004) (describing improper golden rule argument as argument in which "counsel asks jurors to put themselves in the plaintiff's shoes and ask what compensation they would personally expect"); *Metropolitan Dade County v. Zapata,* 601 So.2d 239, 241 (Fla. App. 1992) (golden rule argument is impermissible and grounds for reversal when it "strike[s] at the sensitive area of financial responsibility and hypothetically request[s] the jury to consider how much they would wish to receive in a similar situation"); *Coral Gables Hospital, Inc. v. Zabala,* 520 So.2d 653, 653 (Fla. App. 1988); *SDG Dadeland Associates, Inc. v. Anthony,* 979 So.2d 997, 1003–04 (Fla. App. 2008) (story about disabled boy adopting injured puppy because puppy "is going to need somebody that knows what it is like to feel that bad" was improper golden rule argument although it did not directly ask jurors to put themselves in plaintiff's shoes); *Chin v. Caiaffa,* 42 So.3d 300, 309 (Fla. App. 2010) (finding that only purpose for a number of arguments was to suggest that jurors put themselves in plaintiff's shoes); *Robinson v. Wieboldt Stores, Inc.,* 433 N.E.2d 1005, 1010 (Ill. App. 1982) (argument asking jurors to put themselves in the shoes of the plaintiff was improper); *Boshnakov v. Board of Educ. of Town of Eden,* 716 N.Y.S.2d 520 (N.Y. App. 2000) (describing improper "bag of gold" argument as one which told the jurors, "either directly or by implication, that they should put themselves in plaintiff's place and render such a verdict as they would wish to receive were they in plaintiff's position."); *Wilson v. City of New York,* 885 N.Y.S.2d 279, 281 (N.Y. App. 2009); *Adkins v. Aluminum Co. of America,* 750 P.2d 1257, 1264 (Wash. 1988) (opinion clarified on denial of reconsideration at 756 P.2d 142) (explaining that references to the biblical "golden rule" "or allusions to the rule such as 'urging them to place themselves in the position of one of the parties to the litigation, or to grant a party the recovery they would wish themselves if they were in the same position' constitutes an improper 'golden rule' argument").

[26] *Bocher v. Glass,* 874 So.2d 701, 703 (Fla. App. 2004).

- Arguing for damages based on a per diem or unit of time measure of calculating pain and suffering damages[27] (this is only prohibited in a minority of states)[28]

- Comparing the value of life to artwork or another expensive object (again, this only applies in some states)[29]

- Arguing for punishment of the defendant or asking the jury to "send a message" (especially through increased damages award) where punitive damages are not an issue[30]

---

[27] *Caley v. Manicke,* 182 N.E.2d 206, 208 (Ill. 1962) (*but see Watson v. City of Chicago,* 464 N.E.2d 1100, 1102–03 (Ill. App. 1984) (holding that suggestion of lump sum for pain for remainder of life in conjunction with mention of life expectancy was not improper)); *De Cicco v. Methodist Hosp. of Brooklyn,* 424 N.Y.S.2d 524 (N.Y. App. 1980) (stating that time unit theory of calculating pain and suffering damages is impermissible); *Miller v. Owen,* 709 N.E.2d 378, 379 (N.Y. App. 2000) (*but see Tate v. Colabello,* 445 N.E.2d 1101, 1103 (N.Y. 1983) (declining to address the propriety of a "per diem" argument)).

[28] Arizona, California, Florida, and Washington allow per diem arguments. See *O'Rielly Motor Co. v. Rich,* 411 P.2d 194 (Ariz. App. 1966) (allowing calculation was within trial court's discretion); *Beagle v. Vasold,* 417 P.2d 673, 676–82 (Cal. 1966) (specifically approving of per diem argument); *Ratner v. Arrington,* 111 So.2d 82, 85–89 (Fla. App. 1959); *Jones v. Hogan,* 351 P.2d 153, 159 (Wash. 1960).

[29] *Public Health Trust of Dade County v. Geter,* 613 So.2d 126, 127 (Fla. App. 1993); *Chin v. Caiaffa,* 42 So.3d 300 (Fla. App. 2010); *but see Dotson v. Sears, Roebuck and Co.,* 510 N.E.2d 1208, 1211 (Ill. App. 1987) (argument stating that a million dollars is substantial but that horses, paintings, and computers are bought and sold for that much was proper).

[30] *Acuna v. Kroack,* 128 P.3d 221 (Ariz. App. 2006) (describing argument urging jury to send a message as improper); *Collins v. Union Pacific R. Co.,* 143 Cal. Rptr. 3d 849, 861 (Cal. App. 2012); *State Farm Mut. Auto. Ins. Co. v. Revuelta,* 901 So.2d 377, 379 (Fla. App. 2005); *Kloster Cruise Ltd. v. Grubbs,* 762 So.2d 552, 554–55 (Fla. App. 2000); *Kiwanis Club of Little Havana, Inc. v. de Kalafe,* 723 So.2d 838 (Fla. App. 1998); *Pleasance v. City of Chicago,* 920 N.E.2d 572, 579 (Ill. App. 2009); *Spyrka v. County of Cook,* 851 N.E.2d 800, 812 (Ill. App. 2006); *Halftown v. Triple D Leasing Corp.,* 453 N.Y.S.2d 514, 516 (N.Y. App. 1982); *Broyles v. Thurston County,* 195 P.3d 985, 1003 (Wash. App. 2008); *but see Cota v. Harley Davidson,* 684 P.2d 888, 896 (Ariz. 1984)

- In some jurisdictions, like Florida, arguing that the jury is the conscience of the community[31] (but in most other states, this sort of argument is well accepted)

- Reference to the relative wealth of parties[32] or the defendant's insurance coverage[33]

Improper Arguments—Civil Defense

In addition to the general prohibitions discussed above, civil defense attorneys cannot:

- Argue that plaintiffs commonly ask for more than they think they are entitled to or more than they think the jury would award[34]

(asking jury to send a message to product manufacturer that denied that its product was defective was permissible argument).

[31] *Airport Rent-A-Car, Inc. v. Lewis,* 701 So.2d 893, 896 (Fla. App. 1997) (stating that argument asking jurors to tell everyone what they had awarded was an impermissible conscience of the community argument); *Maercks v. Birchansky,* 549 So.2d 199, 199–200 (Fla. App. 1989); *Decker v. Domino's Pizza, Inc.,* 644 N.E.2d 515, 522 (Ill. App. 1994); *Norton v. Nguyen,* 853 N.Y.S.2d 671, 674 (N.Y. App. 2008); *but see State v. Finch,* 975 P.2d 976, 997 (Wash. 1999) (in criminal case, prosecutor could make conscience of the community arguments provided they were not made to inflame the jury).

[32] *Tyron v. Naegle,* 510 P.2d 768, 772 (Ariz. App. 1973); *Warner Constr. Corp. v. City of Los Angeles,* 466 P.2d 996, 1007–08 (Cal. 1970); *Samuels v. Torres,* 29 So.3d 1193, 1196 (Fla. App. 2010); *Thomas v. Johnson Controls, Inc.,* 801 N.E.2d 90, 99 (Ill. App. 2003); *Nicholas v. Island Indus. Park of Patchoque, Inc.,* 361 N.YS.2d 39, 41 (N.Y. App. 1974); *Kenneth v. Gardner,* 317 N.Y.S.2d 798, 799–800 (N.Y. App. 1971); *Jones v. Hogan,* 351 P.2d 153, 156 (Wash. 1960).

[33] *Copeland v. City of Yuma,* 772 P.2d 1160, 1162 (Ariz. App. 1989); *King v. Kaplan,* 211 P.2d 578, 580–81 (Cal. App. 1949); *Neumann v. Bishop,* 130 Cal. Rptr. 786, 803 (Cal. App. 1976); *Nicaise v. Gagnon,* 597 So.2d 305, 306 (Fla. App. 1992); *Reed v. Johnson,* 204 N.E.2d 136 (Ill. App. 1965); *Johnson v. Lazarowitz,* 771 N.Y.S.2d 534, 536–37 (N.Y. App. 2004).

[34] *Donaldson v. Cenac,* 675 So.2d 228, 229 n.* (Fla. App. 1996); *Laberge v. Vancleave,* 534 So.2d 1176, 1177 (Fla. App 1988); *Hartford Accident & Indemnity Co. v. Ocha,* 472 So.2d 1338, 1342–43 (Fla. App. 1985); *Carlasare v.*

- Ask jurors to place themselves in the defendant's shoes or consider their personal interest[35]
- Refer to settlements outside the record or argue that the plaintiff's settlement with another party shows who is responsible[36]
- State that insurance rates will rise as a result of the verdict[37]
- Comment on or suggest the defendant's financial inability to pay or lack of insurance[38]

Objections to Improper Arguments

Not all improper arguments are particularly effective. If you are on the receiving end of an improper argument, you have two options:

1. Your first option is to immediately object and ask the court to admonish the jury. You will want the court to not just cut off the argument, but also explain to the jury why the argument was unfair.

Wilhelmi, 479 N.E.2d 1073, 1077 (Ill. App. 1985); *Kallas v. Lee*, 317 N.E.2d 704, 710 (Ill. App. 1974).

[35] *Cassim v. Allstate Ins. Co.*, 94 P.3d 513, 522 (Cal. 2004); *Du Jardin v. City of Oxnard*, 45 Cal. Rptr. 2d 48, 51 (Cal. App. 1995); *Norman v. Gloria Farms, Inc.*, 668 So.2d 1016, 1020–22 (Fla. App. 1996); *Offutt v. Pennoyer Merchants Transfer Co.*, 343 N.E.2d 665 (Ill. App. 1976); *Adkins v. Aluminum Co. of America*, 750 P.2d 1257, 1264–65 (Wash. 1988).

[36] *Shepherd v. Walley*, 105 Cal. Rptr. 387, 390 (Cal. App. 1972); *Donaldson v. Cenac*, 675 So.2d 228, 229 n.* (Fla. App. 1996); *Henry v. Beacon Ambulance Serv, Inc.*, 424 So.2d 914, 915 (Fla. App. 1982); *Garcez by and through Chicago Title & Trust Co. v. Mitchel*, 668 N.E.2d 194, 198 (Ill. App. 1996).

[37] *Clark v. Yellow Cab Co.*, 195 So.2d 39, 39 (Fla. App. 1967); *Feder v. Kaufman*, 180 N.Y.S.2d 609, 610 (N.Y. App. 1958).

[38] *Tryon v. Nangle*, 510 P.2d 768 (Ariz. App. 1973); *Hoffman v. Brandt*, 421 P.2d 425, 428 (Cal. 1968); *Rush v. Hamdy*, 627 N.E.2d 1119, 1125 (Ill App. 1993); *Koonce ex re. Koonce v. Pacillo*, 718 N.E.2d 628, 634 (Ill. App. 1999); *Allstate Ins. Co. v. White*, 493 N.Y.S.2d 195, 196 (N.Y. App. 1985); *Miller v. Staton*, 394 P.2d 799 (Wash. 1964); *A.C. ex rel. Cooper v. Bellingham Sch. Dist.*, 105 P.3d 400, 408 (Wash. App. 2004) (discussing *in limine* order barring reference to financial status).

2. Your second option is to *not* object. Perhaps you believe the argument was ineffective. Or perhaps you feel you can counter it in your own argument.[39] That is a judgment call, based on your need to persuade your three audiences (judge, jury, and appellate court). But know this: if you don't object immediately to an improper argument, you have almost certainly waived the objection.[40]

Some appellate courts may consider the argument that your opponent's closing was improper, even though you didn't object to it at the time, *if* it was sufficiently egregious and likely to have caused prejudice.[41] Still, you should not count on such relief.

---

[39] It is improper, however, to tolerate improper argument by your opponent in the hope that it will excuse similar improper conduct by you in response. *United States v. Young,* 470 U.S. 1, 11–13 (1986).

[40] *Copeland v. City of Yuma,* 772 P.2d 1160, 1162–63 (Ariz. App. 1989) (refusing to consider improper argument when no objection was made; court emphasized that objection could have been made anytime before case went to jury); *Horn v. Atchison T. & S.F. Ry. Co.,* 394 P.2d 561, 565–66 (Cal. 1961); *Murphy v. International Robotic Systems, Inc.,* 786 So.2d 1010 (Fla. 2000) (recognizing general rule that objection is not preserved if not made contemporaneously with alleged violation); *Hubbard v. Sherman Hosp.,* 685 N.E. 648, 654 (Ill. App. 1997); *People v. Dien,* 571 N.E.2d 69, 69–70 (N.Y. 1991); *Simpson v. K-Mart Corp.,* 667 N.Y.S.2d 90, 91–92 (N.Y. App. 1997); *Washington State Physicians Ins. Exchange & Ass'n v. Fisons Corp.,* 858 P.2d 1054, 1072 (Wash. 1993).

[41] *Ritchie v. Kraspner,* 211 P.3d 1272 (Ariz. 2009) ("Waiver does not apply when it appears 'that the improper conduct of counsel actually influenced the verdict.'") (quoting *Anderson Aviation Sales Co., Inc. v. Perez,* 508 P.2d 87, 94 (Ariz. App. 1973)); *Murphy v. International Robotic Systems, Inc.,* 786 So.2d 1010, 1028 (Fla. 2000) (discussing standards in other jurisdictions and holding that in civil cases, objection must at least be raised in motion for new trial and the trial courts may order a new trial based on improper closing argument to which no objection was made only when the argument was improper, harmful, incurable, and damaging to the public interest in the fairness of the judicial system); *Limanowski v. Ashland Oil Co., Inc.,* 655 N.E.2d 1049, 1051 (Ill. App. 1995) ("Generally, failure to object to any impropriety in counsel's closing argument results in waiver unless comments are so inflammatory and prejudicial that plaintiff is denied a fair trial."); *City of Bellevue v. Kravik,* 850 P.2d 559, 564 (Wash. App. 1993) ("Absent an objection to counsel's remarks, the issue of misconduct cannot be raised on appeal unless the misconduct is so

In a criminal case, the appellate courts may review improper arguments even if the other side didn't object. This is based on varying standards, such as whether the prosecutor's argument is so prejudicial as to prevent the defendant from receiving a fair trial,[42] or if the defendant can show an objection would have been futile, or that an admonition would not have cured the harm.[43] But in all cases, if your opposition's remarks are so improper that they may be the basis of a later appeal, it is better to object and, where appropriate, ask the court to admonish the jury to disregard the improper statements.[44]

Implementation

What you do *not* want to do in closing argument is repeat the testimony of all the witnesses, which the jurors have just heard. This will bore, insult, and frustrate them. You will want to talk about some of the testimony, but put it in a new context—the context of the reasons you are entitled to win.

There is no single right way to construct a closing argument. The type of case, the legal issues, the way your adversary has conducted her case, and the mood in the courtroom will all influence the closing argument you decide to make. There are infinite variations on closing argument structure, but three will be discussed below, as they are the most common and most useful in thinking about your own closing.

---

flagrant and ill intentioned that no curative instructions could have obviated the prejudice engendered by the misconduct.").

[42] *People v. Fort,* 153 N.E.2d 26, 31–32 (Ill. 1958); *State v. Hoffman,* 804 P.2d 577, 599 (Wash. 1991) ("The failure to object to a prosecuting attorney's improper remark constitutes a waiver of such error unless the remark is deemed to be so flagrant and ill-intentioned that it evinces an enduring and resulting prejudice that could not have been neutralized by an admonition to the jury.").

[43] *People v. Clark,* 261 P.3d 243 (Cal. 2011).

[44] If your opposing counsel is known for making improper arguments, you may want to file a motion *in limine* to prevent such arguments from ever being made.

Jury Instruction Style

The jury instructions provide an easy, commonsense structure for a closing argument. The structure could not be simpler:

- Introduction
- Review of the most important jury instructions and facts relevant to those instructions
- Conclusion summarizing why you deserve to win

For the introduction, quickly summarize your position for the jury. One way to approach this is to think about finishing this sentence: "We are here because . . ." In the case of a defendant charged in California with shooting from a moving vehicle in violation of penal code section 26100(c) and (d), you might start with an introduction like this if you are the prosecutor:

> We are here because Johnny Defendant wanted to prove to his friends what a tough guy he is.

If you are defending the case, you might want to start with:

> We are here because the police pressured known criminals to make a deal so they could close a case. From the beginning of this investigation until today, the police and the prosecutor have been taking shortcuts, conducting an investigation of convenience, and now seeking a conviction of convenience.

After the introduction, it is easy to transition to the jury instructions. You might, for example, say: "Let's look at the jury instructions that you must follow in reaching your verdict."

You do not need to discuss the instructions in the same order they are given by the judge. You might start with the instruction that outlines the elements of the crime or cause of action, the burden of proof instruction, or even some normally unimportant instruction that makes a good beginning for your discussion. You might not discuss most of the boilerplate instructions—those given in virtually every case—at all. There is no single right way to structure an argument using jury instructions. The point is that the instructions themselves are movable pieces of structure that make organizing a closing argument quite easy.

As you go through the elements instructions, you can show the jurors which elements are contested and which are not. If your client is charged with shooting from a moving vehicle, the elements instruction might look like this:

> 968. Shooting From Motor Vehicle (Pen. Code, § 26100(c) & (d))
>
> The defendant is charged with shooting from a motor vehicle at another person in violation of Penal Code section 26100.
>
> To prove that the defendant is guilty of this crime, the People must prove that:
>
> 1. The defendant willfully and maliciously shot a firearm from a motor vehicle;
>
> AND
>
> 2. The defendant shot the firearm at another person who was not in a motor vehicle.
>
> Someone commits an act *willfully* when he or she does it willingly or on purpose.
>
> Someone acts *maliciously* when he or she intentionally does a wrongful act or when he or she acts with the unlawful intent to disturb, defraud, annoy, or injure someone else.[45]

The defense might be that your client fired a pistol out the car window, but just to surprise and impress his friends. You would then argue that yes, your client willfully shot a gun from a vehicle, but he did not do so maliciously, as he wasn't trying to disturb or annoy anyone. You would further argue that he did not shoot at another person. You would point out the evidence that supports your position—or the lack of evidence to support the prosecution's position. Or you might argue that while you agree your client fired the gun out the window to annoy his friends in the car, the prosecution has presented no evidence on a critical element—that he aimed or fired *at* anyone.

---

[45] Cal. Crim. No. 968.

As prosecutor, you might point out that the defense does not dispute any of the elements except that the gun was fired at another person. You could then point out the instruction on circumstantial evidence, and transition by saying,

> So what do we know about whether the gun was shot at another person? We know the defendant said to his friends, right before he fired, "Look at that jerk in the purple coat." The defendant wants you to believe that is a coincidence. How likely is that?

You might then go to the burden of proof/reasonable doubt instruction and explain to the jury why that standard has been met.

In more complex cases, the approach is the same. Show the jurors the jury instructions and describe how the evidence matches or fails to match the instruction. In essence, the formula is simple: instruction + evidence relevant to that instruction = finding in your favor.

Story Style

Just as in a novel, you can start your story-style closing anywhere you want and tell the story from any perspective you like. Your story can have flashbacks, you can switch point of view, and you can have anyone as the hero or protagonist—even the jurors. Some lawyers have gone so far as to tell the story from the point of view of the car that was hit or the medical instrument that did the damage.

As you think about how to tell the story of your case in closing argument, the top priority should be *how to tell the story of the case in the way most likely to convince the jurors to give you the verdict you want.*

The story-style closing is particularly effective when the case involves issues of motivation. *Why* did your client's best friend tell the police your client committed a crime? *Why* did the drug company put a dangerous product on the market? *Why* has the plaintiff not recovered from her injuries when all the doctors say she should be better by now? Often, if the jury agrees with you on such questions of motivation, the verdict in your favor will follow.

Any closing argument needs an introduction, and a story-style introduction may not be any different than the introduction in an instruction-style closing. This could work:

> We are here because the police pressured known criminals to make a deal so they could close a case. From the beginning of this investigation until today, the police and the prosecutor have been taking shortcuts, conducting an investigation of convenience, and now seeking a conviction of convenience.

But then, instead of moving to the jury instructions, you might continue like this:

> Let's look at what happened from the police department's point of view. Detective Perrillo told you about the pressure the department was under with all the drive-by shootings in the Huntsville neighborhood in the previous year. What was that like for him to, "almost every week," as he said, have to read an article in the paper about the department's failure to stop these crimes? And of course it was more personal than that. He was the officer in charge of solving these shootings—and he told you, the pressure kept mounting.

From here, you can walk through the chronology of events, viewed through the prism of this detective's motivation to get these crimes solved and the cases closed.

Again, there are an infinite number of ways to construct a story-style closing. The best of these closings are almost always built around the motivations of one or more people.

Hybrid Closings

Almost all closings will be a mix of the jury instruction style and the story style. It is hard to imagine a good story-style closing that makes no mention of the jury instructions. Conversely, a jury instruction–style closing will of necessity often discuss the motivations of witnesses and parties. The facts in the case, the length of the trial, your opponent's style, and a variety of other factors will dictate the degree to which your closing leans in one direction or the other. Most important, your personality and style will also influence it. Some lawyers are more comfortable telling a story; others are more comfortable explaining and discussing the application of jury instructions. The ultimate, and only important question is: *how can you be most persuasive?*

Points to Include

Regardless of your closing structure, include the following in your closing.

Testimony Highlights

The jury does not need or want you to recite all the testimony you presented at trial (new lawyers often make this mistake). Still, there were high points of the trial for your side, weren't there? Include references to those high points in your closing.

Exhibit Highlights

Don't go through every exhibit, but certain ones may powerfully support your positions. Whether it is a letter, photo, or physical object, talk about it, show it to the jury, and explain why it is important.

Key Jury Instructions

Jurors take jury instructions seriously. So should you. These are the rules of decision. To do their jobs, the jurors must follow the instructions. Show them how the instructions point to—or require—a verdict in your favor. Show them how the instructions your opponent will be relying upon do not entitle your opponent to the verdict.

Most importantly, *explain to the jurors why the instructions you are relying upon are fair.* Most lawyers overlook this, and it is a big mistake. You cannot expect jurors to follow a legal principle they don't understand or don't believe is fair. You have spent a minimum of three years studying and thinking about rules like this; the jurors have not. You know why proof beyond a reasonable doubt is a good idea. You know why the eggshell skull/preexisting condition instruction is fair and right. Most principles and rules given to the jury in instructions are in accord with commonsense fairness—but that is often not self-evident. *So explain to them why the rules you want them to follow make sense and are fair.* Of course, do this in a nonpatronizing, nontechnical way. You will find jurors are actually interested in the reasons behind the rules. You will also find they are more likely to follow you and the instructions to a correct verdict.

Questions to Ask

- Is there any time limit on closing argument?
- Will you read the jury instructions to the jury before or after closing argument?

Suggested Reading

Bettinger, Carl. *Twelve Heroes, One Voice: Guiding Jurors to Courageous Verdicts.* Portland, OR: Trial Guides, 2011.

Levine, Moe. *Moe Levine on Advocacy.* Portland, OR: Trial Guides, 2009.

———. *Moe Levine on Advocacy II.* Portland, OR: Trial Guides and the American Association for Justice, 2012.

Perdue, Jim. *Who Will Speak for the Victim? A Practical Treatise on Plaintiff's Jury Argument.* Austin, TX: Texas Bar Books, 1989.

———. *Winning with Stories: Using the Narrative to Persuade in Trials, Speeches and Lectures.* Austin, TX: Texas Bar Books, 2006.

Spence, Gerry. *Win Your Case: How to Present, Persuade, and Prevail—Every Place, Every Time.* New York: St. Martin's Griffin, 2006.

Your jurisdiction's practice manuals, which often include sections on improper argument.

17

Jury Questions and Taking the Verdict

Your job as a trial advocate does not end with your last words of closing argument. You have two more opportunities to influence the jury: responding to jury questions and responding to the jury's verdict.

Jury Questions

It is quite common for jurors to send out notes to the judge asking questions. The question may be procedural: "Can we have a black marker and an easel?" or "Can we go home at 4:00 today?" In that event, the judge may respond without consulting the lawyers.[1] The question may also be substantive, asking for clarification of jury

---

[1] Procedural rules do, however, sometimes guarantee the right to be notified of jury questions and be provided with an opportunity to comment on any response. *See* Ariz. R. Crim. P. 22.3; Cal C.C.P. § 614; Cal. Penal Code § 1138; Fla. R. Cri, P. 3.410; N.Y CPL § 310.30; Wash. Crim. R. 6.15. Of course, if the question is truly inconsequential, a breach of this right may not be prejudicial. *See, e.g., State v. Jasper,* 245 P.3d 228, 240 (Wash. App. 2010), affirmed on other grounds, 271 P.3d 876 (Wash. 2012).

instructions or for a playback of certain witness testimony. In that event, the judge will consult with the lawyers about how to respond.

How a judge answers a jury question can determine the outcome of your case, or it can have no effect at all. You never know, so you must take each question seriously. Argue for your view of the law if the issue has to do with instructions. Argue for a fair, in-context playback if that is the issue. Make sure your positions are on the record.

Inconsistent Verdict

If there are trial lawyers who enjoy taking the verdict, they have not announced themselves. Most dread it. If the verdict is unfavorable, all you want to do is get out of the courthouse as soon as possible. Resist that impulse. Listen closely to the verdict. *Before the judge discharges the jury,* ask yourself if the verdict makes sense. Is it in some way inconsistent?

An inconsistent verdict is one in which two findings on the verdict form conflict with one another. A verdict that finds a criminal defendant guilty of an offense but not guilty of a predicate offense is inconsistent.[2] In civil cases, a verdict is inconsistent

---

[2] *Brown v. State,* 959 So.2d 218 (Fla. 2007) (explaining that although inconsistent criminal verdicts are generally permitted in Florida, an impermissible "true" inconsistent verdict exists when "an acquittal on one count negates a necessary element for conviction on another count"); *People v. Hill,* 735 N.E.2d 191, 197 (Ill. App. 2000) ("Verdicts are legally inconsistent if they necessarily involve the conclusion that the same essential element or elements of each crime were found both to exist and not to exist."); *People v. Trappier,* 660 N.E.2d 1131 (N.Y. 1995) ("A verdict is inconsistent or repugnant . . . where the defendant is convicted of an offense containing an essential element that the jury has found the defendant did not commit.").

In criminal cases, an inconsistent verdict does not necessarily require a reversal, as the majority of jurisdictions in the United States recognize that an inconsistent acquittal may reflect jury lenity, and therefore does not necessarily show that the jury improperly convicted on another charge. *See, e.g., United States v. Powell,* 469 U.S. 57, 65 (1984); *State v. Zakhar,* 459 P.2d 83, 84–85 (Ariz. 1969); *People v. Avila,* 133 P.3d 1076, 1151–52 (Cal. 2006) ("As a general rule, inherently inconsistent verdicts are allowed to stand."); *State v.*

if it assigns relative fault among the parties in a certain percentage and in another part of the same verdict finds the relative fault for the same accident in different percentages.[3] Likewise, a verdict that says a civil defendant was negligent and that his negligence caused injury to the plaintiff, but then awards no money to the plaintiff, can be considered inconsistent.[4] The more complex the verdict form, the greater the chance of an inconsistency.

Ng, 750 P.2d 632, 639–40 (Wash. 1988) (holding that conviction should not be reversed based on inconsistent acquittal where conviction is supported by sufficient evidence).

[3] *See Remy v. Exley Produce Express, Inc.*, 307 P.2d 65,67 (Cal. App. 1957) (holding that the jury's finding that two codefendants were liable to plaintiff was inconsistent with jury's finding for first codefendant in cross-claim against second, where if first defendant was negligent in action by plaintiff, its negligence should have barred its cross-claim); *Southland Corp. v. Crane*, 699 So.2d 332, 334 (Fla. App. 1997) (verdict finding that both plaintiff and defendant were legal causes of plaintiff's injuries, but assigning 100 percent of fault to defendant, was inconsistent); *Long v. Illinois Power Co.*, 543 N.E.2d 525, 534 (Ill. App. 1989) (verdict finding that driver was 90 percent responsible for property damages and 100 percent responsible for personal injuries was inconsistent); *Mateo v. 83 Post Ave Assocs.*, 784 N.Y.S.2d 520, 521 (N.Y. App. 2004) (verdict finding that plaintiff's negligence was not a substantial factor causing her injuries and assigning 25 percent of total fault to plaintiff was inconsistent); *Alvarez v. Keyes*, 887 P.2d 496, 497–98 (Wash. App. 1995) (verdict finding that first driver was not at fault for injuries to second driver but was 55 percent responsible for her own injuries on counterclaim arising from same accident was inconsistent). *But see Redmond v. Socha*, 837 N.E.2d 883, 897 (Ill. 2005) (holding that verdicts against both plaintiffs and defendants on their respective claims arising from single accident were not inconsistent, as they could reflect finding that both parties failed to carry burden of proof).

[4] *Walsh v. Advanced Cardiac Specialists Chartered*, 273 P.3d 645, 648 (Ariz. 2012) (stating that because "damages are an indispensable element of a common-law negligence claim, . . . a verdict in favor of the plaintiff awarding zero damages is internally inconsistent" but that because damages are not an element of wrongful death claim, award of no damages is not necessarily inconsistent); *Molinari v. Florida Key Electronic Co-op*, 545 So.2d 322 (Fla. App. 1989) (verdict finding defendant 10 percent at fault but awarding no damages, where plaintiff clearly injured in incident, was inconsistent); *Theofanis v. Sarrafi*, 791 N.E.2d 38 (Ill. App. 2003) (verdict for plaintiff but awarding no damages was inconsistent, at least where evidence of some damages was uncontradicted).

You need to object to an inconsistent verdict before the judge discharges the jury; this allows the trial court the opportunity to correct the error.[5] If the verdict form in your case is complex, and your verdict disappointing, you may not be sure whether the verdict is inconsistent. Ask the judge for time to look at the form as the jury filled it out. This is hard to do, with everyone staring at you, but it is your job. If you need more time to figure this out, approach the bench and tell the judge you think the verdict might be inconsistent. Ask her to send the jurors back to the deliberation room while you have a chance to study the form. Make sure you are doing this on the record.

If the verdict appears inconsistent and there is not a strategic reason to accept this inconsistency, point it out to the judge and ask for relief. In this regard, it is helpful to be familiar with what your jurisdiction considers an inconsistent verdict and the relief that is available. The relief might be to send the jury back to work with a new instruction explaining why the verdict is inconsistent. It may be that one part of the verdict would control over another part if no correction is made.[6] Call a partner or friend for advice on what relief to request. Whatever relief you request, make sure you request it on the record. If the judge does not do what you want, you may have created a great point for posttrial motions or appeal.

---

[5] *Gonzalez v. Gonzalez*, 887 P.2d 562, 565–66 (Ariz. 1994); *Zagami, Inc. v. James A. Crone, Inc.*, 74 Cal. Rptr. 3d 235, 243 n.5 (Cal. App. 2008) (stating that a "hopelessly ambiguous" verdict must be reversed regardless of timely objection but failure to object to "merely ambiguous" verdict may constitute waiver); *Tunnage v. Green*, 947 So.2d 686, 689–90 (Fla. App. 2007); *Barry v. Manglass*, 432 N.E.2d 125, 127 (N.Y. 1981); *State v. Barnes*, 932 P.2d 669, 686 (Wash. App. 1997). *But see People v. Ousley*, 697 N.E.2d 926, 930 (Ill. App. 1998) (in criminal case, defendant did not waive claim that verdict was legally inconsistent by failing to raise issue before jury was discharged because it constituted plain error).

[6] *See, e.g.,* Cal. C.C.P. § 625 (stating that, if inconsistent, a special verdict controls over a general verdict).

Polling the Jury

Usually the judge will ask if you want the jury *polled*. This is a process where the judge asks each juror—before they are discharged—if they agree with the verdict. If it is a bad verdict, and the judge doesn't ask, ask her if she will poll the jurors: "Can we poll the jury, Your Honor?"[7] There is a chance—admittedly slim—that some of the jurors did not understand what they were doing and you will find that the required number of jurors do not agree with the verdict. In that event, the jurors will generally be sent back to deliberate some more, but the judge may discharge them and declare a mistrial.

Hung Jury

The jurors may send out a note saying they cannot reach a verdict. Do you want the judge to keep pushing them to reach a verdict? It depends. Maybe a hung jury is a victory of sorts; maybe it is a disaster. The judge has a lot of discretion on how to handle this situation. The important point here is to not be surprised at such a note, and be prepared with your proposed response.

---

[7] The parties have a right to have the jury polled. *See* Ariz. R. Civ. P. 49(f); Ariz. R. Crim. P. 23.4; Cal. C.C.P. § 618; Cal. Penal Code § 1163; Fla. R. Crim. P. 3.450; *Papegeorgiou v. F.W. Woolworth Co.,* 383 N.E.2d 1346, 1352 (Ill. App. 1978); *People v. Herron,* 332 N.E.2d 623 (Ill. App. 1975); *Duffy v. Vogel,* 905 N.E.2d 1175 (N.Y. 2009); N.Y. CPLS 310.80; RCW § 4.44.390; Wash. Crim. R. 6.16(a)(3).

18

Posttrial Motions

When the trial is over, you often still have work to do. In a civil case, the side that won needs to reduce the verdict to a judgment, submit a cost bill in a timely manner, and possibly bring a motion for attorney's fees if allowed under the circumstances. In criminal cases, if the defendant has been convicted on any charge, there will be a sentencing. Procedural rules in your jurisdiction control the timing and content of these issues, and they are beyond the scope of this book. Pay careful attention to deadlines for sentencing, motions, and fees, as well as deadlines for any appeal.

Posttrial motions that could possibly alter the result of your trial or obtain a new trial without an appeal are not beyond the scope of this book. The primary posttrial motions are:

- Motion for judgment of acquittal, on all or some of the charges, in criminal cases.

- In civil cases, renewed motion for judgment as a matter of law (JMOL),[1] sometimes called motion for judgment

---

[1] See chapter 13.

notwithstanding the verdict (JNOV motion).[2] This asks the court to set aside the verdict and enter a judgment in favor of the party who lost at trial.

- Motion for a new trial, which asks the court to set aside the verdict and have a new trial on some or all of the claims. In judge-tried cases, a motion for reconsideration may substitute for a motion for new trial under some circumstances.

- Motion for remittitur, which asks the court to reduce the amount of the jury's verdict.

- Motion for additur, which asks the court to increase the amount of the jury's verdict.

Purpose

These posttrial motions give the court an opportunity to correct any perceived legal or factual error in the verdict or judgment without having an appeal. Trial judges are intimately familiar with what happened at trial and are in a good position to judge whether the verdict was supported by the evidence, whether any error at trial prejudiced one of the parties, and whether the final result was fair.

Advocacy Goals

When you file any of these posttrial motions, your goals will be twofold. First, to convince the trial judge that an error occurred and that it is serious enough to require a change in the result of trial—either asking for the judge to enter a judgment contrary to the jury's decision, or asking for a new trial. Although it may be a long shot, judges grant these motions when they recognize error. Second, you will want to position your case as well as you can for appeal. Not only do you need these motions to preserve certain

---

[2] Some states refer to their equivalent of a renewed JMOL motion by a different name; such states likely differ procedurally from the federal rule as well.

issues for appeal, they also provide a last chance to make sure that the record includes everything you need for appeal and that you have properly articulated the grounds for your objections.

Applicable Law/Implementation

Know your deadlines. You must generally file posttrial motions fairly quickly after either the verdict or entry of judgment. The Federal Rules of Civil Procedure provide for a relatively generous twenty-eight days to file renewed JMOL motions and motions for new trial.[3] Federal Rule of Criminal Procedure 33(b), however, requires that you file a motion for a new trial on any grounds other than newly discovered evidence within fourteen days after the verdict or finding of guilt. State civil and criminal rules also generally provide for a shorter time period than the federal civil rules now allow.[4]

---

[3] Fed. R. Civ. P. 50(b); Fed. R. Civ. P. 59(b).

[4] Renewed JMOL motions, motions for judgment of acquittal, and their equivalent: Ariz. R. Civ. P. 50(b) (fifteen days after entry of judgment); Ariz. R. Crim. P. 20(b) (ten days after verdict); Cal. C.C.P. § 629 (within the time for filing a motion for new trial pursuant to Cal. C.C.P. § 659; no prior motion required); Cal. Penal Code § 1185 (motion in arrest of judgment must be made and determined before judgment pronounced) (*see People v. Morgan*, 141 Cal. Rptr. 863 (Cal. App. 1977) (noting that in California, "motion for a judgment notwithstanding the verdict is unknown in criminal law proceedings" and that proper motion is one for new trial or to arrest judgment)); Fla. R. Civ. P. 1.480(b) (ten days after verdict or discharge of jury); Fla. R. Crim P. 3.380(c) (ten days after verdict or discharge of jury); 735 ILCS 5/2-1202 (thirty days after judgment or discharge of jury if no verdict is reached); 725 ILCS 5/115-4(k) (rule does not expressly provide for a renewed motion although right of court to grant judgment of acquittal after verdict was recognized in *People v. Van Cleve*, 432 N.E.2d 837, 839 (Ill. 1982)); N.Y. CPLR § 4405 (fifteen days after decision, verdict, or discharge of jury); N.Y. CPL § 290.10 (providing that motion not granted is reserved); Wash. R. Civ. P. 50(b) (ten days after judgment); Wash. Crim. R. 7.4 (ten days after verdict).

New trial motions: Ariz. R. Civ. P 59(d) (fifteen days after entry of judgment); Ariz. R. Crim. P. 24.1(b) (ten days after verdict); Cal. C.C.P. § 659 (before or within 15 days after notice of entry of judgment; no later than 180 days after entry of judgment); Cal. Penal Code § 1182 (before judgment,

Many lawyers file renewed JMOL motions and motions for new trial together, seeking alternative relief. Many civil rules reflect this practical reality. Some rules explicitly state that you can bring these motions together, and that if the court grants the renewed JMOL motion, it should also conditionally rule on any motion for new trial.[5] Some other rules provide for unified posttrial motions.[6]

Renewed JMOL motions (or JNOV motions) are the last opportunity for a judge to change the result of your trial without providing for a new trial. At this stage, the evidence is viewed in the light most favorable to the party that didn't file the motion; the judge can only grant the motion if the moving party is entitled to the requested relief as a matter of law.[7] A renewed motion after the verdict is necessary to preserve for appeal the issues raised in the original JMOL or JNOV motion.[8] As discussed in

---

order of probation, or the commitment of defendant as a mentally disordered sex offender or for narcotics addiction or insanity); Fla. R. Civ. P. 1.530(b) (within ten days of verdict or, if judge-tried, entry of judgment); Fla. R. Crim. P. 3.590 (ten days of verdict except in capital cases, in which case it is ten days from entry of judgment); 735 ILCS 5/2-1202 (thirty days after judgment or discharge of jury if no verdict is reached); 735 ILCS 5/1-1203 (thirty days after judgment in nonjury cases); 725 ILCS 5/116-1(b) (thirty days after verdict); N.Y. CPLR § 4405 (fifteen days after decision, verdict, or discharge of jury); N.Y. CPL § 330.30 (made and decided before sentencing); Wash. Civ. R. 59(b) (ten days after judgment); Wash. Crim. R. 7.5 (ten days after verdict).

[5] *See, e.g.,* Fed. R. Civ. P. 50(b) and (c).

[6] *See, e.g.,* 735 ILCS 5/2-1202; N.Y. CPLR § 4405; *see also Mono v. Peter Pan Bus Lines, Inc.,* 13 F.Supp.2d 471, 475 n.2 (S.D.N.Y. 1998) (recognizing that New York law does not distinguish between motions for new trial and motions for judgment notwithstanding the verdict).

[7] *A Tumbling-T Ranches v. Flood Control Dist. of Maricopa County,* 217 P.3d 1220, 1229 (Ariz. App. 2009); *Baker v. American Horticulture Supply, Inc.,* 111 Cal. Rptr. 3d 695, 706 (Cal. App. 2010); *Hancock v. Schorr,* 941 So.2d 409, 412 (Fla. App. 2006); *Sullivan v. Edward Hosp.,* 806 N.E.2d 645, 660 (Ill. 2004); *Winkler v. Giddings,* 190 P.3d 117 (Wash. App. 2008).

[8] *Unitherm Food Systems, Inc. v. Swift–Eckrich, Inc.,* 546 U.S. 394, 407 (2006); *see also Marquette Venture Partners II, L.P. v. Leonesio,* 254 P.3d 418, 422 (Ariz. App. 2011); *Washburn v. City of Federal Way,* 283 P.3d 567, 579–81 (Wash. App. 2012).

chapter 13, under the federal rules and in most states, if you fail to make the original motion, you have waived the right to make the motion after trial. Some states, such as California, do not require a prior motion.[9]

Motions for judgment of acquittal in criminal cases are similar to renewed motions for JMOL in that they are properly reserved for those cases in which the conviction cannot legally stand[10] and often (but not always) require a prior motion.[11]

Like motions for judgment as a matter of law and other directed verdict motions, renewed JMOL motions and motions for judgment of acquittal are based on the legal insufficiency of a claim, charge, or defense. Most commonly, this will be because the evidence offered is insufficient to establish a necessary element, or because the party opposing a claim or defense agreed with the facts necessary to establish all elements of the claim or defense as a matter of law.

Motions for new trial can address a wider variety of issues than a renewed JMOL motion. A motion for new trial is appropriate if the trial result is not fair, either because the process was flawed in some way (for example, evidence was improperly admitted or excluded, there was an error in the instructions, or improper

---

[9] *See* Cal. C.C.P. § 629.

[10] On a motion for judgment of acquittal, the evidence is viewed in the light most favorable to the prosecution, and the motion should be denied if any rational trier of fact could find the elements of the crime beyond a reasonable doubt. *See State v. West*, 250 P.3d 1188 (Ariz. 2011); *Williams v. State*, 967 So.2d 735 (Fla. 2007); *People v. Abdullah*, 785 N.E.2d 863, 870 (Ill. App. 2004); *People v. Brun*, 872 NY.S.2d 188, 189 (N.Y. App. 2009) (reversed on other grounds, 938 N.E.2d 965 (N.Y. 2010)); *State v. Ceglowski*, 12 P.3d 160, 162 (Wash. App. 2000).

[11] Ariz. R. Crim. P 20(b) (providing that a motion for judgment of acquittal made before verdict may be renewed after the verdict is returned); Cal. Penal Code § 1185 (stating that motion for arrest of judgment based on any grounds upon which demurrer may be granted is waived by a failure to demur); Fla. R. Crim P. 3.380(c); N.Y. CPL § 290.10; *but see People v. Robinson*, 556 N.E.2d 1204, 1213–14 (Ill. App. 1989) (prior motion for a directed verdict is not always required before defendant may move for judgment notwithstanding the verdict); Wash. Crim R. 7.4 (no prior motion required).

argument was allowed), the verdict is the result of passion or prejudice, or the verdict is otherwise not supported by the weight of the evidence. Note that in most states, when the question is whether sufficient evidence was presented, a renewed JMOL motion may only be granted if the evidence viewed in the light most favorable to the opposing party cannot support the verdict,[12] but a new trial motion may be granted if the judge concludes that the verdict is not supported by the *weight* of the evidence.[13] As the cases in the preceding note demonstrate, however, some states are more inclined to allow a trial judge to grant a new trial based on the weight of the evidence than others. In some jurisdictions, you must

---

[12] *McBride v. Kieckhefer Assocs., Inc.*, 265 P.3d 1061, 1064 (Ariz. App. 2011); *Hartt v. County of Los Angeles*, 132 Cal. Rptr. 3d 27, 35 (Cal. App. 2011); *Irven v. Department of Health and Rehabilitative Servs.*, 790 So.2d 403, 406 n.2 (Fla. 2001); *Jablonski v. Ford Motor Co.*, 955 N.E.2d 1138, 1155 (Ill. 2011); *Broadie v. St. Francis Hosp.*, 807 N.Y.S.2d 656 (N.Y. App. 2006); *Oregon Mut. Ins. Co. v. Barton*, 36 P.3d 1065, 1069 (Wash. App. 2001).

[13] *See McBride v. Kieckhefer Assocs., Inc.*, 265 P.3d 1061 (Ariz. App. 2011) (holding that trial court improperly granted a renewed JMOL motion because there was some evidence to support the verdict, but properly granted a new trial because trial court exercises greater discretion with respect to such motions and can independently evaluate evidence); Cal. C.C.P. § 657; *Lee v. Hughes Aircraft Co.*, 993 P.2d 388, 392 (Cal. 2000) (stating that trial court on motion for a new trial sits as an independent trier of fact and an order granting a new trial will not be reversed if there is evidence that could have supported a verdict for the moving party, even if there is also conflicting evidence); *Brown v. Estate of Stuckey*, 749 So.2d 490, 495, 497 (Fla. 1999) (stating that trial judge has broad discretion to grant a new trial if he or she concludes that the verdict was contrary to the manifest weight of the evidence) (discussing *Cloud v. Fallis*, 110 So.2d 669, 673 (Fla. 1959); *Poliszczuk v. Winkler*, 899 N.E.2d 1115, 1129 (Ill. App. 2008) (trial judge should grant new trial if verdict is against the manifest weight of the evidence); *Williams v. Pelican Pest Control, Inc.*, 782 N.Y.S.2d 748, 749 (N.Y. App. 2004) (judge should give great deference to jury's fact-finding and not set verdict aside "unless the jury could not have reached the verdict on any fair interpretation of the evidence") (citations omitted). *But see Thompson v. Grays Harbor Community Hosp.*, 675 P.2d 239 (Wash. App. 1983) (holding that while trial court has some discretion with respect to motion for new trial, motion should be denied if there is substantial evidence on both sides).

file a motion for new trial with the trial court in order to raise an *insufficient evidence* argument on appeal.[14]

While neither Federal Civil Rule 59 nor Federal Criminal Rule 33 details the grounds for a new trial, many state rules do. For example, Arizona Rule of Civil Procedure 59(a) provides:

> A verdict, decision or judgment may be vacated and a new trial granted on motion of the aggrieved party for any of the following causes materially affecting that party's rights:
>
> 1. Irregularity in the proceedings of the court, referee, jury or prevailing party, or any order or abuse of discretion, whereby the moving party was deprived of a fair trial.
>
> 2. Misconduct of the jury or prevailing party.
>
> 3. Accident or surprise which could not have been prevented by ordinary prudence.
>
> 4. Material evidence, newly discovered, which with reasonable diligence could not have been discovered and produced at the trial.
>
> 5. Excessive or insufficient damages.
>
> 6. Error in the admission or rejection of evidence, error in the charge to the jury, or in refusing instructions requested, or other errors of law occurring at the trial or during the progress of the action.
>
> 7. That the verdict is the result of passion or prejudice.

---

[14] *See, e.g.*, ARS § 12-2101(C) ("[A] motion for new trial must be made before the scope of the appeal may be enlarged to include the sufficiency of the evidence to sustain the verdict or judgment.").

8. That the verdict, decision, findings of fact, or judgment is not justified by the evidence or is contrary to law.[15]

Even where statute or procedural rules set forth grounds for a new trial, court opinions are useful to explain or supplement those grounds.

As the grounds for a new trial in Arizona illustrate, one of the possible bases for a new trial is excessive or insufficient damages. As an alternative to granting a new trial based on a determination that a damage award is either excessive or insufficient, a trial court may order *remittitur* (reduction in the award) or *additur* (increase in the award).[16] The standard for determining whether a sufficient defect in the damage award exists to require the court to grant a remedy differs from jurisdiction to jurisdiction.[17] When a

---

[15] Ariz. R. Civ. P. 59(a). *See also* Ariz. R. Crim. P. 24.1(c); Cal C.C.P. § 657; Cal. Penal Code § 1181; Fla. R. Crim. P. 3.600; N.Y. CPL § 330.30; Wash. Civ. R. 59(a); Wash. Crim. R. 7.5(a).

[16] Ariz. R. Civ. P. 59(i)(1) (providing for order of new trial on condition that adversely affected party does not accept reduction or increase in damages); Cal. C.C.P § 662.5 (if a new trial on damages would be appropriate, court may issue conditional order granting new trial unless adversely affected party accepts increased or decreased award); Fla. Stat. § 768.74 (calling for "close scrutiny" of damage awards); *Merrill v. Hill,* 783 N.E.2d 152, 156–57 (Ill. App. 2002) ("Additur is appropriate only to rectify the omission of a liquidated or easily calculated item of damages," and is not appropriate where the inadequate damages may reflect a compromise verdict); *O'Connor v. Papertisan,* 131 N.E.2d 883 (N.Y. 1956) ("[T]he trial court may deny a motion for a new trial on condition that the party, other than the movant, stipulate to pay a greater amount or accept a lower amount, as the case may be."); RCW § 4.76.030 (authorizing court, where award is "so excessive or inadequate as unmistakably to indicate that the amount thereof must have been the result of passion or prejudice," to order a new trial unless party adversely affected consents to decreased or increased amount).

[17] *See, e.g., Moorer v. Clayton Mfg. Corp.,* 627 P.2d 716 (Ariz. App. 1981) ("There is no magic formula which tests the excessiveness of damages. . . . Each case turns on its own facts."); *Gonzales v. Arizona Public Serv. Co.,* 775 P.2d 1148 (Ariz. App. 1989) ("To be found excessive, damages must be unreasonable, outrageous, and beyond all measure."); *Gersick v. Shilling,* 218 P.2d 583

court determines that the jury award is excessive or insufficient, it cannot unilaterally enter judgment in the revised amount, however. The party adversely affected by the posttrial motion gets the choice between accepting the remittitur or additur or a new trial on damages.[18]

If you do face a remittitur or additur, you should consider how accepting the reduced or enhanced amount will impact your ability to appeal. If you agree to a remittitur or additur, you often

---

(Cal. App. 1950) ("Whether the contention is that the damages fixed by the jury are too high or too low, the determination of that question rests largely in the discretion of the trial judge."); *Fortman v. Hemco, Inc.*, 259 Cal. Rptr. 311, 321–22 (Cal. App. 1989) ("It is well settled that damages are excessive only where the recovery is so grossly disproportionate to the injury that the award may have been presumed to have been the result of passion or prejudice."); *Aills v. Boemi*, 41 So.3d 1022, 1027–28 (Fla. App. 2010); ("The verdict should not be disturbed unless it is so inordinately large as obviously to exceed the maximum limit of a reasonable range within which the jury may properly operate.") (quoting *Bould v. Touchette*, 349 So.2d 1181, 1184–85 (Fla. 1977)); Fla. Stat. § 768.74(5) (setting forth factors for court to consider); *Poliszczuk v. Winkler*, 899 N.E.2d 1115, 1129–30 (Ill. App. 2008) ("[A] jury's award of damages is entitled to substantial deference by the court and a trial court can upset a jury's award of damages only if it finds that: (1) the jury ignored a proven element of damages; or (2) the verdict resulted from passion or prejudice; or (3) the award bore no reasonable relationship to the loss sustained."); *Prunty v. YMCA of Lockport, Inc.*, 616 N.Y.S.2d 117 (N.Y. App. 1994) (adopting standard that trial court should set aside jury's award of damages where it "deviates materially from what would be reasonable compensation") (quoting N.Y. CPLR 5501(c)); *Bingaman v. Grays Harbor Community Hosp.*, 699 P.2d 1230 (Wash. 1985) (comprehensively discussing standards for reviewing jury verdict and emphasizing that absent some indication of passion or prejudice, jury verdict should not be altered).

[18] Ariz. R. Civ. P. 59(i)(1); Cal. C.C.P. § 662.5; Fla. Stat. § 768.74(4); *Allstate Ins. Co. v. Mahr*, 767 N.E.2d 494, 496 (Ill. App. 2002) ("[A]dditur may be awarded only where the defendant consents to it as an alternative to a new trial, even where the damages are liquidated or the evidence of damages is essentially undisputed."); *Rajeeve Sindhwani, M.D., PLLC v. Coe Business Serv., Inc.*, 861 N.Y.S.2d 705, 708–09 (N.Y. App. 2008) (holding that although damages were inadequate, trial court erred in entering unconditional judgment for increased amount, rather than ordering a new trial, unless the defendant stipulates to the additur); RCW 4.76.030.

cannot appeal the damage award that you accepted,[19] but you may in some jurisdictions raise the issue on cross-appeal.[20]

---

[19] *See Collins v. Union Pacific R. Co.*, 143 Cal. Rptr. 3d 849, 860 (Cal. App. 2012) ("Normally, when the plaintiff has consented to a remittitur he cannot thereafter appeal on any inseverable issue."); *Omni-Vest, Inc. v. Reichhold Chemicals, Inc.*, 352 So.2d 53 (Fla. 1977); *Diaz v. Legat Architects, Inc.*, 920 N.E.2d 582 (Ill. App. 2009) ("[A] party who consents to a remittitur is bound thereby and is precluded from appealing the entry of the remittitur unless the opposing party appeals from the judgment.") (quoting *Haid v. Tingle*, 579 N.E.2d 913, 919–20 (1991)); *Adams v. Genie Industries, Inc.*, 929 N.E.2d 380, 382–83 (N.Y. 2010) ("It has long been and remains the rule that parties who stipulate to a modification of damages as an alternative to a new trial are not aggrieved by that modification and may not appeal from it.").

[20] *See* Ariz. R. Civ. P. 59(i)(2); *Collins v. Union Pacific R. Co.*, 143 Cal. Rptr. 3d 849, 860 (Cal. App. 2012) (holding that plaintiff who accepted remittitur will not be deemed to waive right to appeal after defendant first appeals); ILCS S. Ct. Rule 366(b)(2)(ii) ("Consenting to a remittitur as a condition to the denial of a new trial does not preclude the consenting party from asserting on appeal that the amount of the verdict was proper. No cross-appeal is required."); RCW § 4.76.030. *But see Omni-Vest, Inc. v. Reichhold Chemicals, Inc.*, 352 So.2d 53 (Fla. 1977) (plaintiff who accepted remittitur could not cross-appeal order of remittitur even where defendant appeals the reduced judgment); *Adams v. Genie Industries, Inc.*, 929 N.E.2d 380, 382–83 (N.Y. 2010).

19

You

You are a major element of the trial. Your actions, personality, and spirit are present at and influence every stage.

You spend a lot of time thinking about each element of trial; how much time do you spend thinking about yourself?

A surprising number of trial lawyers are not particularly thoughtful or introspective. Expressed in positive terms, they can be seen as people of action, not contemplation. Expressed in negative terms, they can be seen as people staying supremely busy to hide from parts of themselves that cause them discomfort.

But just as you need to work on your jury instruction or opening statement skills to be the best trial lawyer you can be, you also need to work on yourself. What does it mean to "work on yourself"? It can mean different things for different people. It can also mean different things depending on the role you are filling. Here, we are not concerned with your role as a parent, spouse, or community member, but rather with your role as an advocate. Interestingly though, the same characteristics that can trip you up as a parent, for example, will probably trip you up as an advocate. If hair-trigger anger interferes with your parenting, whether you know it or not, it probably interferes with your being an effective advocate.

So what does it mean to "work on yourself"? It means to focus on that tool you carry into every trial with you—your self. It means to work on making the person you are a more effective aid to your advocacy. How do you do that? Let's look at that question through the same lenses we have used for all the other elements of trial.

Purpose

You are at trial because our system presumes that you can do a better job advocating for your client than your client can for himself. Your education, training, experience, and detachment make you the better advocate. If you use those qualities to the best of your ability, and your opponent does the same, a societal "truth" is announced at the end of the trial—a truth our society is prepared to endorse as fair and just.

Advocacy Goals

Here are four goals for how your personality and style—your self—can influence the trial outcome, in increasing order of difficulty:

- Do no harm.
- Encourage the judge and jurors to trust you as a reliable source of information about the law and the facts of the case.
- Encourage the judge and jurors to like and respect you.
- Encourage the judge and jurors to want to follow you anywhere.

Applicable Law

Legal principles constrain how you can relate to judges and jurors. In the courtroom, you cannot just say and do what you want, when you want. This can feel unnatural and frustrating.

How can your true, good self—your best self—possibly come across in the courtroom?

In this sense, trial work is like an art. How can the painter convey her soul with a two-dimensional canvas and paint? How can a three-minute song move someone to tears? How can a haiku poem convey a lifetime of observation and wisdom in seventeen syllables? The constraints of these art forms also give them their power. Similarly, your true self can indeed come through and find expression in the courtroom, despite the legal constraints.

Implementation

Do No Harm

Many wounds at trial are self-inflicted; thus, our first goal is like the physicians'—to do no harm.

We do harm to our case when we:

- Fail to treat witnesses, judges, jurors, and, yes, even opposing counsel, with respect
- Are dishonest, sneaky, or disingenuous
- Are unprepared on the facts or the law
- Act peevish, defensive, pompous, or arrogant
- Quibble or are petty
- Are mean or bullying
- Lose our temper (except in rare instances, when it can actually help)
- Ignore basic societal principles of hygiene or dress

Think of acts or behaviors that can harm your relationship with another person outside the courtroom. Those same acts or behaviors will harm your relationships with everyone in the courtroom—even those to whom your actions are not directed. It's simple: bully a witness and the jurors will start to side with her; act peevish toward the judge and the jurors will infer that your case is weak; act sneaky and the jurors will conclude they cannot trust your case.

How is it that someone who appears kind, honest, and genial outside the courtroom, becomes sneaky, mean, and peevish inside the courtroom? Sometimes the kind, honest, and genial person believes he has to behave differently because of the courtroom environment. He tries to put on a "lawyer facade," and it does not fit very well.

At other times, the qualities people put out for public consumption in the "real world" are the facade—and the facade crumbles under the pressures and stress of trial. And let's face it, we all have personality and character flaws we are not proud of and that we would prefer others not see. Unless you are an accomplished liar, it is hard to hide these from the jurors or judge.

Here is the hard lesson no one wants to hear: if you are going to be the best trial lawyer you can be, you have to strive to be the best *person* you can be. You have to strive for this inside and outside the courtroom, twenty-four hours a day. It is true that some bad people get good results as trial lawyers; they would get better results if they were better people.

All of us occasionally do harm to our cases because of how we behave in the courtroom. If you can manage to have your personality or self do no harm during most of your trials, you are doing better than many lawyers who try cases.

Encourage the Judge and Jurors to Trust You as a Reliable Source of Information about the Law and the Facts

This may be the simplest of your advocacy goals. You can accomplish this by *hard work* and *vigilance*.

Hard work is obvious: you need to master the facts of your case and the law that applies.

Vigilance is more difficult, but still simple. You need to be vigilant with yourself. There is constant pressure on the advocate to overstate his case. The temptation to exaggerate a case-holding or fact can be hard to resist. Your wish that a case or fact did not exist can make it magically disappear from a presentation. If a juror or judge realizes you have succumbed to this lure of the Sirens, it is likely your credibility will never recover.

Vigilance is necessary against more than just intentional exaggeration or omission; you must also employ it against your own perceptions. As an advocate, it is easy to see things from the vantage point of your own self-interest, or that of your client. Stated another way, you are biased, and that bias can affect your perceptions. You may overstate your case, honestly believing you are being scrupulously objective and accurate. That is a real danger. Many, many lawyers have this blind spot.

A good advocate is able to filter each fact and legal authority through three perspectives:

1. How it can help her case

2. How it can hurt her case

3. Most importantly, how an objective person, such as a judge or juror, would evaluate whether it helps or hurts her case

This is a skill that takes time and vigilance to develop.

To be credible, you need not adopt the worst interpretation of a fact or authority, but you need to recognize that such an interpretation exists. To be credible, you often must deal with such negative interpretations head-on. You can say, "Some might view this case as saying _____, because of footnote 3, but in fact, there is reason to read it another way, and that is _____." Or, "You will hear that my client had been drinking that night, but you will also hear that had nothing to do with this accident because _____." In short, ignoring bad facts and law will not make them go away; it will only give them more power to hurt you.

This whole discussion concerns *important* facts and legal principles. Bring up *every* fact and legal argument that could possibly hurt you, and you will lose your focus as an advocate. You will also actually lose credibility by appearing unable to distinguish the forest from the trees.

Encourage the Judge and Jurors to Like and Respect You

You can win a case without the judge or jurors liking and respecting you—it is just harder. We tend to listen more and be persuaded more easily by people we like and respect. If you follow the suggestions outlined above, you will be well on your way to being liked and respected by the jury.

There is one way to guarantee the jurors and judge won't like or respect you: flatter or pander to them. No one likes or respects a person who is obsequious. They appear weak, phony, or both.

Encourage the Judge and Jurors to Want to Follow You Anywhere

Wouldn't that be great? The force of your presentation would cause you to be the leader, and them, the followers. There would be an electric, magical air in the courtroom. The jurors would want you to win, and would do anything you ask. While rare, this can happen. The formula for such occurrences looks something like this:

- You have followed the suggestions outlined above.
- The other side has behaved badly (see the "Do No Harm" section above).
- You have an appealing client.
- The case has come to be about something bigger than you or your client.
- Luck.

Even for the best trial lawyers, these factors rarely come together in one case. But it is helpful for you to be aware of them.

Being Your Best, Physically, Mentally, and Emotionally

The trial is about to start. Nobody warns us of the single most common mistake beginning trial lawyers make: nervously sipping water during the first hour of trial and then being able to think of nothing but the upcoming bathroom break for the next hour. Even experienced lawyers can find themselves making this mistake on a regular basis. Drink sparingly during the court day.

If you were preparing for an athletic event or a camping trip, you would give a lot of thought to your food and liquids. A trial is as physically demanding as an athletic event and can last as long as any camping trip. Give some thought to how you will sustain yourself. Many lawyers reach the end of trial so exhausted and physically run down, they can hardly stand or—more importantly—think straight.

If you are like most trial lawyers, your bodily systems will be totally out of whack during trial. You will eat too much, or not at all. You will almost certainly have trouble sleeping. Everyone has to find their own way of dealing with these issues. Pay attention to what seems to keep your system on an even keel, and *bring snacks to trial.* Your brain will not function as well as it should without caloric intake.

Bring fruit, PowerBars, nuts, carrots—whatever does not need refrigeration and might be appealing during trial breaks. It almost certainly won't seem appealing in the morning when you leave for court, but bring it anyway. You need to keep your blood sugar up, your stomach settled, and your mind clear. Avoid sugary snacks that will cause your blood sugar to spike and then crash. Force yourself to eat something at every break. Drink water, *but not too much.*

This book began with a paradox about trial practice, so it is fitting that as it comes to an end, we examine yet another paradox: a good trial lawyer is passionate and detached.

Jurors and judges cannot help but watch, listen, and evaluate whether you actually believe what you are saying. If they think you do, you are more persuasive. Even better if they believe you *care* passionately about what you are saying. Of course, you can't communicate your passionate belief directly (see chapter 16). You must do it through tone of voice, facial expression, and body language. All of these things will take care of themselves if you in fact do believe in and care about your cause.

Advocacy without belief will erode your soul. Over time, it will make you cynical and callous. This is not to say you must believe in the ultimate rightness of your client's case (although that is optimal). We are not always fortunate enough to have a case we can believe in wholeheartedly. Even clients with difficult or problematic positions deserve vigorous representation. But they are not entitled to anyone lying for them.

A criminal defense lawyer may know his client is guilty, but still believe the state does not have adequate proof to justify conviction. More likely, he has serious doubts about his client's innocence but doesn't know for sure. Either way, he can passionately believe in the presumption of innocence and fight for that in court in a way that communicates that belief. Either way, he can believe in his client's humanity and insist that a court of law recognize it.

Simply stated, if you find things about your client's case to believe in, you will be a better advocate. But belief and caring bring with them a cost. They make the trial infinitely more stressful. They give you a personal, emotional stake in the outcome. The boundary between your client's interests and emotions and your own can become blurred. When the inevitable unfair ruling arrives, it is hard not to take it personally. (And is the ruling really unfair, or are you biased by your emotional involvement?) When the other side appears to misrepresent facts or law, it can feel like a personal affront. (And are they really misrepresenting, or just seeing things from their own perspective?)

Under the stress of your own belief and caring, you are more likely to take things personally, and more likely to harm your own case. Remember, we do that when we:

- Fail to treat witnesses, judges, jurors, and, yes, even opposing counsel, with respect

- Are dishonest, sneaky, or disingenuous

- Act peevish, defensive, pompous, or arrogant

- Quibble or are petty

- Are mean or bullying

- Lose our temper (except in rare instances, when it can actually help)

Caring and belief can make the client's trial feel like your own personal life-or-death struggle. Most of us can handle a few trials like that, if we must. But if you regularly go to trial, and every trial feels like that, it will wear you down, make you crazy, or both. A worn-out, crazed advocate is not an effective advocate.

This, then, is the paradox: we must care and believe to be effective, and we must be detached to be effective.

Detachment involves the ability to separate ourselves from our clients, their issues, and their emotions. A large part of our job is to take calculated risks on behalf of our client. It is detachment that allows us to clearly see the reality of a situation and objectively evaluate our strategic and tactical options. If you are detached, you are less likely to be thrown off balance when a hard blow lands at trial; you are less likely to panic or overreact.

Detachment, of course, has its own risks and costs. If you are detached, you may have difficulty seeing, hearing, and feeling the emotional reality of a situation. And emotional reality drives many courtroom decisions by both judges and juries.

Excessive detachment can also lead to a cold, aloof, even cynical presentation—such presentations are rarely effective.

Finally, detachment can deprive you of some of the richest rewards of being a trial lawyer. It is when we emotionally engage with our clients, the witnesses, the judge, and jurors that we transcend pedestrian advocacy and achieve something beautiful that can actually nurture our souls.

In the end, being an emotionally healthy and effective trial lawyer requires embracing the paradox of caring, believing, and detachment.

Questions to Ask

- What are my strengths and weaknesses as a trial lawyer?
- How can I work to improve each one?
- Do I tend to care too much or too little about my clients and their cases?
- What can I do to work on that?
- How hard am I willing to work to become a good trial lawyer?

Suggested Reading

Ball, David. "The Leading Character: You." In *Theater Tips and Strategies for Jury Trials.* 3rd ed. Boulder, CO: National Institute for Trial Advocacy, 2003.

Friedman, Rick. *Rick Friedman on Becoming a Trial Lawyer.* Portland, OR: Trial Guides, 2008.

Spence, Gerry. *Win Your Case: How to Present, Persuade, and Prevail—Every Place, Every Time.* New York: St. Martin's Griffin, 2006.

Conclusion

Legal combat is the clash of values. Beneath every legal issue, competing values strive for dominance. When can we say that a product is defective? Is it fair to allow the jury to hear of a client's drunk driving conviction? What is the value of human pain? What is a child's life worth? The work of the trial lawyer is thus the work of applied philosophy.

Fighting for values requires training, discipline, stamina, and courage. In that sense, the work of the trial lawyer is much like the work of a soldier.

Moment by moment, the trial lawyer makes decisions that develop and reveal her own character. Through her actions she demonstrates her belief and understanding about the meaning of human existence. In this sense, the work of the trial lawyer is the work of an artist.

As a trial lawyer, you have abundant opportunities to develop and embody the qualities of integrity and intellectual rigor, courage, and compassion. You also have abundant opportunities to betray these qualities. It is these opportunities that in the end make trial work so exciting and rewarding.

Who will you be when you step into court?

INDEX

83 Post Ave Assocs., Mateo v. 203

A

ABA Model Rules of Professional Conduct 31, 95
Abdullah, Illinois v. 211
Abel, United States v. 131
Acuna v. Kroack 190
Adams v. Genie Industries, Inc. 216
Adcox, California v. 185
Addison, Seaboard Coastline R.R. Co. v. 16
additur, motion for 208, 214–216
Adkins v. Aluminum Co. of America 189, 192
admitting exhibits 119–123
Advanced Cardiac Specialists Chartered, Walsh v. 203
adverse witnesses. *See* hostile witnesses
advocacy goals
  about 2
  for charging conference 178
  for closing argument 181–182
  compelling cases as 52
  for cross-examination 129
  for directed verdict 163–164
  for direct examination 108
  for jury instructions 15–16
  for jury selection 76, 84–90
  for motions *in limine* 59
  for opening statement 93–94
  for posttrial motions 208–209
  for rebuttal case 171
  for record of proceedings 148–150
  for trial briefs 59
  for trial lawyers 218
affirmative defense 11, 97, 107
Agnew, Arizona v. 108
Agnich, Naleway v. 172
Aills v. Boemi 215

Airport Rent-A-Car, Inc. v. Lewis 185, 191
Alabama, J.E.B. v. 80
Alaska, Davis v. 128, 130
Albert F. Amling Co., De Rosa v. 20
Albertson, Faust v. 165, 166
Aldridge v. United States 77
Alford v. United States 128, 131
Allen v. Blyth 165
Allstate Ins. Co., Cassim v. 183, 189, 192
Allstate Ins. Co. v. Gonzalez 166
Allstate Ins. Co. v. Mahr 215
Allstate Ins. Co. v. White 192
Al-Site Corp v. Della Croce 186
Alston, New York v. 186
Aluminum Co. of America, Adkins v. 189, 192
Alvarado v. California Superior Court 128
Alvarez v. Keyes 203
American Dist. Telegraph Co., Kurrack v. 129
American Horticulture Supply, Inc., Baker v. 210
Amtower v. Photon Dynamics, Inc. 62
analyzing cases. *See* case analysis
Anderson, Arizona v. 79
Anderson Aviation Sales Co., Inc. v. Perez 193
Anderson, Washington v. 188
Anfinson v. FedEx Ground Package System, Inc. 20
Anthony, DG Dadeland Associates, Inc. v. 189
In re Anthony P. 131
Anthony, SDG Dadeland Associates, Inc. v. 184, 186
appellate courts
  on closing arguments 183
  influencing 149–151
  on plain error exception 150

229

record of proceedings and 146, 150
applicable law
  about 2
  for charging conference 178
  for closing argument 182–194
  for cross-examination 129–132
  for directed verdict 164–168
  for direct examination 108–110
  for jury instructions 16–20
  for jury selection 76–81
  for motions *in limine* 60–62
  for opening statement 94–99
  for posttrial motions 209–216
  for rebuttal case 172–173
  for record of proceedings 150–152
  for trial briefs 60–62
  for trial lawyers 218–219
approaching the bench 69, 123, 154
argumentative instructions 19, 23
argumentative opening statement 94, 96
argumentative questions 132
Arias, California v. 187
Arizona paper instructions 21
Arizona Public Serv. Co., Gonzales v. 214
Arizona, Stephens v. 19
Arizona Superior Court, Berger v. 60
Arizona Superior Court, Pool v. 132
Arizona v. Agnew 108
Arizona v. Anderson 79
Arizona v. Belcher 147, 151
Arizona v. Cota 168
Arizona v. Davis 183
Arizona v. Dunlap 128
Arizona v. Eisenlord 93
Arizona v. Gonzales 185, 186
Arizona v. Jessen 146
Arizona v. King 94, 187
Arizona v. Lavers 120
Arizona v. Lee 185
Arizona v. Lichon 61
Arizona v. Lujan 61
Arizona v. Maloney 20
Arizona v. Mathers 166
Arizona v. Melendez 77
Arizona v. Morris 187
Arizona v. Mosley 165
Arizona v. Newell 186
Arizona v. Rothe 130
Arizona v. Skaggs 77
Arizona v. Spears 165
Arizona v. Sucharew 98
Arizona v. VanWinkle 187
Arizona v. West 166, 211
Arizona v. Zakhar 202
Armstrong, Illinois v. 151
Arnold, Stryzinski v. 20
Arrington, Ratner v. 190
Ashland Oil Co., Inc.. Limanowski v. 193
Ash v. Flieger 167
Ashwal, New York v. 183
Atchison T. & S.F. Ry. Co., Horn v. 193
Atkins v. Florida 187
A Tumbling-T Ranches v. Flood Control Dist. of Maricopa County 168, 210
audiovisual recordings 145
Avila, California v. 202

B
Bachman, Trillet v. 168
bad facts in cases, neutralizing 53–54
Bahman v. Estes Homes 173
Bailey, Kelley v. 130
Bailey, New York v. 187
Bakersfield (California), McCleery v. 151
Baker v. American Horticulture Supply, Inc. 210
Ball, Sisk v. 184
Baltes, New York v. 99
Bangs, Walker v. 148
Bankers Multiple Line Ins. Co. v. Farish 20
Banks, Illinois v. 187
Barnes, New York v. 165
Barnes, Washington v. 204
Barrett v. Lucky Seven Saloon, Inc. 17, 21

Barry v. Manglass 204
Barton, Bill 88
Barton, Juhasz v. 94
Barton, Oregon Mut. Ins. Co. v. 212
Basiliere, Florida v. 130
Bates numbering or stamping 41
Batson v. Kentucky 76, 79
Baum, New York v. 188
Baxter v. Jones 128, 129
Beacon Ambulance Serv., Inc., Henry v. 192
Beagle v. Vasold 190
Bean, Tomlinson v. 151
Beeche Systems Corp., Saratoga Spa & Bath, Inc. v. 146
Belcher, Arizona v. 147, 151
Belgarde, Washington v. 185, 187
believability of stories 6–8, 51–52
Bellevue (Washington) v. Kravik 193
Bellingham Sch. Dist., Cooper v. 192
Bellsouth Human Resources Admin., Inc. v. Colatarci 187
Bell v. Greissman 79
bench conferences 69, 123, 154
bench copy 24
In re Restraint of Benn 128
Berger v. Arizona Superior Court 60
Berry v. Dumdai 168
Better Business Brokers & Consultants, Inc., Brewer v. 166
bias of witnesses 130–131, 136, 141
Billip, New York v. 60
Bingaman v. Grays Harbor Community Hosp. 215
Birchansky, Maercks v. 191
Bishop, Neumann v. 191
Blyth, Allen v. 165
Board of Educ. of Town of Eden, Boshnakov v. 189
Board of Regents of University of New York, Friedel v. 128, 129
Bocher v. Glass 189
Boemi, Aills v. 215
boilerplate instructions 13
Boshnakov v. Board of Educ. of Town of Eden 189
Bould v. Touchette 215

Boyette, California v. 184
Brady, Washington v. 77
Brandt, Hoffman v. 192
breach of contract instruction 13–14
Brett, Washington v. 185
Brewer v. Better Business Brokers & Consultants, Inc. 166
Briscoe, Washington v. 132
Broadie v. St. Francis Hosp. 212
Brock v. G.D. Searle & Co. 62
Brooklyn E.I. R.R. Co., Williams v. 183
Brown v. Estate of Stuckey 212
Brown v. Florida 20, 202
Brown v. Moawad 183
Brown v. Spokane County Fire Protection Dist. No. 1 131
Broyles v. Thurston County 190
Brun, New York v. 211
burden of proof 197
burying the case in documents 52
Byford, Deal v. 17
Byrd, King v. 186

C
Cabellero, Illinois v. 187
Caiaffa, Chin v. 189
Calabria, New York v. 186
Caley v. Manicke 190
California Dept. of Transp., McCarty v. 17
California, Griffin v. 187
California pattern instructions 21
California Superior Court, Alvarado v. 128
California Superior Court, County of Los Angeles v. 117
California Superior Court, Jennings v. 130
California Superior Court, Nienhouse v. 147
California Superior Court, Press–Enterprise Co. v. 73
California v. Adcox 185
California v. Arias 187
California v. Avila 202
California v. Boyette 184

232 The Elements of Trial

California v. Castaneda 187
California v. Chatman 132
California v. Clark 186, 194
California v. Cleveland 77
California v. Cuevas 165
California v. Earp 19, 186
California v. Eli 132
California v. Estrada 20
California v. Farnam 93, 97
California v. Green 98
California v. Harris 183
California v. Johnson 166
California v. Krug 131
California v. Lake 165
California v. Mattson 79
California v. Mayfield 132
California v. McManus 94
California v. Millwee 97
California v. Milosavljevic 18
California v. Morgan 209
California v. Ramos 132
California v. Redd 185
California v. Riley 168
California v. Smith 129
California v. Solomon 61
California v. Taylor 77
California v. Thomas 187
California v. Vance 186, 187
California v. Ward 183, 184, 185
California v. Wash 98
California v. Williams 78
California v. Woods 188
California v. Yarbrough 60
Calva, Espinoza v. 147
In re Candido B. 151
Cannon v. William Chevrolet/Geo, Inc. 62
Carlasare v. Wilhelmi 191
case analysis
  comparing stories 8
  jury instructions and 8, 11
case-in-chief
  about 47–48, 107
  addressing bad facts 53–54
  admitting exhibits 119–122
  believability quality of 51–52
  burying the case in documents 52
  compelling nature of 52
  consistency quality of 49–51
  determining order of proof 119
  determining witness testimony 110–119
  easy-to-understand quality of 49
  ideal qualities for 48–52
  overtrying the case 48, 52, 117
  preparing 110–112
  presenting 107–125
  rebuttal case and 173
  suggested reading 55
Casiar Min. Corp., Gutierrez v. 146
Cassim v. Allstate Ins. Co. 183, 189, 192
Castaneda, California v. 187
C.D. Plastics, Haves v. 62
Ceglowski, Washington v. 211
Cenac, Donaldson v. 191, 192
Cervantes v. Rijlaarsdam 129
challenges during jury selection
  for-cause challenges 74–76, 78–79, 86, 88–89
  peremptory challenges 74, 79–81, 85, 89
Chandler Ins. Agency, Inc., ITT Real Estate Equities, Inc. v. 120
Chapman v. Hubbard Woods Motors, Inc. 173
charging conference
  advocacy goals 178
  applicable law 178
  implementing goals and strategy 178–179
  purpose of 177
  qustions to ask 180
  suggested reading 180
Chatman, California v. 132
Chavez v. Tolleson Elementary School Dist. 168
Cheney, Warfel v. 151
Chicago, Pleasance v. 190
Chicago Transit Authority, Krywin v. 164, 166
Chicago, Watson v. 190
Chin, New York v. 130
Chin v. Caiaffa 189

chronological order
    organizing documents and
        exhibits in 43–44
    in storytelling 43, 100
citations in trial notebooks 137
*City of Yuma (Arizona), Copeland
    v.* 191
civil defense, improper arguments
    191–192
Clafflin, Washington v. 184
Clancy v. Dawe 19
Clark, California v. 186, 194
Clarke, Illinois v. 188
Clark v. Yellow Cab Co. 192
Clay, Illinois v. 132
Clayton Mfg. Corp., Moorer v. 214
Cleveland, California v. 77
In re Click 128
closing argument
    advocacy goals 181–182
    applicable law 182–194
    hybrid closings 198–199
    implementing goals and strategy
        194–200
    improper 183–194
    jury instructions and 195–197,
        199–200
    points to include 199–200
    purpose of 181
    questions to ask 200
    story style 197–198
    suggested reading 200
Cloud v. Fallis 212
Coco v. Florida 130
*Coe Business Serv., Inc., Rajeeve
    Sindhwani, M.D., PLLC v.* 215
Cohen, Lioce v. 185
Colabello, Tate v. 190
*Colatarci, Bellsouth Human Resources
    Admin., Inc. v.* 187
Colby, Paul 48
Collins, New York v. 188
*Collins v. School Board of Broward
    County* 164
Collins v. Union Pacific R. Co. 190, 216
Compton v. Ubilluz 61
Confrontation Clause 128, 131

*Consolidated World Investments, Inc.
    v. Lido Preferred Ltd.* 165
Contes, New York v. 166
Cook County (Illinois), Spyrka v. 190
Cooper, Romero v. 179
Cooper v. Bellingham Sch. Dist. 192
Copeland v. City of Yuma 191, 193
Coral Gables Hospital, Inc. v. Zabala
    188, 189
Cota, Arizona v. 168
Cota v. Harley Davidson 190
*Crane, Owens Corning Fiberglass
    Corp. v. Crane* 186
Crane, Southland Corp. v. 203
credibility
    jury instructions and 16
    of trial lawyers 51–52, 59,
        101–102
    of witnesses 50, 130–131, 133–
        134, 136
criminal defense, improper
    arguments 188
Croskery, New York v. 17, 19
cross-examination
    advocacy goals 129
    applicable law 129–132
    collecting and organizing
        134–137
    exercising judgment in
        138–139
    implementing goals and strategy
        133–143
    leading questions in 127,
        139–142
    losing cases on 141–143
    organizing material related to 38
    planning and writing 137–139
    preparing for trial 134–137, 143
    purpose of 127–129
    questions to ask 143
    re-cross-examination 143
    story inconsistencies coming out
        in 50
    suggested reading 143
Cuevas, California v. 165
*Cunningham v. Millers General Ins.
    Co.* 60

D

Dailey v. Multicon Development, Inc. 60
Dale v. Ford Motor Co. 173
Darden, Washington v. 129, 130
Davis, Arizona v. 183
Davis v. Alaska 128, 130
Davis v. Early Const. Co. 166
Dawe, Clancy v. 19
Days Inn Management Co., Lagestee v. 173
dealth penalty 75
Deal v. Byford 17
De Cicco v. Methodist Hosp. of Brooklyn 190
Decker v. Domino's Pizza, Inc. 191
Decker v. St. Mary's Hosp. 98
defense
    affirmative 11, 97
    afirmative 107
    cross-examination and 128
    improper closing arguments 188, 191–192
    presenting case-in-chief 107
    reserve opening 104
de Kalafe, Kiwanis Club of Little Havana, Inc. v. 185, 190
Delaware v. Van Arsdall 128, 131
Della Croce, Al-Site Corp v. 186
Delonda R., Kenneth C. v. 117
Department of Health and Rehabilitative Servs., Irven v. 212
depositions, filing in witness books 40
De Rosa v. Albert F. Amling Co. 20
De Vito v. Katsch 93, 99
DG Dadeland Associates, Inc. v. Anthony 189
Dhaliwal, Washington v. 187
Diaz v. Legat Architects, Inc. 216
Dien, New York v. 193
directed verdict. *See also* specific motions
    about 161
    advocacy goals 163–164
    applicable law 164–168
    implementing goals and strategy 168–169
    purpose of 162–163
    questions to ask 168–169
direct examination
    about 107
    advocacy goals 108
    applicable law 108–110
    implementing goals and strategy 110–125
    leading questions in 108–110, 115
    preparing for trial 110
    purpose of 107
    questions to ask 125
    story inconsistencies coming out in 50
    suggested reading 125
DiRico, Taylor v. 189
discovery
    numbering documents produced in 41
    organizing documents 43
    resreve opening and 104
discovery books (notebook system)
    about 38–40
    handing unique materials 40–41
discrediting stories 7
documents
    annotating in timeline 46
    burying the case in 52
    chronological order for 43–44
    creating inconsistencies with 50
    filing with court 24
    intended for impeachment 67
    jury boredom and 52
    making copies within notebook system 38, 39
    multiple roles in litigation 39
    numbering 41
    organizing for trial 35–36, 42–45
    overtrying the case 52
Domino's Pizza, Inc., Decker v. 191
Donaldson v. Cenac 191, 192
Dotson v. Sears, Roebuck and Co. 190
double jeopardy 188
Dover Union Free School Dist., Rondout Elec., Inc. v. 62

Doyle v. Ohio 187
drunk driving cases 124–125
Duffy, New York v. 132
Duffy v. Vogel 205
Du Jardin v. City of Oxnard 192
Dumdai, Berry v. 168
Dunlap, Arizona v. 128
Duran v. Safeway Stores, Inc. 178

E

Early Const. Co., Davis v. 166
Earp, California v. 19, 186
Edgar v. Workmen's Compensation Appeals Bd. 172
Edmonson v. Leesville Concrete Co. 80
educating jurors 100
Edward Hosp., Sullivan v. 210
83 Post Ave Assocs., Mateo v. 203
Eisenlord, Arizona v. 93
elements of trial
    about 5–9, 227
    assessing case-in-chief 47–56
    charging conference 177–180
    closing argument 181–200
    cross-examination 127–144
    directed verdict 161–170
    direct examination 107–125
    investigation 27–34
    jury instructions 11–26
    jury questions 201–202
    jury selection 73–92
    jury verdict 202–206
    motions *in limine* 57–64
    opening statement 93–106
    posttrial motions 207–216
    pretrial hearing 65–72
    rebuttal case 171–176
    record of proceedings 145–160
    system of organization 35–46
    trial briefs 57–64
    trial lawyers as 217–226
Eli, California v. 132
Emerson, Illinois v. 185
Emery, Washington v. 188
Ernst & Young, Gemstar Ltd. v. 16
Espinoza v. Calva 147

Estate of Stuckey, Brown v. 212
Estes Homes, Bahman v. 173
Estrada, California v. 20
ethical rules when dealing with witnesses 33
Evans, Washington v. 60
evidence
    absence of 182
    chronological order for 43–44
    exclusion of 7
    insufficient evidence argument 213
    jury instructions on 16, 148, 152, 158–160
    moving exhibits into 70
    offers of proof 123–125, 147, 151, 155–157
    opening statement on 93, 96–98
    overtrying the case with 48, 52
    rebuttal 107, 171–176
    in record of proceedings 146–147
exclusion of evidence 7
exhibit books (notebook system) 36, 42–45
exhibits
    admitting 119–123
    annotating in timeline 46
    assessing case-in-chief 48
    chronological order for 44–45
    closing argument on 199
    identifying 122
    introducing 119
    laying a foundation for 119–122
    moving into evidence 70
    in opening statement 98
    organizing for trial 36, 42–45
Exley Produce Express, Inc., Remy v. 203

F

Fallis, Cloud v. 212
Farish, Bankers Multiple Line Ins. Co. v. 20
Farnam, California v. 93, 97
Faust v. Albertson 165, 166
federal pattern instructions 22

Federal Rules of Civil Procedure
  on directed verdict 162
  on documents intended for
    impeachment 67
  on jury instruction 17
  on motions 167, 209
  on objections 146–147
Federal Rules of Criminal Procedure
  on directed verdict 162
  on motions 209
  on objections 17
  on offers of proof 147
Federal Way (Washington), Washburn v. 210
Feder v. Kaufman 192
FedEx Ground Package System, Inc., Anfinson v. 20
Fehringer v. Florida 151
Feliciano v. School Bd. of Palm Beach County 178
Ferri v. Ferri 108
Fifth Amendment 188
filing. *See also* organizing for trial
  motions *in limine* 58
  pleadings or documents 24
Finch, Washington v. 191
In re Firestorm 1991 117
first degree murder elements 14–15
First Nat. Bank of Arizona, La Bonne v. 165
Fisons Corp., Washington State Physicians Ins. Exchange & Ass'n v. 193
Fleming, Washington v. 188
Flieger, Ash v. 167
Flood Control Dist. of Maricopa County, A Tumbling-T Ranches v. 168, 210
Flores v. Miami-Dade County 131
Florida, Atkins v. 187
Florida, Brown v. 20, 202
Florida, Coco v. 130
Florida Farm Bureau Ins. Co., Swan v. 60
Florida, Fehringer v. 151
Florida, G.A. v. 151
Florida, Geralds v. 130
Florida, Gore v. 188
Florida, Harding v. 185
Florida, Hawker v. 60
Florida, Hoskins v. 73
Florida Key Electronic Co-op, Molinari v. 203
Florida, Mendez v. 77
Florida, Occhicone v. 93
Florida, Pagan v. 165, 166
Florida pattern instructions 21
Florida, Penn v. 130
Florida, Phillips v. 151
Florida, Porter v. 108
Florida, Ruiz v. 184, 187
Florida, Sanders v. 77, 79
Florida, Steinhorst v. 128
Florida, Stockton v. 183
Florida, Urbin v. 185
Florida v. Basiliere 130
Florida v. Smith 187
Florida, Wicklow v. 186, 187
Florida, Williams v. 165, 211
for-cause challenges 74–76, 78–79, 86, 88–89
Ford Motor Co., Dale v. 173
Ford Motor Co., Jablonski v. 212
Ford Motor Co., Mikolajczyk v. 17
Fort, Illinois v. 184, 194
Fortman v. Hemco, Inc. 215
foundation objections 121
Foutch v. O'Bryant 146
Frederiksen, Washington v. 78
Fred Hutchinson Cancer Research Center, Goehle v. 178
Fremont Indemnity Co. v. Workers' Comp. Appeals Bd. 128
Friedel v. Board of Regents of University of New York 128, 129
Frost, Washington v. 183
Fuentes v. Fuentes 182
F.W. Woolworth Co., Papegeorgiou v. 205

G

Gagnon, Nicaise v. 191
Gallagher, Washington v. 99
Garcez by and through Chicago Title & Trust Co. v. Mitchel 192

Gardner, Kenneth v. 191
G.A. v. Florida 151
Gazarosian, Mayo v. 185
G.D. Searle & Co., Brock v. 62
Gemstar Ltd. v. Ernst & Young 16
General Motors Corp., Soule v. 16
Genie Industries, Inc., Adams v. 216
Gentry, Washington v. 166
George v. Mann 186
Georgia v. McCollum 80
Geralds v. Florida 130
Gerber v. Iyengar 173
Gersick v. Shilling 214
Geter, Public Health Trust of Dade County v. 190
Gibian, New York v. 183
Giddings, Winkler v. 210
Glass, Bocher v. 189
Gloria Farms, Inc., Norman v. 187, 192
Goehle v. Fred Hutchinson Cancer Research Center 178
golden rule argument 188
Goldstein, New York v. 185, 186
Gonzales v. Arizona Public Serv. Co. 214
Gonzales, Washington v. 79
Gonzalez, Allstate Ins. Co. v. 166
Gonzales, Arizona v. 185, 186
Gonzalez, Illinois v. 130, 131
Gonzalez v. Gonzalez 204
Gore v. Florida 188
Grace Community Church, Nally v. 164, 166
Graves, Illinois v. 183
Grays Harbor Community Hosp., Bingaman v. 215
Grays Harbor Community Hosp., Thompson v. 212
Green, California v. 98
Green, Tunnage v. 204
Green, Washington v. 165
Greissman, Bell v. 79
Griffin, New York v. 130
Griffin, Tesoro Del Valle Master Homeowners Ass'n v. 173
Griffin v. California 187

Grubbs, Kloster Cruise Ltd. v. 190
Gutierrez v. Casiar Min. Corp. 146

H
Haid v. Tingle 216
Hales v. Pittman 183, 185, 186
Hale, United States v. 187
Halftown v. Triple D Leasing Corp 190
Hamdy, Rush v. 192
Hamilton v. Raftopoulos 178
Hancock v. Schorr 210
Harding v. Florida 185
Harley Davidson, Cota v. 190
Harris, California v. 183
Hartford Accident & Indemnity Co. v. Ocha 191
Hartt v. County of Los Angeles 212
Haves v. C.D. Plastics 62
Hawker v. Florida 60
hearsay 152, 153
Hemco, Inc., Fortman v. 215
Henry Mayo Newhalll Memorial Hosp., Semsch v. 151
Henry v. Beacon Ambulance Serv, Inc. 192
Hernandez v. New York 80
Herring v. New York 183
Herron, Illinois v. 205
Hill, Illinois v. 202
Hill, Merrill v. 214
Hockett, Watson v. 19
Hoffman v. Brandt 192
Hoffman, Washington v. 194
Hogan, City of Hollywood v. 167
Hogan, Jones v. 183, 190, 191
Hollywood v. Hogan 167
Homestead (Florida), Young-Chin v. 173
Horn v. Atchison T. & S.F. Ry. Co. 193
Hoskins v. Florida 73
hostile witnesses
  about 31–33
  cross-examination tactic for 50, 133
housekeeping instructions 12–13
Hubbard v. Sherman Hosp. 193

*Hubbard Woods Motors, Inc.,
    Chapman v.* 173
Hughes Aircraft Co., Lee v. 212
hung jury 205
Hurley, McArdle v. 186
Hyatt v. Sierra Boat Co. 58

I
*Illinois Board of Fire and Police
    Commissioners, Launius v.* 108
Illinois pattern instructions 21
Illinois Power Co., Long v. 203
Illinois v. Abdullah 211
Illinois v. Armstrong 151
Illinois v. Banks 187
Illinois v. Cabellero 187
Illinois v. Clarke 188
Illinois v. Emerson 185
Illinois v. Fort 184, 194
Illinois v. Gonzalez 130, 131
Illinois v. Graves 183
Illinois v. Herron 205
Illinois v. Hill 202
Illinois v. Kirchner 186
Illinois v. Kirkman 130
Illinois v. Kliner 93, 97
Illinois v. Lake 130
Illinois v. McCord 166
Illinois v. Mulero 187
Illinois v. Ngo 184
Illinois v. Ousley 204
Illinois v. Reinhold 79
Illinois v. Rinehart 73, 77, 78
Illinois v. Robinson 211
Illinois v. Sims 78
Illinois v. Spreitzer 187
Illinois v. Thompkins 147, 151
Illinois v. Thurman 17
Illinois v. Tiller 185, 186
Illinois v. Triplett 128
Illinois v. Van Cleve 209
Illinois v. Withers 165
impeachment, documents intended
    for 67
implementing goals and strategy
    about 2
    for charging conference 178–179
    for closing argument 194–200
    for cross-examination 133–143
    for directed verdict 168–169
    for direct examination
        110–125
    for jury instructions 21–25
    for jury selection 82–90
    for motions *in limine* 62–63
    for opening statement 99–105
    for posttrial motions 209–216
    for rebuttal case 173–174
    for record of proceedings
        152–160
    for trial briefs 62–63
    for trial lawyers 219–225
improper closing arguments
    about 183–184
    civil defense 191–192
    criminal defense 188
    objections to 192–194
    plaintiff 188–191
    prosecutor 187–188
    universally improper 184–187
inconsistent jury verdicts
    202–204
*Innovative Transmission & Engine
    Co., LLC v. Massaro* 60
insufficient evidence argument 213
*International Robotic Systems, Inc.,
    Murphy v.* 181, 183, 193
interviewing witnesses
    hostile witnesses 31–33
    importance of 28–29
    recording interviews 32
"in the record" 146
introducing exhibits 119
investigation
    jury instructions and 16
    suggested reading 34
    working with witnesses 27–34
*Irven v. Department of Health and
    Rehabilitative Servs.* 212
*Island Indus. Park of Patchoque, Inc.,
    Nicholas v.* 191
*ITT Real Estate Equities, Inc. v.
    Chandler Ins. Agency, Inc.* 120
Iyengar, Gerber v. 173

Index   239

J

Jablonski v. Ford Motor Co. 212
Jackson v. Virginia 166
Jackson, Washington v. 163
Jacobsen, Brandvik & Anderson, Ltd., Profit Management Development, Inc. v. 184
Jacobs v. Wainwright 147
James A. Crone, Inc., Zagami, Inc. v. 204
Jamison v. Lindsay 17
Jansen v. Lichwa 172
Jasper, Washington v. 201
J.E.B. v. Alabama 80
Jennings v. California Superior Court 130
Jessen, Arizona v. 146
JMOL (judgment as a matter of law) 161–168, 207–212
JNOV (judgment notwithstanding the verdict) 167, 207, 210
Jodhan, New York v. 132
John Caddell Const. Co., Mendez v. 173
Johnson, California v. 166
Johnson Controls, Inc., Thomas v. 191
Johnson, Reed v. 191
Johnson v. Lazarowitz 191
Jones, Baxter v. 128, 129
Jones, Trower v. 131
Jones v. Hogan 183, 190, 191
journalistic device
    preparing for cross-examination 134–137
    preparing for direct examination 110
judgment *non obstante veredicto* 167
Juhasz v. Barton 94
juror education 100
jury instructions. *See also* pattern instructions
    about 11–12, 12
    advocacy goals 15–16
    applicable law 16–20
    boilerplate instructions 13
    case analysis and 8, 11
    categories of 12

    closing argument on 195–197, 199–200
    on evidence 16, 148, 152, 158–160
    finalizing 177–180
    housekeeping instructions 12–13
    implementing goals and strategies for 21–25
    instruction conference with attorneys 24
    language in 16, 20
    limiting instruction 159
    midtrial 148, 151–152, 158–160
    objections to 24
    organizing 24, 42
    preparing case-in-chief and 110–111
    purpose of 12–15
    questions to ask 25
    record of proceedings on 148, 151–152, 158–160
    statement of the case 23–24
    substantive instructions 13–15
    suggested reading 26
    summary of the case 23–24
    trial briefs and 15
    verdict reversals and 22
jury questions 201–202
jury selection
    advocacy goals 76, 84–90
    applicable law 76–81
    arguing case in 87
    for-cause challenges 74–76
    identifying and eliminating bad jurors 85–87
    implementing goals and strategy 82–90
    organizing 89–90
    organizing materials 42
    purpose of 73–76
    questions to ask 84–87, 90
    seating charts during 89
    statement of the case instructions and 23–24
    suggested reading 91
    where to sit 84

240   *The Elements of Trial*

jury verdicts
   explaning legal and moral basis
      for   103
   guiding juries to   6
   hung jury   205
   inconsistent   202–204
   influencing   148–149, 182
   polling the jury   205
   reversals of   22

K
Kallas v. Lee   192
Kaplan, King v.   191
Kass, New York v.   148
Katsch, De Vito v.   93, 99
Kaufman, Feder v.   192
Kay Foundation v. S & F Towing Serv. of Staten Island, Inc.   168
Kelley v. Bailey   130
Kelly v. New West Federal Savings   58, 60
Kenneth C. v. Delonda R.   117
Kenneth v. Gardner   191
Kentucky, Batson v.   76, 79
Keyes, Alvarez v.   203
Kieckhefer Assocs., Inc., McBride v.   212
killing with premeditation   14–15
King, Arizona v.   94, 187
Kingston v. Turner   20
King v. Byrd   186
King v. Kaplan   191
Kirchner, Illinois v.   186
Kirkman, Illinois v.   130
Kiwanis Club of Little Havana, Inc. v. de Kalafe   185, 190
Kliner, Illinois v.   93, 97
Kloster Cruise Ltd. v. Grubbs   190
K-Mart Corp., Simpson v.   193
Knight, New York v.   79
Konoff, Robert   48
Koonce v. Pacillo   192
Krack Corp., Mad River Orchard, Inc. v.   151
Kraspner, Ritchie v.   193
Kravik, City of Bellevue v.   193
Kroack, Acuna v.   190
Kroll, Washington v.   93, 94

Krug, California v.   131
Krywin v. Chicago Transit Authority   164, 166
Kurrack v. American Dist. Telegraph Co.   129

L
Laberge v. Vancleave   191
La Bonne v. First Nat. Bank of Arizona   165
Lagestee v. Days Inn Management Co.   173
Lake, California v.   165
Lake, Illinois v.   130
Lane v. Lane   173
language
   in jury instructions   16, 20
   in opening statements   94–99
La Paz County (Arizona) v. Yakima Compost Co.   166
Latham, Washington v.   60
Lauman v. Vandalia Bus Lines, Inc.   19
Launius v. Illinois Board of Fire and Police Commissioners   108
Lavers, Arizona v.   120
laying a foundation for exhibits   119–122
Lazarowitz, Johnson v.   191
leading questions
   in cross-examination   127, 139–142
   in direct examination   108–110, 115
Lee, Arizona v.   185
Lee, Kallas v.   192
Leesville Concrete Co., Edmonson v.   80
Lee v. Hughes Aircraft Co.   212
legal or procedural purpose.
   See purpose, legal or procedural
Legat Architects, Inc., Diaz v.   216
Leonesio, Marquette Venture Partners II, L.P. v.   210
Lewis, Airport Rent-A-Car, Inc. v.   185, 191
Liberatore v. Thompson   61
Lichon, Arizona v.   61
Lichwa, Jansen v.   172

Lido Preferred Ltd., Consolidated World Investments, Inc. v. 165
Limanowski v. Ashland Oil Co., Inc. 193
limiting instruction 159
Lindsay, Jamison v. 17
Lioce v. Cohen 185
Long v. Illinois Power Co. 203
Lopez-Stayer v. Pitts 73
Los Angeles County, Hartt v. 212
Los Angeles County v. California Superior Court 117
Los Angeles, Warner Constr. Corp. v. 191
losing cases on cross-examination 141–143
Louisiana, Snyder v. 80
Lucky Seven Saloon, Inc., Barrett v. 17, 21
Lujan, Arizona v. 61

M
Mad River Orchard, Inc. v. Krack Corp. 151
Maercks v. Birchansky 191
Mahr, Allstate Ins. Co. v. 215
Major v. Western Home Ins. Co. 19
Maloney, Arizona v. 20
Manglass, Barry v. 204
Manicke, Caley v. 190
Mann, George v. 186
Marquette Venture Partners II, L.P. v. Leonesio 210
Martinez, United States v. 80
Massaro, Innovative Transmission & Engine Co., LLC v. 60
Mateo v. 83 Post Ave Assocs. 203
Mather, New York v. 108
Mathers, Arizona v. 166
Mattson, California v. 79
Mayfield, California v. 132
Mayol v. Summers, Watson & Kimpel 20
Mayo v. Gazarosian 185
McArdle v. Hurley 186
McBride v. Kieckhefer Assocs., Inc. 212

McCarty v. California Dept. of Transp. 17
McCleery v. City of Bakersfield 151
McCollum, Georgia v. 80
McCord, Illinois v. 166
McGill v. Virginia 79
McKenzie, Washington v. 186
McManus, California v. 94
medical malpractice cases
 opening statement in 103
 organizing documents in 43
Melendez, Arizona v. 77
Mendez v. Florida 77
Mendez v. John Caddell Const. Co. 173
Merlo v. Standard Life & Acc. Ins. Co. 20
Merrill v. Hill 214
Methodist Hosp. of Brooklyn, De Cicco v. 190
Metropolitan Dade County v. Zapata 189
Metz, New York v. 60
M. Furuya Co., Moy Quon v. 130
Miami-Dade County, Flores v. 131
midtrial jury instructions 148, 151–152, 158–160
Mikolajczyk v. Ford Motor Co. 17
Millers General Ins. Co., Cunningham v. 60
Miller v. Owen 190
Miller v. Staton 192
Millwee, California v. 97
Milosavljevic, California v. 18
minor impact cases 53–54
Mitchel, Garcez by and through Chicago Title & Trust Co. v. 192
Moawad, Brown v. 183
model instructions. *See* pattern instructions
Molinari v. Florida Key Electronic Co-op 203
Mono v. Peter Pan Bus Lines, Inc. 210
Moorer v. Clayton Mfg. Corp. 214
Mora v. Phoenix Indem. Ins. Co. 18
In re Detention of Morgan 146
Morgan, California v. 209
Morris, Arizona v. 187

Mosley, Arizona v. 165
motion for additur 208, 214–216
motion for a new trial 208
motion for directed verdict.
    See directed verdict
motion for judgment as a matter of law 161–168, 207–212
motion for judgment notwithstanding the verdict 167, 207, 210
motion for judgment of acquittal 161, 165, 207
motion for remittitur 208, 214–216
motions *in limine*
    about 2
    advocacy goals 59
    anticipating issues 152
    applicable law 60–62
    cross-examination and 141
    filing with court 58
    implementing goals and strategies 62–63
    offers of proof in 156
    oral arguments on 65–72
    organizing 42
    purpose of 57–59
    questions to ask 63–64
    suggested reading 64
motivation of witnesses 135, 141
Motor Vehicle Acc. Indemnification Corp., Nunez v. 165
Moye, New York v. 185
Moy Quon v. M. Furuya Co. 130
Mulero, Illinois v. 187
Multicon Development, Inc., Dailey v. 60
Mu'Min v. Virginia 73
murder, first degree 14–15
Murphy v. International Robotic Systems, Inc. 181, 183, 193

N
Naclerio v. Naclerio 151
Naegle, Tyron v. 191
Naleway v. Agnich 172
Nally v. Grace Community Church 164, 166
Nangle, Tryon v. 192
Neumann v. Bishop 191
Newell, Arizona v. 186
New West Federal Savings, Kelly v. 58, 60
New York City, Wilson v. 189
New York, Hernandez v. 80
New York, Herring v. 183
New York pattern instructions 21
New York v. Alston 186
New York v. Ashwal 183
New York v. Bailey 187
New York v. Baltes 99
New York v. Barnes 165
New York v. Baum 188
New York v. Billip 60
New York v. Brun 211
New York v. Calabria 186
New York v. Chin 130
New York v. Collins 188
New York v. Contes 166
New York v. Croskery 17, 19
New York v. Dien 193
New York v. Duffy 132
New York v. Gibian 183
New York v. Goldstein 185, 186
New York v. Griffin 130
New York v. Jodhan 132
New York v. Kass 148
New York v. Knight 79
New York v. Mather 108
New York v. Metz 60
New York v. Moye 185
New York v. Pereyra 148
New York v. Robinson 185
New York v. Smith 184
New York v. Spruill 187
New York v. Stanard 128
New York v. Trappier 202
New York v. Weinberg 185
New York v. Whipple 168
Ngo, Illinois v. 184
Nguyen, Norton v. 191
Nicaise v. Gagnon 191
Nicholas v. Island Indus. Park of Patchoque, Inc. 191

Nienhouse v. California Superior Court 147
Nishihama v. City and County of San Francisco 189
Norle Properties, Corp., Zanoletti v. 172
Norman v. Gloria Farms, Inc. 187, 192
Northern Pac. R.R. Co., W. E. Roche Fruit Co. v. 171
Norton v. Nguyen 191
notebook system
    about 36–37, 45
    citations organized in 137
    different colored spines 45
    discovery books 38–40
    exhibit books 42–45
    making copies of documents within 38, 39
    pleadings books 37–38
    research books 41
    trial brief books 41–42
    witness books 40, 134–137
Nunez v. Motor Vehicle Acc. Indemnification Corp. 165

O
objections
    about 17, 146–147
    bench conferences 69, 123, 154
    charging conference and 179
    foundation 121
    to improper arguments 192–194
    to jury instructions 24
    to laying a foundation for exhibits 121
    leading questions 115
    offers of proof and 124–126
    one-phrase/one-rule 68–69, 123, 153–154
    to opening statement 97, 104
    plain error exception 150
    record of proceedings and 146–147, 149–150, 152–155, 179
    risk-benefit analysis for 149–150
    speaking 67–68, 123, 153
    waiving 150
    writing 155

O'Bryant, Foutch v. 146
Occhicone v. Florida 93
Ocha, Hartford Accident & Indemnity Co. v. 191
O'Connor v. Papertisan 214
offers of proof for evidence
    direct examination and 123–125
    record of proceedings and 147, 151, 155–157
Offshore Systems, Inc., Rice v. 120
Offutt v. Pennoyer Merchants Transfer Co. 192
Ohio, Doyle v. 187
Ohio, Powers v. 80
Ohler v. United States 60
Omni-Vest, Inc. v. Reichhold Chemicals, Inc. 216
one-phrase/one-rule objections 68–69, 123, 153–154
"on the record" 146
open-ended questions 30
opening statement
    advocacy goals 93–94
    applicable law 94–99
    implementing goals and strategy 99–105
    objections to 97, 104
    practical considerations 104–105
    purpose of 93
    questions to ask 105
    reserve opening 104
    stating contentions in 96
    suggested reading 105
oral arguments on motions *in limine. See* pretrial hearing
Oregon Mut. Ins. Co. v. Barton 212
organizing for trial
    corss-examination 134–137
    creating timelines 46, 135
    documents and exhibits 35–36, 42–45
    jury instructions 24, 42
    jury selection 89–90
    notebook system 36–45
    one-page trial summary 46
    questions to ask 46
    trial system for 35–36

O'Rielly Motor Co. v. Rich 190
Orme School v. Reeves 164
Ousley, Illinois v. 204
overtrying the case 48, 52, 117
Owen, Miller v. 190
Owens Corning Fiberglass Corp. v. Crane 186
Oxnard (California), Du Jardin v. 192

P
Pacillo, Koonce v. 192
Pagan v. Florida 165, 166
Papegeorgiou v. F.W. Woolworth Co. 205
Papertisan, O'Connor v. 214
Parkhouse Tire Serv., Inc., Torres v. 20
pattern instructions
 about 12, 22–23
 applicable law 18
 citing leading cases and statutes 22–23
 frequently referenced 21–22
 modifying 12, 16, 22
Pelican Pest Control, Inc., Williams v. 212
Pennoyer Merchants Transfer Co., Offutt v. 192
Penn v. Florida 130
peremptory challenges 74, 79–81, 85, 89
Pereyra, New York v. 148
Perez, Anderson Aviation Sales Co., Inc. v. 193
personal injury cases 54
personal opinion, expressing 95–96
Peter Pan Bus Lines, Inc., Mono v. 210
Phillips v. Florida 151
Phoenix Indem. Ins. Co., Mora v. 18
Photon Dynamics, Inc., Amtower v. 62
Pierce, Washington v. 187
Pilat, Szczerbiak v. 164
Pittman, Hales v. 183, 185, 186
Pitts, Lopez-Stayer v. 73
plain error exception 150
plaintiff
 elements to prove in trial 11

improper closing arguments 188–191
presenting case-in-chief 107
planning cross-examination 137–139
pleadings
 filing with court 24
 organizing 37–38
 in record of proceedings 145
pleadings books (notebook system) 37–38
Pleasance v. City of Chicago 190
police reports
 annotating in timeline 46
 inconsistency with testimony 138
 organizing 39
Poliszczuk v. Winkler 212, 215
polling the jury 205
Pool v. Arizona Superior Court 132
Porter v. Florida 108
posttrial motions
 about 207–208
 advocacy goals 208–209
 applicable law 209–216
 implementing goals and strategy 209–216
 purpose of 208
Powell, United States v. 202
Powers v. Ohio 80
Prado, Washington v. 185
preexisting conditions 53–54
premeditation 14–15
preparing for trial
 case-in-chief 110–112
 cross-examination 134–137, 143
 direct examination 110–112
 drafting jury instructions 11–13
 importance of 143
 jury instructions 110
 witness testimony 117–119
Press–Enterprise Co. v. Superior Court of Cal. 73
pretrial hearing
 about 65–67
 moving exhibits into evidence 70
 questions to ask 66–67
 signaling unusual issues 70

suggested reading 71
Price Waterhouse, Standard Chartered PLC v. 167, 184, 185
Probkevitz v. Velda Farms, LLC 173
procedural purpose. *See* purpose, legal or procedural
Profit Management Development, Inc. v. Jacobsen, Brandvik & Anderson, Ltd. 184
prosecution
   elements to prove in trial 11
   improper closing arguments 187–188
   presenting case-in-chief 107
Prunty v. YMCA of Lockport, Inc. 215
Public Health Trust of Dade County v. Geter 190
purpose, legal or procedural
   about 2
   charging conference 177
   closing argument 181
   cross-examination 127–129
   directed verdict 162–163
   direct examination 107
   jury instructions 12–15
   jury selection 73–76
   motions *in limine* 57–59
   opening statement 93
   posttrial motions 208
   rebuttal case 107, 171
   record of proceedings 145–148
   trial briefs 57–59
   trial lawyers 218

Q
quality of life 54
questions to ask
   about 3
   argumentative questions and 132
   charging conference 180
   closing argument 200
   cross-examination 143
   directed verdict 168–169
   direct examination 125
   identifying weak points in stories 142
   jury instructions 25

jury selection 84–87, 90
leading questions 108–110, 115, 127, 139–142
motions *in limine* 63–64
open-ended for witnesses 30
opening statement 105
organizing for trial 46
pretrial hearing 66–67
rebuttal case 175
record of proceedings 160
about stories 5–9
trial briefs 63–64
trial lawyers 226

R
Raftopoulos, Hamilton v. 178
Rainbow Ambulance Serv., Inc., Scott v. 99
Rajeeve Sindhwani, M.D., PLLC v. Coe Business Serv., Inc. 215
Ramos, California v. 132
Ratner v. Arrington 190
reasonable doubt 197
rebuttal case
   advocacy goals 171
   applicable law 172–173
   implementing goals and strategy 173–174
   purpose of 107, 171
   questions to ask 175
record of proceedings
   about 145
   advocacy goals 148–150
   applicable law 150–152
   audiovisual recordings 145
   charging conference and 179
   implementing goals and strategy 152–160
   "in the record" 146
   on midtrial jury instructions 148, 151–152, 158–160
   on objections 146–147, 149–150, 152–155, 179
   on offers of proof 147, 151, 155–157
   "on the record" 146
   purpose of 145–148

questions to ask 160
re-cross-examination 143
Redd, California v. 185
Redmond v. Socha 203
Reed v. Johnson 191
Reeves, Orme School v. 164
Reichhold Chemicals, Inc., Omni-Vest, Inc. v. 216
Reinhold, Illinois v. 79
remittitur, motion for 208, 214–216
Remy v. Exley Produce Express, Inc. 203
research books (notebook system) 41
reserve opening 104
reversals of jury verdicts 22
Revuelta, State Farm Mut. Auto. Ins. Co. v. 190
Rice v. Offshore Systems, Inc. 120
Rich, O'Rielly Motor Co. v. 190
Rijlaarsdam, Cervantes v. 129
Riley, California v. 168
Rinehart, Illinois v. 73, 77, 78
Ritchie v. Kraspner 193
Roberts, Washington v. 132
Robinson, Illinois v. 211
Robinson, New York v. 185
Robinson v. Wieboldt Stores, Inc. 189
Romero v. Cooper 179
Rondout Elec., Inc. v. Dover Union Free School Dist. 62
Rothe, Arizona v. 130
Ruiz v. Florida 184, 187
Rush v. Hamdy 192
Ruskin v. Travelers Ins. Co. 20
Russell, Inc. v. Trento 185

S

Safeway Stores, Inc., Duran v. 178
Saka v. Saka 146
Salica v. Tucson Heart Hosp.-Carondelet, LLC 166
Samuels v. Torres 191
Sanders v. Florida 77, 79
Sandoval, Washington v. 185
San Francisco, Nishihama v. 189
Saratoga Spa & Bath, Inc. v. Beeche Systems Corp. 146

Sarrafi, Theofanis v. 203
scheduling issues 70
School Board of Broward County, Collins v. 164
School Board of Palm Beach County, Feliciano v. 178
Schorr, Hancock v. 210
Scott v. Rainbow Ambulance Serv., Inc. 99
Scott v. Virginia 79
Scott, Washington v. 108
SDG Dadeland Associates, Inc. v. Anthony 184, 186
Seaboard Coastline R.R. Co. v. Addison 16
Sears, Roebuck and Co., Dotson v. 190
seating charts during jury selection 89
self-defense 7
Semsch v. Henry Mayo Newhalll Memorial Hosp. 151
S & F Towing Serv. of Staten Island, Inc., Kay Foundation v. 168
Shepherd v. Walley 192
Sherman Health Systems, Studt v. 178
Sherman Hosp., Hubbard v. 193
Shilling, Gersick v. 214
Sierra Boat Co., Hyatt v. 58
Sierra v. Winn Dixie Stores, Inc. 19
Simpson v. K-Mart Corp. 193
Sims, Illinois v. 78
Sisk v. Ball 184
Sixth Amendment confrontation right 128, 131
Skaggs, Arizona v. 77
Smith, California v. 129
Smith, Florida v. 187
Smith, New York v. 184
Snyder v. Louisiana 80
Socha, Redmond v. 203
Solomon, California v. 61
Soule v. General Motors Corp. 16
Southland Corp. v. Crane 203
Spain, California v. 108
speaking objections 67–68, 123, 153
Spears, Arizona v. 165
Spence, Gerry 86
Spencer, Washington v. 130

Spokane County Fire Protection Dist. No. 1, Brown v. 131
Spreitzer, Illinois v. 187
Spruill, New York v. 187
Spyrka v. County of Cook 190
Stanard, New York v. 128
Standard Chartered PLC v. Price Waterhouse 167, 184, 185
standard instructions 13
Standard Life & Acc. Ins. Co., Merlo v. 20
standard of care 103
State Farm Mut. Auto. Ins. Co. v. Revuelta 190
statement of the case instructions 23–24
Staton, Miller v. 192
status conference. *See* pretrial hearing
Steinhorst v. Florida 128
Stephens v. Arizona 19
St. Francis Hosp., Broadie v. 212
St. Mary's Hosp., Decker v. 98
Stockton v. Florida 183
stories and storytelling
   believability of 6–8, 51–52
   chronological order in 43, 100
   closing argument and 197–198
   comparing with opponent's 8
   consistency of witnesses' 49–51
   credibility of 50
   determining which ones to tell 6–7
   exclusion of evidence from 7
   factual discredit to 7
   ideal qualities for 48–52
   identifying weak points in 142
   list of questions for 5–6
   in opening statement 97
   preparing witness outlines 112–117
   separate ponts in 115–117
   showing entitlement to legal results 7–8
   stringing together 116–117
   suggested reading 9
   undermining opponent's case 102–103

vulnerable parts of 7
witness testimony 27–28, 32–33
Stryzinski v. Arnold 20
Studt v. Sherman Health Systems 178
substantive instructions
   about 13
   on breach of contract 13–14
   first degree murder elements 14–15
Sucharew, Arizona v. 98
suggested reading
   about 3
   case-in-chief 55
   charging conference 180
   closing argument 200
   cross-examination 143
   direct examination 125
   investigation 34
   jury instructions 26
   jury selection 91
   motions *in limine* 64
   opening statement 105
   pretrial hearing 71
   stories 9
   trial briefs 64
   trial lawyers 226
Sullivan v. Edward Hosp. 210
Sullivan, Washington v. 61
summary judgment motion 39
summary of the case instructions 23–24
summary, trial 46
Summers, Watson & Kimpel, Mayol v. 20
Swan v. Florida Farm Bureau Ins. Co. 60
Swift–Eckrich, Inc, Unitherm Food Systems, Inc. v. 210
Szczerbiak v. Pilat 164

T
table of contents
   for discovery books 38–39
   for exhibit books 42–43
   for pleadings books 37
Tacoma, Turner v. 20

Tate v. Colabello 190
Taylor, California v. 77
Taylor v. DiRico 189
technical information, explaining 100
Tesoro Del Valle Master Homeowners Ass'n v. Griffin 173
Theofanis v. Sarrafi 203
third-party witnesses 31–33
Thomas, California v. 187
Thomas v. Johnson Controls, Inc. 191
Thompkins, Illinois v. 147, 151
Thompson, Liberatore v. 61
Thompson v. Grays Harbor Community Hosp. 212
Thorgerson, Washington v. 183, 186
Thurman, Illinois v. 17
Thurston County (Washington), Broyles v. 190
Tiller, Illinois v. 185, 186
timelines, creating 46, 135
Tingle, Haid v. 216
Tolleson Elementary School Dist., Chavez v. 168
Torres, Samuels v. 191
Torres v. Parkhouse Tire Serv., Inc. 20
Touchette, Bould v. 215
Trappier, New York v. 202
Travelers Ins. Co., Ruskin v. 20
Trento, Russell, Inc. v. 185
trial brief books (notebook system) 41–42
trial briefs
   advocacy goals 59
   applicable law 60–62
   implementing goals and strategies 62–63
   jury instructions and 15
   offers of proof in 156
   purpose of 57–59
   questions to ask 63–64
   suggested reading 64
trial lawyers
   about 217–218
   advocacy goals 218
   applicable law 218–219
   behavior toward court personnel 66
   being your best 222–225
   credibility of 51–52, 59, 101–102
   do no harm 219–220
   encouraging followers 222
   encouraging respect 222
   encouraging trust 220–221
   exercising judgment 138–139
   implementing goals and strategy 219–225
   obnoxious manner 87, 142
   purpose of 218
   questions to ask 226
   suggested reading 226
   Younger's commandments for 140–141
trial readiness conference. *See* pretrial hearing
trial summary 46
trial system for organization. *See* organizing for trial
Trillet v. Bachman 168
Triple D Leasing Corp, Halftown v. 190
Triplett, Illinois v. 128
Trower v. Jones 131
Tryon v. Nangle 192
Tucson Heart Hosp.-Carondelet, LLC, Salica v. 166
Tunnage v. Green 204
Turner, Kingston v. 20
Turner v. City of Tacoma 20
Tyron v. Naegle 191

U

Ubilluz, Compton v. 61
undermining opponent's case 102–103
Union Pacific R. Co., Collins v. 190, 216
United States, Aldridge v. 77
United States, Alford v. 128, 131
United States, Ohler v. 60
United States v. Abel 131
United States v. Hale 187
United States v. Martinez 80
United States v. Powell 202

United States v. Young 184, 185, 193
Unitherm Food Systems, Inc. v. Swift–Eckrich, Inc. 210
unrepresented persons 31–33
Urbin v. Florida 185

V

Van Arsdall, Delaware v. 128, 131
Vance, California v. 186, 187
Vancleave, Laberge v. 191
Van Cleve, Illinois v. 209
Vandalia Bus Lines, Inc., Lauman v. 19
VanWinkle, Arizona v. 187
Vasold, Beagle v. 190
Velda Farms, LLC, Probkevitz v. 173
verdicts. *See* jury verdicts
Virginia, Jackson v. 166
Virginia, McGill v. 79
Virginia, Mu'Min v. 73
Virginia, Scott v. 79
Vogel, Duffy v. 205
voir dire. *See* jury selection
vulnerable parts of stories 7

W

Wainwright, Jacobs v. 147
waiving objections 150
Walker v. Bangs 148
Walker v. Washington 17
Walley, Shepherd v. 192
Walsh v. Advanced Cardiac Specialists Chartered 203
Ward, California v. 183, 184, 185
Warfel v. Cheney 151
Warner Constr. Corp. v. City of Los Angeles 191
Washburn v. City of Federal Way 210
Wash, California v. 98
Washington pattern instructions 22
Washington State Physicians Ins. Exchange & Ass'n v. Fisons Corp. 193
Washington v. Anderson 188
Washington v. Barnes 204
Washington v. Belgarde 185, 187
Washington v. Brady 77
Washington v. Brett 185

Washington v. Briscoe 132
Washington v. Ceglowski 211
Washington v. Clafflin 184
Washington v. Darden 129, 130
Washington v. Dhaliwal 187
Washington v. Emery 188
Washington v. Evans 60
Washington v. Finch 191
Washington v. Fleming 188
Washington v. Frederiksen 78
Washington v. Frost 183
Washington v. Gallagher 99
Washington v. Gentry 166
Washington v. Gonzales 79
Washington v. Green 165
Washington v. Hoffman 194
Washington v. Jackson 163
Washington v. Jasper 201
Washington v. Kroll 93, 94
Washington v. Latham 60
Washington v. McKenzie 186
Washington v. Pierce 187
Washington v. Prado 185
Washington v. Roberts 132
Washington v. Sandoval 185
Washington v. Scott 108
Washington v. Spencer 130
Washington v. Sullivan 61
Washington v. Thorgerson 183, 186
Washington v. Whelchel 98
Washington v. White 171, 172, 173
Washington, Walker v. 17
Watson v. City of Chicago 190
Watson v. Hockett 19
Weinberg, New York v. 185
W. E. Roche Fruit Co. v. Northern Pac. R.R. Co. 171
West, Arizona v. 166, 211
Western Home Ins. Co., Major v. 19
Whelchel, Washington v. 98
Whipple, New York v. 168
White, Allstate Ins. Co. v. 192
White, Washington v. 171, 172, 173
Wicklow v. Florida 186, 187
Wieboldt Stores, Inc., Robinson v. 189
Wigmore, John Henry 127
Wilhelmi, Carlasare v. 191

William Chevrolet/Geo, Inc., Cannon v. 62
Williams, California v. 78
Williams v. Brooklyn E.I. R.R. Co. 183
Williams v. Florida 165, 211
Williams v. Pelican Pest Control, Inc. 212
Wilson v. City of New York 189
Winkler, Poliszczuk v. 212, 215
Winkler v. Giddings 210
Winn Dixie Stores, Inc., Sierra v. 19
Winning Jury Trials (Klonoff and Colby) 48
Withers, Illinois v. 165
witness books (notebook system)
  about 40
  collecting and organizing information 134–137
  filing depositions in 40
  making copies of documents for 38, 39
witnesses
  annotating statements in timeline 46
  asking open-ended questions 30
  assessing case-in-chief 48
  bias of 130–131, 136, 141
  as building blocks in stories 27–28
  changing their stories 32–33
  clients as 31
  closing argument on 199
  consistency in stories of 49–51
  credibility of 50, 130–131, 133–134, 136
  cross-examination of.
    See cross-examination
  determining order of proof 119
  direct examination of. *See* direct examination
  ethical rules when dealing with 33
  forming relationships with 29–30
  hostile 31–33, 50, 133
  interviewing 28–29, 31–33
  leading questions and 108–110
  listening to answers of 117
  meeting at different locations 31
  motivation of 135, 141
  moving exhibits into evidence and 70
  objections to testimony by 121
  organizing material related to 38, 39, 40
  overtrying the case 52, 117
  preparing for testinmony 111–119
  scheduling issues 70
  signing statements 32, 39
  spending time with 28–30
  stating opinions of 95
  summaring impressions of 40
  understanding the big picture 29, 118
witness outlines 112–117, 136–137
Woods, California v. 188
Workers' Comp. Appeals Bd., Fremont Indemnity Co. v. 128
Workmen's Compensation Appeals Bd., Edgar v. 172
writing
  cross-examinations 137–139
  objections 155

Y

Yakima Compost Co., County of La Paz v. 166
Yarbrough, California v. 60
Yellow Cab Co., Clark v. 192
YMCA of Lockport, Inc., Prunty v. 215
Young-Chin v. City of Homestead 173
Younger, Irving 140–141
Young, United States v. 184, 185, 193
Yuma (Arizona), Copeland v. 193

Z

Zabala, Coral Gables Hospital, Inc. v. 188, 189
Zagami, Inc. v. James A. Crone, Inc. 204
Zakhar, Arizona v. 202

Zanoletti v. Norle Properties, Corp. 172
Zapata, Metropolitan Dade County v. 189

About the Authors

Rick Friedman conducts a national trial practice representing individuals and small businesses in tort and business cases. He has tried cases in over ten different states, and four times has obtained verdicts ranked in the annual top ten verdicts by *Lawyers USA*. He is a member of the Inner Circle of Advocates and the author of *Rules of the Road, Polarizing the Case,* and *Rick Friedman on Becoming a Trial Lawyer.*

Bill Cummings practices with Rick at Friedman | Rubin. After graduating from the University of Pennsylvania Law School, he clerked for Justice Warren Matthews of the Alaska Supreme Court. Bill was in private practice in Anchorage, representing businesses, landowners, and individuals in both litigation and transactional matters, before joining Friedman | Rubin in 2007. His role includes helping prepare cases for trial and briefing issues in trial courts and on appeal.